"Douglas O'Donnell writes with [...]
of the Bible. At a time when m[...]
the rest of Scripture, O'Donnell's call to pay close attention to these books and his gripping introduction to them should be widely read."

Peter J. Williams, Warden, Tyndale House, Cambridge, England

"Rarely does an individual combine the precision of an exegete, the passion of a poet, and the pulse of a pastor. But Doug O'Donnell demonstrates all of these qualities in his most recent book. What is even more impressive is that O'Donnell focuses his attention on the Old Testament Wisdom Literature, one of the sections of the Bible most neglected by scholars and pastors alike. His model sermons and the hermeneutical discussions that undergird them are sure to inspire many others to follow the path that he has blazed so well."

Daniel J. Estes, Distinguished Professor of Bible, Dean of the School of Biblical and Theological Studies, Cedarville University

"I have long thought that the Wisdom Literature of the Old Testament is a good grid on which to introduce our unbelieving and troubled world to the gospel—it is so down-to-earth and practical. Douglas O'Donnell does this in an appealing way. His homiletical exercises in Proverbs, Ecclesiastes, and Job, conveyed in fresh conversational prose, lead the preacher from the text to the pulpit to the pew. If a sermon is like a painting, it should always be like a Rembrandt with the famous beam of light that characterizes his portraits. O'Donnell's model sermons glow with that beaming light of the gospel. And he helpfully instructs his readers on the hermeneutical principles that can engage the text and enlighten the preacher for the awesome task of gospel proclamation, yes, even from the Wisdom Literature!"

C. Hassel Bullock, Franklin S. Dyrness Professor of Biblical Studies Emeritus, Wheaton College

"Since these days I am as likely to be sitting in a pew (or preferably, of course, a comfortable chair) as standing in a pulpit, I am now part of that great hungry multitude hoping for help, heart nourishment for the week ahead, a true word from the Lord that a lively exposition from Holy Scripture can bring, and above all a fresh sense of the greatness of the God we know in and through Christ. These sermons of Doug O'Donnell's, as well as the practical instructions he provides, have enriched me, as they will surely do for many others."

R. C. Lucas, Retired Rector, St. Helen's Church, Bishopsgate, London

"Doug O'Donnell's sermons in this volume are all that a preaching commentary should be—analytic of the biblical text, wide-ranging in biblical scholarship, containing a wealth of 'bridge building' to everyday life, and stylistically excellent."

Leland Ryken, Professor of English, Wheaton College

"The Wisdom Literature of the Old Testament poses one of the most daunting challenges for preachers whose resolve is to preach Christ from all the Scriptures. Pastor Douglas O'Donnell offers invaluable modeling and coaching to help us explore, in practical terms, how to preach Proverbs, Ecclesiastes, and Job in a way that both expounds the biblical texts with integrity and sets them into the larger context of the Bible's unified witness to Christ, in whom are hidden all the treasures of wisdom and knowledge."

Dennis E. Johnson, Professor of Practical Theology,
Westminster Seminary, California

"The church very much needs to hear preaching from Old Testament wisdom, and for that preaching to be Christian, it must be faithful to the text and also point people to Christ. O'Donnell's vision for wisdom preaching, and the sermons themselves, serve as excellent guideposts for those who want to preach through Old Testament wisdom books. They inspire other preachers to work through the texts on their own with a clear vision for preaching the gospel through the wisdom God has given in Scripture."

Michael Graves, Associate Professor of Old Testament, Wheaton College

"This lively, contemporary introduction to the Old Testament Wisdom books provides an ideal way for today's Christian readers to share their wealth, learn their secrets, and discern the glories of Christ in their pages. For the biblical preacher, O'Donnell's book is packed with helpful models and practical advice on how to preach this often-neglected material with fresh power and effectiveness."

David Jackman, Former President, Proclamation Trust, London, England

"In an age of endless self-help courses, books, and psychobabble there are few parts of the Bible more needed than the Wisdom Literature. Christians need to learn from our Creator how to live wisely in his world and, in learning it, discover how this literature leads to the gospel and points to Christ. Doug O'Donnell's book seeks to show how we may know and enjoy the Wisdom Literature and preach Christ from it. Such an enterprise is timely and helpful for those who wish to live God's way in his world."

Phillip Jensen, Senior Minister, St Andrew's Cathedral, Sydney,
Australia; Director, Sydney Diocesan Ministry Training and Development

THE BEGINNING AND END OF
WISDOM

THE BEGINNING AND END OF
WISDOM

*Preaching Christ from the First and Last Chapters
of Proverbs, Ecclesiastes, and Job*

Douglas Sean O'Donnell

FOREWORD BY SIDNEY GREIDANUS

WHEATON, ILLINOIS

The Beginning and End of Wisdom: Preaching Christ from the First and Last Chapters of Proverbs, Ecclesiastes, and Job
Copyright © 2011 by Douglas Sean O'Donnell
Published by Crossway
    1300 Crescent Street
    Wheaton, Illinois 60187

Cover design: Spire2 Communications
Interior design and typesetting: Lakeside Design Plus
First printing 2011
Printed in the United States of America

Trade paperback ISBN:	978-1-4335-2334-2
PDF ISBN:	978-1-4335-2335-9
Mobipocket ISBN:	978-1-4335-2336-6
ePub ISBN:	978-1-4335-2337-3

Library of Congress Cataloging-in-Publication Data
O'Donnell, Douglas Sean, 1972–
    The beginning and end of wisdom : preaching Christ from the first and last chapters of Proverbs, Ecclesiastes, and Job / Douglas Sean O'Donnell ; foreword by Sidney Greidanus.
    p. cm.
    Includes bibliographical references (p.   ) and index.
    ISBN 978-1-4335-2334-2 (tp)
    1. Bible. O.T. Proverbs—Sermons. 2. Bible. O.T. Ecclesiastes—Sermons. 3. Bible. O.T. Job—Sermons. 4. Sermons, American—21st century. 5. Presbyterian Church—Sermons. I. Title.

BS1465.54.O36   2011
223'.06—dc22

                                                   2011005644

To my son, Simeon Joseph,
who looks in awesome wonder at God's power
throughout the universe displayed

"Look, Da Da, the moon!
Look, look, flowers. Look!"

CONTENTS

LIST OF TABLES

FOREWORD

I feel honored that Doug O'Donnell invited me to review his new book, *The Beginning and End of Wisdom*, and, he said, if I liked it, to write the foreword. I do indeed like the book: it is well researched and written and fills a real need for preachers and seminary students.

The contemporary need is this: Old Testament Wisdom Literature is one of the more difficult genres to interpret and preach. This need is heightened by the fact that many modern preachers do not know how to preach Christ from these books. Many, therefore, think it the better part of wisdom to omit Wisdom Literature from their preaching schedule.

It is telling that the *Revised Common Lectionary* in its three-year cycle of some 230 Old Testament readings (not including the Psalms) has only eleven readings from Wisdom Literature: four readings from Proverbs (Year B, sixteenth, seventeenth, and eighteenth Sundays after Pentecost, and Year C, first Sunday after Pentecost); five from Job (Years A, B, and C, Holy Saturday, and Year B, twentieth, twenty-first, twenty-second, and twenty-third Sundays after Pentecost); one from Ecclesiastes (Years A, B, and C, New Year); and one from the Song of Solomon (Year B, fifteenth Sunday after Pentecost). This arrangement suggests the possibility of a three-sermon series on Proverbs and a four-sermon series on Job once every three years. I am not faulting the *Lectionary* for so few wisdom passages as it seeks to follow the life of Christ through the church year; after all, there are numerous beautiful passages in the Old Testament. But these statistics do indicate that congregations whose preachers follow the *Lectionary* closely will be undernourished with respect to Old Testament wisdom. This is where *The Beginning and End of Wisdom* can provide the needed dietary supplements for the church.

At first reading, the book's title may seem presumptuous, as if this book is *the beginning and end of wisdom*. But in reading the book you will discover what a wonderfully apt title this is. This title resonates on no less than three levels. First, O'Donnell presents six sermons, one on the beginning and one on the end of three wisdom books: Proverbs, Ecclesiastes, and Job. Second, the wisdom passages all begin in the Old Testament and all end with Jesus Christ, the very "wisdom of God" (1 Cor. 1:24), "in whom are hidden all the treasures of wisdom and knowledge" (Col. 2:3). And third, in preaching this Old Testament wisdom today, pastors begin with this wisdom so that its end may be transformed lives that *live* this wisdom. As you read this delightful book, you may discover even more levels where this title resonates.

O'Donnell has a twofold aim with this book: "First, I wish to light a fire beneath you; that is, I desire to help you know and enjoy the Wisdom Literature of the Bible so that you might preach on it more often. Second, I wish to show you how to build a fire; that is, how to preach such literature" (from the preface). He accomplishes both aims. In text, endnotes, quotations, and illustrations, his book witnesses to wide readings and interests (history, theology, biblical hermeneutics, literature, art, current events, preaching), thorough research, and wise judgments. The sound expository sermons are written in a fresh, sometimes witty, oral style, including dialogue with the congregation. But this book consists of much more than six excellent sermons.

In writing these six sermons on Proverbs, Ecclesiastes, and Job, O'Donnell set himself a major task of research, for each of these books is a different form (sub-genre) of Wisdom Literature; that is, each has a different mix of wisdom forms such as proverb, reflection, instruction, anecdote, and autobiographical narrative. Therefore, each book requires a specific hermeneutical approach (see the separate bibliographies on Proverbs, Ecclesiastes, Job, and "Other Resources"). Moreover, preaching a sermon on the beginning as well as the end of each book requires a thorough acquaintance with the *whole* book. In addition, he seeks not only to preach the Old Testament texts in their Old Testament contexts but to link each message to Jesus Christ in the New Testament: "I want us to put on gospel glasses and look at this text again so that we might see clearly how what we have in Christ . . . changes a buried seed into a budding flower." This desire for Christocentric sermons requires additional research into the connections between the Old Testament and the New as well as into the New Testament itself. O'Donnell accomplishes these multiple tasks very well. His sermons are biblical, expository, relevant, and interesting. In fact, they sing! At appropriate times the preacher smoothly slides into a higher key and preaches Jesus Christ.

These six sermons are model sermons that will inspire and teach you how to preach Christ from Old Testament wisdom. The many endnotes provide further information and insights. The sermons are followed by a seventh chapter, "How Shall Wisdom Be Preached?" This chapter gives specific tips on how to move from an Old Testament wisdom text to Jesus Christ in the New Testament. Since much of Wisdom Literature is written as poetry, an appendix, "Preaching Hebrew Poetry," provides more hints for interpreting and preaching this literature. A final appendix offers a brief summary of each book and valuable suggestions for preaching sermon series on Proverbs, Ecclesiastes, and Job.

Before Doug invited me to write a foreword for his new book, I did not know him at all. In fact, our life paths have been remarkably different. But now that our paths have crossed, I recognize in him a kindred spirit whose zeal is the same as mine. This stimulating book will drive you from your study to the pulpit in order to preach Christ from "all the Scriptures" (Luke 24:27, 44).

Sidney Greidanus
Author, *Preaching Christ from Ecclesiastes*;
Professor Emeritus of Preaching, Calvin Theological Seminary

ACKNOWLEDGMENTS

I am grateful to God for wisdom. I am grateful to God for an all-wise Savior, the very wisdom of God incarnate. I am grateful to God for wise editors. Thank you, my wonderful editorial "staff," starting with Emily Gerdts, Matt Newkirk, and John Seward, and ending with Lydia Brownback and the team at Crossway. Good editing has made my sentences sing! I am grateful to God for a wise wife, Emily; thanks again for the time and encouragement to read, think, and write. I am grateful to God for wise (or growing-in-wisdom) children—Sean, Lily, Evelyn, Charlotte, and, oh, yes, my little man, Simeon, to whom I dedicate this book. Simeon, you remind me daily to look up and look around at the un-ordinariness of God's creation. May you find the wisdom of Christ even more awe-inspiring!

THE BEGINNING OF WISDOM FOR BEGINNERS

M y midlife crisis came early. Unless, of course, I live to be seventy; in that case, it came right on time. While it was a "crisis" in the sense of a decision, it didn't involve choosing between buying a red corvette or dyeing my gray hairs brown. I was deciding if I should seek ordination as a Presbyterian pastor. After nineteen years as a devout Roman Catholic and sixteen years as an even more devout nondenominational evangelical, this decision wasn't easy. In my left ear I could hear my dear Scottish Catholic mother's voice, still sad about me leaving the one true church and still going on about those wicked Glasgow Presbyterian boys who tossed stones over the fence at her and the other poor, innocent, minding-their-own-business girls of St. Saviour's. In my right ear was the voice of professional prudence and discretion: "As an established evangelical pastor, are you willing to leave the theological flexibility of nondenominationalism and be publically enjoined with those who fervently defend Calvinism, infant baptism, and the spiritual presence of Christ in the sacramental wine?" Eventually I quelled these voices, cleared my head, and made a decision.

I enrolled in "the most perfect school of Christ,"[1] and thus began my journey to Geneva.

The road toward ordination, however, was more arduous than expected. It would require college and seminary transcripts, a letter from my church, and then a good deal of personal and academic writing. I had to submit a summary of my Christian experience and call to ministry, paragraphs on thirteen issues in theology, six exams, an exegetical essay, a theological paper, and a sermon manuscript. Once completed, all my work would then be reviewed by the Candidates and Credentials Committee of the regional Presbytery. If approved, I would twice stand before the Presbytery for oral examinations, where I could be asked any and all relevant questions:

How did you come to Christ?
What is the chief end of man?
What is justification?
Name the five points of Calvinism.
What is a censure?
When did the PCA and the RPCES become one?
What is the square root of the year J. Gresham Machen left Princeton?

On the morning I took my first three oral exams—on the English Bible, the Westminster Standards (theology), and *The Book of Church Order* (church polity)—I also handed my sermon manuscript to the Candidates and Credentials Committee and proceeded to preach the text of the manuscript before them. All the members of that committee looked so tired, dour, and slightly irritated, much like that fêted picture of John Knox. They sat on brown folding chairs around a brown folding table, all folding their white arms. A few of them lay back in their chairs. Others slumped forward. I stood as straight as I could behind a shorter-than-I'd-wished music stand, my sermon manuscript seemingly seven miles beneath my eyes. The only positive sign was that one member (the head of the committee no less) had long hair. The almost-always-correct equation (long hair = leniency) quickly soothed my mind.

I started the sermon.

I finished.

Amen and Amen.

They looked up. I looked up. Our eyes met.

"Okay, that's it. Thanks. Good job," the long-haired guy said and smiled. I was right about him.

A few hours later, after I stood before the Presbytery for examination, I was asked to wait in the adjoining room as they voted. I leaned nervously at the doorway of a dingy church kitchen (perhaps "dingy" is redundant). The only barrier between their voices and my ears was new drywall and those out-of-date accordion blinds. In other words, when I listened closely enough, I could hear every word of the "secret counsel" of their predetermined-before-the-foundation-of-the-world determination. I felt as guilty eavesdropping on my inquisitors as I had felt that time years ago when I had lied to Father McLaughlin about how many months it had been since my last confession. And so, after overhearing the first four questions they posed about me, which were addressed to the long-haired guy, the one man who now stood as the only mediator between me and ordination, I decided to retreat into the even dingier but well insulated tan-tiled bathroom. The dialogue of the first few overheard questions, however, still rang in my ears:

How was his sermon?

It was good.

What did he preach on?

He preached on Job 28. (Pause.) It's not every day that someone preaches on Job 28.

How was his exegetical essay?

Good.

What was it on?

He wrote on Proverbs 31.

Interesting?!

Yes.

Poets and Poems, Words and Wisdom

I'm not sure why it is that when I feel most pressed to prove myself, I turn to the Wisdom Literature of the Bible. Perhaps it has something to do with my natural disposition. I would, for example, scribble lines of poetry while my high school algebra teacher taught on variables or binary operations or vectors or imaginary numbers or a + b = b + a or whatever else goes on in such a class. And I have continued, without the algebra-teacher background noise, both to write my own poetry and to dwell on the poetry of others, most notably that of God.

Eleven years ago, I "contributed to scholarship" with my thesis on John Donne's interpretation of the Song of Solomon in light of the history of biblical interpretation.[2] My first published book, *God's Lyrics,* is on the songs of Moses, Deborah, Hannah, David, and Habakkuk. And I am currently working on two commentaries, one on Ecclesiastes and another on the Song of Solomon. In my brief decade of pastoral ministry I have taught through all of Ecclesiastes, much of Proverbs, and some of Job. My library is filled with rows of commentaries on Proverbs, Ecclesiastes, Job, the Song of Solomon, and the Psalms, and also with titles such as *Gospel and Wisdom*, *The Way of Wisdom*, *Old Testament Wisdom*, *Hear and Be Wise*, and *Where Shall Wisdom Be Found?*

These are indications not only of a passionate obsession but also of an oddity. I say "oddity" because from my survey of available literature and of other pastors' libraries and sermons, it appears to me that most men of the cloth today have left these texts and topics in the closet.[3] I find such neglect disappointing yet at the same time invigorating, for if every pastor loved such literature as I do, you wouldn't be holding the book you have in your hands. (And I wouldn't be earning a royalty, which keeps the "wealth" dicta of the Wisdom Literature very much in mind!)

Rubbing Sticks and Lighting Fires

The aim of this book, if I may be as forthright (yet unambiguous) as the preceding parenthesis, is twofold. First, I wish to light a fire beneath you; that is, I desire to help you know and enjoy the Wisdom Literature of the Bible so that you might preach on it more often. Second, I wish to show you how to build a fire, that is, how to preach such literature. In short this is a book on *what* the Wisdom Literature is,[4] *why* we should delight in it, and *how* we should preach it.

Since this task before us is not simple, you will be relieved to know that this book is laid out quite simply. There are only seven chapters, a number that is both *small* and, as you probably know, *perfect*. If I went with more than seven chapters (eight, nine, ten, or so) or less than seven (six, five, or four), we would then find ourselves in a precarious numerological conundrum, of which no poet (especially of the biblical mind) wants to find himself. I say that, of course, tongue in cheek. I do think and hope, however, (with tongue now out of cheek) that seven chapters will *perfectly* suffice to achieve my twofold aim. Specifically, I hope that the first six chapters, which were originally sermons on the first and last portions of Proverbs, Ecclesiastes, and Job,[5] will inform and inspire, and that the final chapter will be a practical aid in your calling to declare the excellencies of Jesus Christ from the whole counsel of God's Word (Acts 20:27; cf. 8:35).[6]

WHY CHRISTIANS ARE FOOLS

f I knew it would require dropping out of school, I probably would
have said no. While in graduate school (but not for graduate
school), I vowed to read the entire *Works of Jonathan Edwards*
in a year.[1] Yes, the entire works! Stamped on the inside cover of the
first volume was this inscription:

> These volumes are the gift of John H. Gerstner to Douglas O'Donnell
> who has vowed to God that he will complete their reading within
> one year of receiving them. Soli Deo Gloria!

That was the deal: Dr. Gerstner gave me the books for free; I vowed
to read them.

When the books came in the mail, I opened them with eager
excitement. Free books! Free Edwards! *Freedom of the Will!* I was
converted to Christ when I was nineteen and converted to reading
shortly thereafter. My job helped form and feed this new obsession.
I worked as an overnight security guard at ServiceMaster's corporate headquarters. Every three hours I did my rounds. This took
about ten minutes each time. The rest of the time—other than eating leftover shrimp in the kitchen from some fancy corporate party,

playing intercom games with the other security guards, strumming my guitar, and doing homework—I read. For four straight years for at least four hours a night, I read dead theologians. I read Augustine. I read Luther. I read Aquinas. I read Calvin. I read Chrysostom. I read Wesley. I read Boethius, for goodness sake. And, yes, I read America's most renowned theologian.

My fellow security guard, the son of an Iowa farmer, called me a "plower." He likened my reading habits to his father's work. "You plow through books slowly but surely, like a plow overturning the soil," he would say with some affection and subtle admiration. "Next thing I know, you're done with this huge book."

Plower or not, half a year into reading Edwards the plow got stuck. I realized that at the pace I was going—the only pace I could go with such complex and interesting material—my vow would be impossible to keep. Something had to give: the rounds? The shrimp? The intercom? The guitar? School?

School! I became a grad school dropout in order to remain a full-time security guard/Edwardsian reader. With a thin yellow highlighter wedged atop my left ear and a red pencil in my right hand, I read, marked, and learned. I underlined and asterisked every important sentence, and then, in the back of each volume, I scribbled my favorite quotes. I finished on December 20, 1994, which I know because I joyfully inscribed it on the front plate beneath Gerstner's Soli Deo Gloria.

Just the other day I pulled these volumes off my shelf, and I relived that year for a moment. Like rereading the Bible that I first read cover to cover and marked up with obnoxious colors and mutilating markings, these volumes revealed so much of my early Christian life. In those back pages, I saw how much I valued Edwards's majestic view of God, salvation, and the church:

> God is the highest Good of the reasonable creature; and the enjoyment of Him is the only happiness with which our souls can be satisfied.

The church is the completeness of Christ, the fullness of Him that filleth all in all.

Surely, the more the sinner has an inward, an immediate, and sole, and explicit dependence upon Christ, the more Christ has the glory of his salvation from him.

The man Jesus Christ, who is the head of all creatures, is the most humble of all creatures.

I am bold to say that the work of God in the conversion of one soul . . . is a more glorious work of God than the creation of the whole material world.

To take on yourself to work out redemption is a greater thing than if you had taken it upon you to create a world.

The gospel of the blessed God does not go abroad begging for its evidence, so much as some think: it has its highest and most proper evidence in itself.

There is not so much difference before God, between children and grown persons, as we are ready to imagine; we are all poor, ignorant, foolish babes in His sight. Our adult age does not bring us so much near to God as we are apt to think.

That final quote I liked best. (It has five stars next to it.) And today I still like it in its depiction of how we relate to, explain, and apply the Wisdom Literature of the Bible. In all my study of the Christian faith over these last twenty years, and especially in my recent work on Proverbs, Ecclesiastes, and Job, I find Edwards's thought here instructive. I have gained enormous insight about God, his Word, and his world, and yet *I know* that *I know* so little. I have plumbed the depths of the riches of the wisdom and knowledge of God only to learn that I am still but a poor, ignorant, foolish babe in his sight. I have climbed the mountains of his unsearchable judgments and inscrutable ways only to find myself not as near to God as I am apt to think.

Where Shall Wisdom Be Found?

The Wisdom Literature is helpful in humbling us before God. It is more helpful, I dare say, than any other part of the Bible. These three books put us in our place. We can dig deep into the recesses of human knowledge. We can mine diamonds from the caverns of human existence, experience, and observation. But we cannot find wisdom, that wisdom which is heavenly—"from above"—from the one who "is above all" (John 3:31). We have "earthly wisdom" (2 Cor. 1:12). But the Lord alone has heavenly wisdom. He alone is wise (Job 28:23–27; 37:1–42:6).

God's wisdom wearies us if we try to grasp it through humanly means (Prov. 30:1b). Knowledge of the Holy One cannot be found within (vv. 2–3). Knowledge of the Holy One cannot be obtained by climbing Jacob's ladder to peek our heads through the clouds (v. 4a). We cannot wrap our minds around the one who "wrapped up the waters in a garment" (v. 4c), who "gathered the wind in his fists" (v. 4b). We can only see flickers of light in the night sky. Streaks of lightning that dance in the storm. And such light—momentary light—comes only through open eyes and hands and hearts, and with faces to the ground.

"Where shall wisdom be found?" (Job 28:12b; cf. v. 20). That is the foundational question of the Wisdom Literature. And Wisdom Literature answers: "The fear of the Lord, that is wisdom" (Job 28:28). This wisdom from above comes only "to those who take refuge in him" (Prov. 30:5b).[2] This wisdom only comes to those who echo John the Baptist's words about God incarnate: "He must increase, but I must decrease" (John 3:30).

So the Wisdom Literature teaches us that the door to the kingdom is open to those whose childlike faith understands how the wisdom of God comes only from the fear of God. But it also teaches us about the gospel, illustrating the wisdom of God in *the sufferings of our Savior.*

At least that's how Paul saw it. The knowledge of God's plan of salvation—the mystery of the gospel revealed (Eph. 1:7–10)—is found in Christ and his cross. Christ, in whom are hidden all the treasures of wisdom (Col. 2:2–3), brings "wisdom from above"— God's peaceable, gentle, merciful wisdom (James 3:17) down to earth. And such wisdom was demonstrated through Christ's growth in wisdom and his teaching of wisdom, but ultimately through his sacrificial death.[3]

> For the word of the cross is folly to those who are perishing, but to us who are being saved it is the power of God. For it is written, "I will destroy the *wisdom* of the wise, and the discernment of the discerning I will thwart." Where is the one who is wise? Where is the scribe? Where is the debater of this age? Has not God made foolish the *wisdom* of the world? For since, in the *wisdom* of God, the world did not know God through *wisdom,* it pleased God through the folly of what we preach to save those who believe. For Jews demand signs and Greeks seek *wisdom,* but we preach Christ crucified, a stumbling block to Jews and folly to Gentiles, but to those who are called, both Jews and Greeks, Christ the power of God and the *wisdom* of God. (1 Cor. 1:18–24)

Christians are fools. That's Paul's argument to the Corinthians. That is, those who trust that God through the crucifixion made Christ "who became to us wisdom from God, righteousness and sanctification and redemption" (v. 30), appear foolish to the unwise—to the overly-wise-in-their-own-eyes—world. Yet he is no fool who abandons human pride and power to find the "secret and hidden wisdom of God" (2:7) now revealed in "Christ and him crucified" (2:2). The seeming folly of a crucified God is God's wisdom perfected. That is where wisdom is ultimately found.

Christocentric Wisdom

In his commentary on Isaiah, the church father Jerome wrote, "To be ignorant of the Scripture is to be ignorant of Christ."[4] Jerome was right. If we know nothing of the Word of God, we will know nothing of the Son of God. Put positively, the more we know the Bible, the better we will know the person and work of Jesus Christ.

Jerome's saying, however, can be reversed to make just as pointed a point: "To be ignorant of Christ is to be ignorant of Scripture." For isn't this the claim of Jesus himself? In John 5:39–40 Jesus rebuked the Pharisees with these words: "You search the Scriptures because you think that in them you have eternal life; and it is *they that bear witness about me*, yet you refuse to come to me that you may have life." Life does not come through Bible literacy. Life comes through Jesus. And a right understanding of Scripture comes through knowledge of Jesus and trust in him. As Paul wrote:

> For to this day, when [unconverted Jews] read the old [testament], that same veil remains unlifted, because *only through Christ* is it taken away. Yes, to this day whenever Moses is read a veil lies over their hearts. But *when one turns to the Lord,* the veil is removed. (2 Cor. 3:14b–16)

Such knowledge understands that just as every book of the Old Testament adds light to our understanding of Jesus, so the revelation of God in the person of Christ enlightens our understanding of the Old Testament. Martin Luther put it this way: "We can only read the Bible forwards, but we have to understand it backwards."[5] Jesus spoke of this forwards-backwards reading of the Word in Luke 24:44, where he taught his disciples how every book of the Old Testament canon—the "Law of Moses and the Prophets and the Psalms"—attested to his person and work, notably his death and resurrection. Most significant for our study is when he mentioned "the Psalms," referencing the *ketuvim* or "Writings," which consists of eleven books, the first being the book of Psalms and the last

Chronicles (1 and 2 Chronicles). Also included in "the Psalms" are the books of Proverbs, Ecclesiastes, and Job.[6]

So, are the books of Proverbs, Ecclesiastes, and Job about Jesus? Jesus says so. And this book aims to show *how so*. In the preface, I stated my twofold aim: (1) to help you know and enjoy the Wisdom Literature so that you might preach on it more often; and (2) to show you how to preach Christ from this genre. I hope by reading and applying this book your mind will be "opened . . . to understand" (Luke 24:45) perhaps something, if not "everything [!] written about [Christ]" (v. 44) in the Wisdom Literature.

May it be so to God's glory and the good of the church.

1

SHIP OF FOOLS

Proverbs 1:1–7

The fear of the LORD is the beginning of knowledge; fools despise wisdom and instruction.

—Proverbs 1:7

Thank God I didn't vow to God. Last year I began a decade-long process of reading the Pulitzer Prize–winning novels from the last century. Yet, after drudging through four more recent winners and finding drab protagonists and meatless plots, I abandoned my aren't-I-eccentric? ambition for a less lofty but more rewarding one: *The Adventures of Robin Hood, The Jungle Book, Robinson Crusoe, Kidnapped, Sleeping Beauty,* and *Aladdin and Other Tales from the Arabian Nights.* These six children's classics—beautifully bound, sitting patiently, un-eccentrically atop the black desk in my family room—beckoned me. Take and read. Take and read.

I took and read—six classics in one year.

And what fun it was. Three cheers for plots and protagonists. Hurray for stealing from the rich. Hurray for shipwrecks. Hurray for talking animals. And hip, hip, hurray *Aladdin*, my favorite of the six. Hurray for medieval Arabian (Islamic) folktales!

The Disney version leaves out anything and everything Islamic (too bad). Yet, like the book, the movie covers Aladdin's discovery of the magic lamp, the emergence of an all-powerful genie, and that genie's willingness to fulfill his master's every wish. How exciting! With the ability to request anything, Aladdin asks for what most sensible single men would ask: to marry the most beautiful woman in the kingdom, the sultan's daughter. Yet he takes a roundabout way. I would have commanded that genie, "Give me the princess now!" and let the genie work out the details. But Aladdin asks for riches to impress the princess's father. He gets the riches, which opens the door to the sultan's approval. Our hero gets the girl. Now, there's more to the story (much more), but that's the first and most important half of it.

I begin with that folktale because an Aladdin-like moment occurs in King Solomon's life. In 1 Kings 3:5 we read not of some magic genie but of the Lord God Almighty coming to David's son, the author of the book of Proverbs.[1] In a dream, God speaks to him: "Ask for whatever you want me to give you" (NIV). Now, that's not "Your wish is my command," but it's fairly close.

And how did Solomon reply? Did he say, "Show me the money"? No. How about, "Give me the girl"? No. Solomon wanted wisdom. After praising the Lord for the Lord's steadfast love, he asked for the ability to discern right from wrong—for wisdom. He wanted wisdom so that he might govern his life and his kingdom in a fitting manner.

This so pleased the Lord—that Solomon didn't ask for long life, riches, or military victory (or for Pharaoh's daughter or any other "sultan's" daughter)—that God bestowed upon him "a wise and discerning mind" (v. 12b) and gave to him "wisdom and understanding beyond measure . . . so that Solomon's wisdom surpassed the wisdom of all" (4:29–30a).[2]

We All Need Wisdom

When I was a newborn Christian (for me—age nineteen), I remember the first time I came across James 1:5: "If any of you lacks wisdom, let him ask God, who gives generously to all without reproach, and it will be given him." At the time, I considered wisdom to be the icing on the cake of Christian discipleship. I reasoned, "Oh, things are going pretty well in my Christian life, but now and then I need a bit of wisdom to make an important decision—what girl I should marry; what college I should attend—and so that's when I'll ask for it." That's when I rub the lamp, if you will. Yet now I realize, as Solomon did much earlier, that I need wisdom like I need oxygen and water—and love.

Isn't this true for you? We all need wisdom. And not just wisdom in the massive decisions of life but in our everyday relationships with their moment-by-moment choices—at home, in the workplace, in our neighborhoods. Thankfully, our gracious God has not left us to our own devices. He has given us the Wisdom Literature of the Bible, especially the book of Proverbs, where its short and salty Solomonic sayings teach us God's mind on many matters under the sun.

How do I find a good wife? It's in there. How do I raise godly children? It's in there. Why should I deal honestly in business? It's in there. What I am to do with this tongue, which sometimes likes to fib, gossip, and yell? It's in there. Why is it important to roll out of bed each morning and work hard? It's in there. How do I become a wise and respected leader within my community? It's in there.

Here at the very start of Proverbs (1:2–6), Solomon calls everyone who needs everyday wisdom—the young, the simple, and those already wise—to listen up. Do you need *practical* wisdom: "instruction in wise dealing" and "prudence . . . knowledge and discretion" (vv. 3–4)? Well, then, listen up. Do you need *intellectual* wisdom: insight into insightful words (vv. 2b, 4b)? Well, then, listen up. Do you need *moral* wisdom: "instruction . . . in righteousness, justice, and equity" (v. 3b)? Well, then, listen up. And do you need *mysterious* wisdom: "guidance" and the ability to understand or comprehend "the words of the wise and their riddles" (vv. 5–6), difficult or complex concepts and sayings?[3] Well, then, listen up. If you want wisdom—practical, intellectual, moral, and mysterious wisdom—well, then, listen now to what God's Word has to say. Listen to what Proverbs has to say about where to *begin*.[4]

In the Beginning

If you closed your Bible but kept your mind open, where would you begin? What would be your starting point? What would be your first controlling principle?[5] Just fill in the blank:

_____ is the beginning of knowledge.[6]

Perhaps you would jot down *natural intelligence*, or *acquired intelligence*, or *experience*. Is it the man with the high IQ, or the woman with the elite education, or the kid with street smarts? The Bible says it's none of the above. Its answer: genuine wisdom begins with the fear of the Lord.

In Proverbs, Ecclesiastes, and Job, this is *the* answer we are given. At the very end of Ecclesiastes, after Solomon speaks of the frivolities of this life, he writes in 12:13: "[This is] the end of the matter. . . . Fear God." In Job 28, the thematic middle of this narrative poem, the dialogue between Job and his friends is interrupted with a question: "Where shall wisdom be found?" (v. 12; cf. v. 20). What is the answer? "Behold, the fear of the Lord, that is wisdom" (v. 28). Then in Proverbs, right from the start, we are introduced to this foundational concept: "the fear of the LORD" (1:7)—that's the *beginning*.[7] If we don't start here (and stay here) we'll get nowhere.

You see, the book of Proverbs is not God's version of Ben Franklin's *Poor Richard's Almanac*—"Early to bed and early to rise, makes a man healthy, wealthy, and wise." Proverbs is not ancient Israel's version of the ancient Chinese sayings of Confucius. Confucius says, "Silence is a friend who will never betray." And Proverbs is not just a less humorous version of Murphy's Law—"Never argue with a fool, people might not know the difference." Proverbs has some of the characteristics of these other famous compilations of practical wisdom, but what sets it apart is its teaching that knowledge begins with an appropriate disposition toward God. This is not to say that Proverbs contains no practical truisms, but rather that it sets these truisms upon the foundation of a relationship with a specific God, "the LORD" (Yahweh), the true and living God who has covenanted with Israel. Proverbs claims that the acquisition of true wisdom comes from a right relationship with Yahweh and an appropriate attitude toward him: fear.

The Beginning of Wisdom

Okay. Fine. That's the "beginning." But what then does it mean to fear the Lord? Well, let me give you my definition, which I derived from studying all the references to "fear of the LORD" exclusively in Proverbs. I will give my definition, briefly explain it, and then thoroughly illustrate it. Here's the definition:

> According to the book of Proverbs, "the fear of the LORD" is a continual (23:17), humble, and faithful submission to Yahweh, which compels one to hate evil (8:13) and turn away from it (16:6) and brings with it rewards better than all earthly treasures (15:16)—the rewards of a love for and a knowledge of God (1:29; 2:5; 9:10; 15:33), and long life (10:27; 14:27a; 19:23a), confidence (14:26), satisfaction, and protection (19:23).

So the fear of the Lord isn't as fearful a concept as it sounds. (Although, don't take all the fright out of fear.) It is simply a way (both an Old *and* New Testament way; see Acts 9:31) of talking about one's *attitude* toward God, an attitude of submission, respect, dependence, and worship.[8]

The Fear of the Lord—Illustrating the Idea

As I thought about illustrating this idea, human-angelic encounters came to mind. In the Bible, what often happened when an angel appeared to a human being? What was Mary's response to the angel Gabriel (Luke 1:29–30)? Fear. And how did the guards who saw the angel that rolled back the stone of the tomb react? Fear. Matthew tells us that they "trembled and became like dead men" (Matt. 28:4). Do you remember what Samson's father said after the angel of the Lord visited him? He said, in great trepidation, "We shall surely die" (Judg. 13:22). Angelic encounters are fearful, and that is why it's not uncommon that the first words an angel says are, "Fear not."

As I thought about those angelic encounters, I thought they might be the perfect illustration of what it means to fear God. The point being: if we fear even angels, mere creatures, how much more ought we to fear God?[9] But since such encounters involved fear mostly in the sense of fearing for one's life—i.e., "I'm scared"—I decided against that. It gets part of the idea, but not all of it. It touches on the holiness aspect, which demands our respect and awe, but touches little on faith, which is also necessary for "fearing" the Lord.

So, next, I thought about using one of the many examples of encounters with God from the Old Testament narratives. I thought about Moses at the burning bush (Exodus 3). I thought about Isaiah's vision of the thrice-holy God in whose presence the purest of angels veil their eyes (Isaiah 6). I thought about Daniel's vision, where he describes himself as having "no strength" left in him and falling with his face to the ground (Dan. 10:8–9). I thought about righteous Job's repentance after he "sees" God in his holiness and sovereignty over creation (Job 38–41), where he says, "I despise myself, and repent in dust and ashes" (42:6).

These divine theophanies—better than the angelic encounters—illustrate the balance of fear (fright of God) and faith (trust in and obedience to God). So they work well to illustrate the idea. Yet I have found that the best, fullest, and clearest pictures of "the fear of God" occur in the incarnation, when people encountered God in the flesh, the Lord Jesus Christ. So, it is to the Gospels we turn next.

Although Jesus's humanity often veiled his divinity, we nevertheless have scenes in the Gospels where the brilliant light—the terrible majesty of God—shines through. What does it mean to fear the Lord? Well, let's look to Jesus and at Jesus. Let's look at when the Lord became a human and dwelt among us.

Can you think of times in the Gospels when a person shows the fear of the Lord to our Lord, this attitude of submission and respect and dependence and worship? Think about the wise men. When the star of Bethlehem led them to the King of kings asleep in a lowly manger, what did they do? "When they saw the star" resting over the place where the child was, "they rejoiced exceedingly with great joy" (Matt. 2:10). But then, once they entered into the room and saw the child, what did they do? "They fell down and worshiped him" (v. 11). Or think of the various reactions to Jesus's miracles. After our Lord spoke to the dead son of a widow, "Young man, I say to you, arise," and the boy sat up and began to speak, how did the mother, the boy, the disciples, and the crowd react? "Fear," we are told, "seized them all . . ." (Luke 7:14, 16).

Or think of the time when Jesus told Simon Peter and the others to put down their nets once again into the water after a fruitless night of fishing. Reluctantly but faithfully Peter agreed. And then what happened? They caught so many fish that the "nets were breaking" (Luke 5:6). They filled two boats full of fish. Now, how would you respond to such a miracle? Leap for joy? Throw a party? Give Jesus a high-five? How did Peter respond? Look at this: "But when Simon Peter saw it [this miracle], he fell down at Jesus' knees, saying, 'Depart from me, for I am a sinful man, O Lord'" (v. 8).

Or think about the time when Jesus's frightened disciples woke him in the middle of a storm at sea, and he simply rebuked the wind and the waves with his word. He said, "Peace! Be still" (Mark 4:39), and the wind ceased and there was a great calm. Now, there was a great calm outside the boat, but inside there was a new fear, a greater fear—not a fear of drowning or of death but of God. "And they were filled with *great fear* and said to one another, 'Who then is this, that even the wind and the sea obey him?'" (v. 41). Or think of when that very question was answered at the Transfiguration—by God! "This is my beloved Son, with whom I am well pleased; listen to him" (Matt. 17:5). How did Peter, James, and John respond? "When the disciples heard this, they fell on their faces and were terrified" (v. 6).

While each of these Gospel narratives illustrates only part of what is meant by "fear of the Lord," each frame seen together fills in the picture. Seen together we see fear and faith.[10] Seen together we see Jesus's greatness, power, and holiness, along with our recognition of lack of greatness, power, and holiness. Seen together we see the attitude of submission and respect and dependence and worship. Seen together we see "the fear of the Lord."

No Fear of God before Their Eyes

And seen together, we see why today such a sight is unseen. As it was in Paul's day, so it is in ours: "There is no fear of God before their eyes" (Rom. 3:18).[11] For most people today there is no fear of God because, as I see it, they don't understand who they are dealing with. Jesus has been raised from the dead. Jesus has ascended into heaven. Jesus now sits exalted at the right hand of God the Father. This is the Jesus to whom heaven's highest creatures fall down and worship (Revelation 4–5). There is no fear of God in people's eyes today because they have the wrong Jesus before their eyes! They don't understand who he is, what he has done, and what he will do. They treat him like a pauper when he is the prince, the heir of David's eternal kingdom, the very God to whom they ought to bow down and adore.

In this way they are like that one thief on the cross next to Jesus who joins the crowd in taunting and teasing our Lord: "If you are the Christ of God, the king, his chosen one, then save me and save us and save yourself." People are just like that today. They don't understand who Jesus is. They don't understand the purpose and the power of the cross. And that is why they won't heed the words of the other thief, who recognized his sin and his need for Jesus as savior and therefore turned to his thieving buddy and said, "Don't you *fear God*, and don't you understand we deserve to die?" And it is why they won't follow this thief's example of faith: "Jesus, remember me when you come into your kingdom."[12]

This thief understood his need for Jesus as did former slave trader turned hymn writer John Newton, who wrote:

> Amazing grace! How sweet the sound
> That saved a wretch like me!
> I once was lost, but now am found;
> Was blind, but now I see.
> 'Twas grace that taught my heart *to fear* . . .

Is that what you need today? Are you ready to begin the way of wisdom? Do you need this amazing grace, a grace which teaches our hearts to fear, to fall before the Lord, even our Lord Jesus Christ, and cry out, "I'm a wretch, I'm blind, I'm lost; cure me, find me, open these eyes"?

The End of Fools

"The fear of the LORD is the beginning of knowledge." But that's not the end of it. Proverbs 1:7, which has been the focus of this chapter, has another lesson to teach us, for it continues, "*Fools* despise wisdom and instruction." What does it mean to fear the Lord? We've spent most of our time thus far answering that question. But there are two other important questions raised by the second half of this verse: first, who doesn't fear the Lord? Answer: fools! "Fools despise wisdom and instruction."[13] Second, what does it matter? Fools despise wisdom. So what? The fear of the Lord is the beginning of knowledge, but what is the end of fools? What becomes of those who reject God's wisdom? Well, that's what much of Proverbs and some of the rest of Scripture is all about. And that's what I want to explore with you now briefly.

Seven Deadly Sins

I imagine you're familiar with the phrase "ship of fools." It was a common medieval motif used in literature and art, especially religious satire.[14] One such satire is Hieronymus Bosch's famous oil painting by that name (c. 1490–1500), which now hangs in the Louvre in Paris. In this marvelous work, which is filled with wonderful symbolism, it shows ten people aboard a small vessel and two overboard swimming around it. It is a ship without a pilot (captain), and everyone onboard and overboard is too busy drinking, feasting, flirting, and singing to know where on earth the waves are pushing them. They are fools because they are enjoying all the sensual pleasures of this world without knowing where it all leads. Atop the mast hangs a bunch of dangling carrots, and a man is climbing up to reach them. Yet above those carrots we find a small but significant detail: a human skull. This is the thirteenth head in the painting, unlucky in every imaginable way. The idea is that these twelve fools, who think all is perfect, are sailing right to their demise. The only pilot on board, the only figure leading the way, is death.

In its own artistic way, the book of Proverbs takes us onboard this ship and shows us what happens when the sins common but fatal to us are the wind beneath our sails.[15] It shows us the destination—what normally happens *in this world*—of those who reject wisdom.

There are a number of points to the Christian worldview that are hard for a non-Christian to comprehend, but this one, I believe, isn't one of them. Christian and non-Christian alike know what usually happens to the man who loves himself too much (pride) or eats too much (gluttony) or works too little (sloth) or can't keep his head (anger). Does this world, even this fallen world, rise up and call him "blessed"? No. Even this world, with its upside-down values, knows it does not profit a man to do whatever his heart and hands and mouth so desire.

For example, if a woman cannot control her tongue and quarrels with everyone, soon she will find that whatever friends she once had are now gone and that even her dear husband has decided, as Proverbs puts it in three different places, that it would be better for him to live on the corner of the roof than in the house with her (21:9; 25:24; 27:5; cf. 12:4b). Or if a man thinks that he can "carry fire next to his chest and his clothes not be burned" (6:27), that is, if he thinks he can indulge his every sexual fantasy and appetite void of any consequence, he is a fool: "He who commits adultery lacks sense; he who does it destroys himself" (v. 32). He also destroys others—his wife, his family, his workplace, and his society. Just think about how freeing the sexual revolution of the 1960s has been. Oh, it's been as freeing to the United States as Castro to Cuba. Sexual freedom has reaped a harvest of bondage and destruction: relationships severed, trust forever lost, families torn apart, and diseases spreading as delicately but as deadly as a sunrise upon the Saharan sand.

Seven Damning Sins

God's Word teaches us that sin has temporal consequences, and the realities of this world confirm this truth. But God's Word doesn't stop here. It also speaks of how sin has eternal consequences: judgment and everlasting separation from God.

Now, you might say, "Well, that's fine, but I don't believe in any of that stuff. I can believe that 'sin' (if you want to call it that) exists. And I can believe that 'sin' has certain consequences. But I can't believe that 'sin' has consequences beyond this life."

Well, let's think about this. I don't know, maybe you're right. Maybe you're right and the Bible is wrong. Maybe you're right and Jesus is wrong. Someone has to be right and someone wrong. Either I speak of hell with great seriousness, or I use "hell" as a swear word. Either there are eternal consequences for sin or there are not. But think about it this way. First, if what the Bible says about sin and its temporary consequences is true (which I think can be proven by shared experience), then might it be possible that what this book says about the eternal consequences for sin is also true? Second, if Jesus is who he claims to be, then might he possibly have more wisdom than, I don't know, every Tom, Dick, and Harry you know, and every Jane, Phil, and Oprah I know?

Greater Than Solomon?

Jesus made many striking claims. Perhaps the most striking was when he referenced the queen of Sheba's visit to King Solomon. Our Lord said, "The queen of the South will rise up at the judgment with this generation and condemn it, for she came from the ends of the earth to hear the wisdom of Solomon, and behold, something greater than Solomon is here" (Matt. 12:42). I love that. Really, Jesus, you are greater and wiser than the wisest man ever to live? Well, what if he is? What if Jesus is, as the apostles testify, wisdom truly and fully and ultimately embodied? What if, as Paul says in Colossians 2:3, "all the treasures of wisdom and knowledge" are hidden in Christ?

Let's think about this a bit further. Jesus certainly spoke like a sage, the sage *par excellence*:

Nothing is covered up that will not be revealed.

The sick need doctors, not the well.

No one can serve two masters.

The measure you give will be the measure you get back.

Many are called, but few are chosen.

A tree is known by its fruits.

One's life does not consist in the abundance of one's possessions.

A city set on a hill cannot be hid.

All that defiles comes from within.

Out of the abundance of the heart the mouth speaks.

Where your treasure is, there your heart will be also.

Do not worry about tomorrow, for tomorrow will bring troubles of its own.

All who exalt themselves will be humbled, and those who humble themselves be exalted.

Whoever seeks to save his life will lose it, but whoever loses it will save it.

The first shall be last, and the last first.[16]

Jesus's proverbial sayings, parables, beatitudes, and many other figures of speech—including his allegories and hyperboles—we might call Proverbs 2.0: conventional wisdom style, unlimited wisdom capacity.[17] Like the sage of Proverbs 1:2–6, Jesus taught practical (Matt. 22:17–22), intellectual (22:23–33), moral (6:1–18), and mysterious wisdom (13:36–40) to the young (18:1–4), the simple (John 9:27–31), and the already wise (3:1–15). And like Israel's wisdom teachers, he used nature analogies and similes to explain the nature of the kingdom of God. As Alyce M. McKenzie illustrates:

> He heard the sound of seeds hitting the earth. . . . He noticed foxes crawling into their holes, birds settling in their nests, and trees barren of fruit. He noticed . . . reeds blowing in the wind, the beauty of lilies, and the behavior of vultures.[18]

Jesus certainly was a wisdom teacher, surpassing even Solomon. But he was and did more than that: he also lived a life of wisdom, far better than Solomon did. Unlike Solomon (or any Old Testament character), our Lord, in his human nature, perfectly and perpetually feared the LORD. From the cradle to the cross, he walked the way of wisdom. Even denying himself the usual rewards of godliness—long life, a good reputation, a strong marriage, healthy children, material prosperity—he submitted to the wise but inexplicable will of his Father, enduring a crown of thorns, a humiliating death, and spiritual abandonment, so that in his sufferings he might become for us the very wisdom and power of God (1 Cor. 1:24).

Jesus taught wisdom, lived wisdom, and finally was Wisdom.[19] Like Lady Wisdom of Proverbs, Jesus invited all to embrace him to find life.[20] Jesus—as the bread of life; the living water; the light of the world; the true vine; the door; the resurrection and the life; the way, and the truth, and the life—invited people to eat, drink, see, bear fruit, open the door, and find eternal life.[21]

So, if it is true that Jesus taught, lived, and was/is Wisdom, then wouldn't you listen to what he has to say? Wouldn't you hear and heed his warm words of invitation—"Come to me, all who labor and are heavy laden, and I will give you rest" (Matt. 11:28)—as well as his merciful words of warning—"Do not fear those who kill the body but cannot kill the soul. Rather *fear him* who can destroy both soul and body in hell" (10:28)?

You see, if you are onboard the ship of fools, don't be fooled into thinking that just because there's no pilot, there's no destination. The beginning of knowledge is the fear of the Lord. But the end of fools (what happens to those who despise such wisdom) is destruction, in this world and in the next.

"Give Me Repentance"

I mentioned at the beginning of this chapter those six children's classics, one of which is *Aladdin* and another which is *Robinson Crusoe*. The climax of the latter story is when Crusoe, shipwrecked on an island, begins to recognize God's afflicting yet delivering providences in his life. At this time, he starts reading the Bible until finally he comes to the end of himself and prays, for the first time in many years, not for rescue from the island but from his sin. "Jesus, Thou Son of David," he prays, "Jesus, Thou exalted Prince and Saviour, give me repentance!"

Perhaps that is what you need, and perhaps with God's kind providential hand he has led you not to the shore of a remote island, but here to read what his Word has to say. Call out to him today—not for riches, not for a beautiful prince or princess, not for success, not for fame—but for wisdom, for wisdom which comes from above and begins with you and me on our knees.

2

IMPERISHABLE BEAUTY

Proverbs 31:10–31

Many women have done excellently, but you surpass them all.

Charm is deceitful, and beauty is vain, but a woman who fears
the Lord is to be praised.

Give her of the fruit of her hands, and let her works praise her
in the gates.

—Proverbs 31:29–31

What should a man look for in a wife? How does a woman earn the praise of the world around her? Those are the two questions this text tackles, questions which are as relevant today as they were three thousand years ago.

If you look at the first verse of Proverbs 31, you will see that the author here is not King Solomon (1:1), but King Lemuel or, more specifically, his mother: "The words of King Lemuel. An oracle that *his mother* taught him."[1] Lemuel's mother taught him three timeless truths. She taught him to let mercy and justice uphold his throne, to be the voice of the voiceless (31:6–9). She taught him to keep his head clear and sober, so as to rule righteously (vv. 4–5). And she taught him to marry well (and marry once).

In verse 3 she says, "Do not give your strength to *women*" (plural). This command is in stark contrast to Solomon, who "loved many foreign women" (1 Kings 11:1)—seven hundred princesses and three hundred concubines—who turned his heart from God (v. 3), which in turn divided his kingdom (v. 11ff). "Do not give your strength to *women*," but rather (and here's how verses 1–9 in Proverbs 31 relate to the poem in vv. 10–31[2]), give your strength to a *woman* (singular)—"an excellent wife" (v. 10). In essence, the wise mother says to her son, "My son, find a woman, one wise woman who fears the Lord and the Lord alone (not false and foreign deities); and she will bring you blessing and honor all the days of your life."

What Should a Man Look for in a Wife?

I don't know if you have ever realized this (I hadn't until recently), but Proverbs is primarily addressed to men, or more specifically, young men.[3] In fact, the word *son* is used forty-four times. Compare that to the word *daughter*, which is never used, and you start to get this point.[4] That's not to say that Proverbs has nothing to say to daughters, women, old men, or children, but it is to say that *boys* are the target audience here. That is why I call it, as others have called it, a *book for boys*. I think of it as a young man's devotional, for as there are thirty-one days in many months, so there are thirty-one chapters—a chapter a day to keep foolishness away.

Stay away from the trap and snares of the adulterous woman (eight chapters focus to some extent on that topic).[5] Stay away from the quarrelsome woman (there are five different references to her—you don't want her). But don't stay away from the wise woman, the excellent wife.[6] Listen for her voice. Find her. Embrace her. Hold on to her like you would a rare and precious pearl.

This emphasis on Proverbs being a book for boys is apparent throughout in the language and themes of the book but especially in this final chapter with its poem (31:10–31). In fact, the very structure of this skillfully crafted poem makes this point literally.[7]

First, this poem is an *acrostic*. That is, each verse begins with a successive letter of the Hebrew alphabet (see Table 2.1).[8] In the Hebrew, verse 10 starts with the letter aleph (א), verse 11 with the letter beth (ב), verse 12 with the letter gimmel (ג), and so on, all through the twenty-two letters in this alphabet.

Table 2.1: An Acrostic of Proverbs 31:10–31

א	10 An excellent wife who can find? She is far more precious than jewels.
ב	11 The heart of her husband trusts in her, and he will have no lack of gain.
ג	12 She does him good, and not harm, all the days of her life.
ד	13 She seeks wool and flax, and works with willing hands.
ה	14 She is like the ships of the merchant; she brings her food from afar.
ו	15 She rises while it is yet night and provides food for her household and portions for her maidens.
ז	16 She considers a field and buys it; with the fruit of her hands she plants a vineyard.
ח	17 She dresses herself with strength and makes her arms strong.
ט	18 She perceives that her merchandise is profitable. Her lamp does not go out at night.
י	19 She puts her hands to the distaff, and her hands hold the spindle.
כ	20 She opens her hand to the poor and reaches out her hands to the needy.
ל	21 She is not afraid of snow for her household, for all her household are clothed in scarlet.
מ	22 She makes bed coverings for herself; her clothing is fine linen and purple.
נ	23 Her husband is known in the gates when he sits among the elders of the land.
ס	24 She makes linen garments and sells them; she delivers sashes to the merchant.
ע	25 Strength and dignity are her clothing, and she laughs at the time to come.
פ	26 She opens her mouth with wisdom, and the teaching of kindness is on her tongue.
צ	27 She looks well to the ways of her household and does not eat the bread of idleness.
ק	28 Her children rise up and call her blessed; her husband also, and he praises her:
ר	29 "Many women have done excellently, but you surpass them all."
ש	30 Charm is deceitful, and beauty is vain, but a woman who fears the LORD is to be praised.
ת	31 Give her of the fruit of her hands, and let her works praise her in the gates.

Second, and more importantly, this poem is a *chiasm*. A chiasm is a structural device often employed in Hebrew poetry in which the point of the poem is highlighted both by its separateness (it alone has no parallel) and by its central placement (it is found in the middle).[9] Look at Table 2.2 and you will see what I am saying.

Table 2.2: The Chiastic Structure of Proverbs 31:10–31[10]

A. The high value of an excellent wife (v. 10)
  B. Her husband's benefits (vv. 11–12)
    C. Her industrious work (vv. 13–19)
      D. Her doing kindness (v. 20)
        E. Fearless [of the present] (v. 21a)
          F. Clothing her household and herself (vv. 21b–22)
            G. Her husband's renowned respect (v. 23)
          F´. Clothing herself and others (vv. 24–25a)
        E´. Fearless [of the future] (v. 25b)
      D´. Her teaching kindness (v. 26)
    C´. Her industrious work (v. 27)
  B´. Her husband's (and children's) praise (vv. 28–29)
A´. The high value of an excellent wife (vv. 30–31)

Do you see how the poet takes several similar themes and, starting from both ends, works his way to the center? If we begin from the outside, the themes in the first and last lines are identical: the high value of an excellent wife. Then, as we continue to move from the outside inward, we see how the theme of an earlier section parallels a later theme. This "narrowing-in" on the main theme takes us to the center: the poetic and practical point of the passage. What is the central point of Proverbs 31:10–31? It is verse 23: "Her *husband* is known in the gates when *he* sits among the elders of the land."

Now, you might think, "Her husband? How is that so? How can this poem be about 'him'? That doesn't make sense! Just look at the start and the subject of almost every sentence. Look at all those verses where 'she' is the subject (vv. 12, 13, 14, 15, 16, 17, 18, 19, 20, 21, 22, 24, 25, 26, 27). This poem is not about the husband but about the wife! And then verse 23, well maybe it's just some kind of poetic digression, or maybe this 'husband' is just a foil. Yes, that's it! He's a foil to the strong, effective, and successful woman.[11] For while she is running to and fro, busy about all her work, what's he doing? Sitting! He sits at the city gate. While she is working her hands to the bone—planting, buying, selling, weaving, sowing—he appears to be sitting on his."

It is natural to think this. Yet whatever our initial impression might be, we must recognize that verse 23 is no digression from the author's aim. "She" might be the main character, but "he" is the author's audience.[12] He is the one who is to see the point of this *point*: this woman, the one described in every verse but one, is "the kind of wife a man needs in order to be successful in life."[13] Verse 23, which declares the respect her husband receives by the most important leaders of the city—"the elders"—is no mistake. Instead, it is the bull's-eye of this poem's target, striking at the heart of its intended audience, young men. This is a book for boys, and this is a poem for boys.

This doesn't mean that the poem has nothing to teach a single woman, married woman, married man, or very young child. If you just read along like you are peeking over the shoulder as someone writes in his journal, you'll find plenty of thoughts that you can apply directly to yourself. But it is the young man, the single man, who especially needs to listen, to heed God's Word here.[14] He must let what is taught here be like corrective eye surgery, removing whatever blocks his vision of true beauty—of what to look for in a wife.[15]

The Beauty Marks of the Excellent Wife

So what should young men be looking for? What are the essential beauty marks of an excellent wife? The first mark to notice comes in verse 10. The question, "An excellent wife who can find?" implies an answer not of impossibility but of rarity. In other words, it is hard to find and obtain a godly wife. The second half of verse 10 follows naturally. It describes her value: "She is far more precious than jewels." Like a colorless, clear, carefully cut, two-carat diamond, an excellent wife is both rare and valuable.

Verse 11 tells us that she is trustworthy and profits her husband: "The heart of her husband trusts in her, and he will have no lack of gain." Martin Luther said, "The greatest gift of God is a pious spouse who fears God and loves his [church], and with whom one can live in perfect confidence."[16] The blessed husband of the woman described here has full confidence in his wife in every area of life.[17] He trusts in her good sense, her fidelity, and her labor.

Beyond being trustworthy, this woman is likewise enriching. As we will see later, she is enriching in an economic, social, and spiritual sense. She is the type of woman who brings in more money than she spends, gains respect *for* her husband, and strengthens and encourages her husband's faith. In sum, "She does him good, and not harm, all the days of her life" (v. 12).

Despite this description, we need not think that a good wife must be perfectly good. This is, after all, an idealized portrait in which all blemishes have been intentionally and artistically left out. So we don't see her flaws. What we see, though, is that she is good to him—not perfectly good but consistently good.

So, according to the first three verses, we see that the excellent wife is trustworthy, enriching, and consistently good. These characteristics are likely not a surprise to anyone. But when we come to the next part of our text (vv. 13–19), we find something perhaps surprising. We find that the majority of this poem highlights this woman's work ethic and industry.

I can tell you from experience that when a group of high school or college guys get together they almost inevitably talk about girls. And I can tell you that the last thing you will hear from such an assemblage of young men, whether or not they are Christian, is their praising the industriousness of a particular member of the opposite sex. Verses 13–19, which describe this significant aspect of a godly woman, are likely not what makes most young men brim with excitement. Yet the point here is that it should!

Boys, what should you look for? Well, look at all the action verbs in these verses:

> She *seeks* wool and flax, and *works* with willing hands. She is like the ships of the merchant; she *brings* her food from afar. She *rises* while it is yet night and *provides* food for her household and portions for her maidens. She *considers* a field and *buys* it; with the fruit of her hands she *plants* a vineyard. She *dresses* herself with strength and *makes* her arms strong. She *perceives* that her merchandise is profitable. Her lamp does not go out at night. She *puts* her hands to the distaff, and her hands *hold* the spindle. . . . She *makes* linen garments and *sells* them; she *delivers* sashes to the merchant. (vv. 13–19, 24)

I know these verses describe the typical labors of a middle- or upper-class woman before the Industrial Revolution, but I'm convinced that her work attitude and work ethic should transcend time.[18] The wife you want should be industrious. Period. Exclamation point!

At my in-laws' house there is an old portrait of the family. Within the large frame there are six smaller frames that contain the names and meanings of the various family members. One of those names is Emily, a name that goes well, in my opinion, with the surname O'Donnell. "Emily O'Donnell"—it's quite lovely. The first time I saw this portrait, I laughed when I observed that my wife's name, Emily, means not "delicate summer rose" or "pure as mountain water" but rather "industrious." Industrious? Yes, industrious! Yet, after twelve years of marriage, I now know there is no more fitting word than that one for my delicate, beautiful, and pure wife.

Boys and men, we are to marry an Emily (not my Emily, get your own), that is, an industrious woman; a woman who, as verse 27 puts it, "looks well to the ways of her household and does not eat the bread of idleness" (cf. 14:1). You see, the virtuous wife is a "Mary no less than a Martha," as Charles Bridges nicely words it.[19] She sits at the feet of Christ in utter devotion, but she also stands upon her feet showing her devotion to him through her service to others.

It is as a result of her industry, demonstrated in her business and domestic skills, that we find next (quite naturally) that she is fearless of the future: "She is not afraid of snow for her household, for all her household are clothed in scarlet" (31:21). "Strength and dignity are her clothing, and she laughs at the time to come" (v. 25). Her industry in the past and present gives her a healthy hope for the future. She fears nothing, least of all what is to come. Even the arrival of winter does not chill her optimism, for her children are "clothed in scarlet" and she with "fine linen and purple" (v. 21–22). Her household is dressed like royalty because the woman of the house is dressed in the virtues of "strength and dignity."

Self-Sufficient yet Selfless

So far we've seen that a Proverbs 31 woman is trustworthy, profitable, reliable, industrious, and fearless of the future. She is also, as verse 20 tells us, compassionate and selfless: "She opens her hand to the poor and reaches out her hands to the needy."

Throughout this poem we see a woman who is self-sufficient in the best sense of the word; as verse 22 states, "She makes bed coverings *for herself*." Yet, while she is *self-sufficient*, she is not *selfish*. Every activity mentioned in these twenty-two verses entails her work on behalf of others. Her hands are busy working for her husband and household but also for those who are most needy in her society. Even the wisdom she possesses she distributes freely to all who will listen. As verse 26 says, "She opens her mouth with wisdom, and the teaching of kindness is on her tongue."

So it is partly upon the foundation of *her* rich reputation that her husband's reputation has developed and flourished; as verse 23 says, "Her husband is known" (or "respected" or "esteemed" or "made famous," cf. 12:4). Her husband is well known at the gates where he sits among the elders of the land.

In the ancient world, it was "at the gates"—the main opening in the city wall—that "business was transacted, affairs were settled, and the news of the community circulated."[20] Men in most ancient societies traveled to the city gates to perform their livelihood. The man in this poem, however, is so respected by his peers that "he sits among the elders of the land" (31:23). He sits on the city council. He sits in a position of rule and judgment over the affairs of the city. In case we miss it, the point is captured well in the familiar but so often true cliché: behind every great man is a great woman. This man's *sitting* is very much related to his wife's *serving*.[21]

In view of her godly reputation, it's no wonder that everyone who knows her ends up praising her (cf. 11:16a). Her city praises her: she is praised "in the gates" (31:31; cf. Job 29:7ff.). Her children praise her: "Her children rise up and call her blessed" (Prov. 31:28a). Her husband also gives her praise, saying, "Many women have done excellently, but you surpass them all" (v. 29). To those who know her best, she is considered "the greatest wife and mother in the world."[22] The author of Proverbs holds the same opinion: "Charm is deceitful, and beauty is vain, but a woman who fears the LORD is to be praised" (v. 30). Here's the summary and conclusion: charm and beauty and personality and prettiness are "inadequate reasons to marry a girl."[23] A young man on the move to find a wife should move in the direction of a woman who "fears the LORD."[24]

It's not that attractiveness has nothing to do with love. (*Eros* and *agape* are not inseparable loves.) We need only flip a few pages forward in our Bibles to the Song of Solomon to find another divinely inspired poem that extols the physical beauty of a woman and highlights, with vivid description, the attractiveness of her body (Song 4:1–15; cf. Prov. 5:18–19).[25]

Nice legs are nice. Tan skin is tantalizing. But the point of this poem in Proverbs is this: to select a wife based on these characteristics (alone) is a foolish decision. Charm is so *often* deceitful. Beauty is *always* fleeting. But a woman who fears the Lord has temporary and eternal value. Her husband will reap benefits from her in this life and the next.

So while the Song of Solomon, we might say, opens our eyes to the physical beauty of the love relationship between man and woman, Proverbs 31 in a sense closes our eyes in order that we might look not upon the outward appearance but "on the heart" (1 Sam. 16:7b).[26]

I know how hard it is for men, especially young men, to see things this way. It's easy to be like Samson, not in his strength but in his stupidity. Samson let his eyes be his demise. When he saw a nice-looking woman—first a lovely little Philistine and then the delightful-to-the-eyes Delilah—he had to have her. Ah, but they always had him, didn't they? Do you remember the end of Samson's story? After he finally gave up the secret of his strength to that woman, what happened? Well, he was quickly captured, and then ironically but quite intentionally (in God's providence) his eyes were gouged out.

Don't be like Samson.

Be like Boaz.

When Boaz came on the scene in the second chapter of the book of Ruth,[27] he was kind, gracious, and intrigued by this poor, young widow because of what he *heard* about her. All that she had done for her mother-in-law and how she had left her homeland to come to Bethlehem—to make the Lord her God[28]—was all "fully told" to him (see Ruth 2:8–12). Boaz liked what he heard. He selected a wife, as one of our best English poets put it, "by his ear" rather "than [by] his eye."[29] Oh, that we men would look at women through our ears first!

The book of Proverbs is a book that seeks to teach young men how to pursue, find, and embrace wisdom. The similarities between the "excellent wife" at the end of Proverbs and the various descriptions of wisdom throughout the book are not accidental.[30] Near the beginning of the book (in 1:20–23 and later in chapter 8) stands a female personification of wisdom. We find Lady Wisdom calling out for young men to embrace her. At the end of the book, Lady

Wisdom has come to life in the character of the excellent wife, calling all young men to embrace her.[31] Duane Garrett nicely summarizes: "In Proverbs wisdom is not merely or even primarily intellectual; it is first of all relational."[32] (We talked about this in the last chapter.) Through fearing God, heeding his parents' teaching, and finding a good wife, a young man obtains wisdom.

Every man faces the same choice: the choice between Lady Folly and Lady Wisdom. If you embrace the adulterous or quarrelsome woman, you will obtain folly. But if you embrace the godly woman, you will obtain wisdom:

> Wisdom cries aloud in the street, in the markets she raises her voice; at the head of the noisy streets she cries out; at the entrance of the city gates she speaks: "How long, O simple ones, will you love being simple?" (1:20–22a)

How Does a Woman Earn the Praise of the World Around Her?

So, what should a man look for in a wife? That is the first question this text tackles. The second, more indirect, but ever so pertinent question is, how does a woman earn the praise of the world around her? Think for a minute: how would *Cosmopolitan* magazine answer that question? How would CNN, most college professors, or the neighbors next door answer it? How would you answer it? Most people would say a woman earns praise (the same way a man does) through obtaining power, amassing her own personal fortune, or reaching a high level of professional success—by climbing the corporate, political, social, or academic ladder.

But God's Word says something very different. It says a woman is not praiseworthy simply for holding a powerful position, making lots of money, or being extraordinarily famous. She is to be praised because she is a *servant,* a servant of all—her husband, her children, her city, and the poor. She is praised because she has sacrificed and submitted self and self-glory. That is why everyone stands up and applauds her at the end of this poem.[33]

In this way Christianity turns the world on its head. Contrary to popular thought, both then and now, the Word of God teaches that women (and men) were not created for self-fulfillment. Can you believe that? Jesus summarized this teaching quite well when he said, "If anyone would come after me, let him deny himself and take up his cross and follow me" (Matt. 16:24). How do those three steps to success sound to you? Would you like to sign up to be a Christian today? "Let's see, Jesus, you want from me self-denial, sacrifice, and submission. Is that right?" Yeah, that's right!

Self-denial, sacrifice, and submission—how contrary to the way we're wired. Do you ever have a tough time motivating yourself to be selfish? Do you ever wake up in the morning and say, "Today I need to think more about me. I'm really struggling to put myself first"? Late last December did you make a New Year's resolution similar to this: "I resolve to get out of this rut of putting others first. This year it's all about me! Me first, me second, and me third"? Selfishness is natural. Servanthood is supernatural.

Do you see this supernatural woman before your eyes today? And doesn't she encourage you when you're "stuck" with those often thankless and seemingly mundane jobs? Changing diapers. Cleaning house. Loading laundry. Cooking dinner. Disciplining children. Your labor is not in vain! "Beauty is vain"—it's slowly going bye-bye—but service to others, there is nothing fleeting or frivolous about it. And nothing is more fulfilling, praiseworthy, and liberating than that.

Those you have bent down to serve will rise up to praise God for you. That's the strange twist of it. "Whoever finds his life will lose it, and whoever loses his life," says Jesus, "for my sake will find it" (Matt. 10:39). That's the paradox of Christian living. The exalted will be humbled, the humbled will be exalted (cf. Prov. 3:34 lxx; James 4:10; 1 Pet. 5:6), eventually and eternally. On the last day, God will say to those who have followed this program of self-denial, sacrifice, and submission, "Well done, [my] good and faithful servant" (Matt. 25:21, 23; cf. John 13:1–17). It's okay to be a servant. In God's kingdom it's the greatest job of all!

A Servant Like Christ

I know that pride is the deadliest sin, but I just can't help it as I think about this concept of humble service—I'm so proud of Christianity's view of greatness. I'm so proud because it's so spot-on. Jesus taught, "But many who are first will be last, and the last first" (Mark 10:31). And he said to his disciples who were fighting with one another about who was the greatest, "If anyone would be first, he must be last of all and servant of all" (9:35). That's so remarkable, isn't it? Yet what is even more remarkable than the teachings of Jesus *is Jesus himself.*

We Americans love equality, don't we? It's a big deal to us, and there are good, historical reasons for that. We have our Equal Rights Amendment and our Declaration of Independence, which states that "all men are created equal." But what is extraordinary about Jesus—one of the many extraordinary things about our Lord—is that he, in the language of Philippians 2,

> did not count equality with God a thing to be grasped, but *made himself nothing*, taking the form of *a servant*, being born in the likeness of men. And being found in human form, [what is more] *he humbled himself* by becoming obedient to the point of death, even death on a cross. (vv. 6–8)

Jesus embodied his own teaching. He walked his talk. But that's not the end of the story. This humble descent was a descent into greatness. Philippians 2 continues and concludes:

> Therefore God has highly exalted him and bestowed on him the name that is above every name, so that at the name of Jesus every knee should bow, in heaven and on earth and under the earth, and every tongue confess that Jesus Christ is Lord, to the glory of God the Father. (vv. 9–11)

We serve a king, our Lord Jesus Christ, who was exalted because of his servanthood. In his humility, Jesus took the punishment for all our arrogance, enmity, and vainglorious desire for equality with God—"God made him who had no sin to be sin for us" (2 Cor. 5:21a NIV)—so that through faith in this gospel (Phil. 1:27), "we might die to sin and live to righteousness" (1 Pet. 2:24); so that we might clothe ourselves with all humility (Col. 3:12; cf. 1 Pet. 3:8).[34]

So don't be fooled into thinking greatness comes from receiving power and prestige or fame and fortune here and now. The wisdom of God's Word teaches us that a woman (and a man) earns praise from God and from those around her through self-denial, sacrifice, and submission.

Two Very Different Questions, One Very Similar Answer

What should a man look for in a wife? He should look for someone who models the servanthood of Christ. And how does a woman earn the praise of the world around her? Well, nearly the same way: by being a servant like Christ, by putting self last and others first.

WHY WORK?

Ecclesiastes 1:1–11

The words of the Preacher, the son of David, king in Jerusalem.

Vanity of vanities, says the Preacher, vanity of vanities! All is vanity.

What does man gain by all the toil at which he toils under the sun?

A generation goes, and a generation comes, but the earth remains forever.

—Ecclesiastes 1:1–4

n her poem *The Orchard*, contemporary American poet Mary Oliver writes:

> I have dreamed
> of accomplishment.
> I have fed
>
> ambition.
> I have traded
> nights of sleep

for a length of work.
Lo, and I have discovered
how soft bloom

turns to green fruit
which turns to sweet fruit.
Lo, and I have discovered

all winds blow cold
at last,
and the leaves,

so pretty, so many,
vanish
in the great, black

packet of time,
in the great, black
packet of ambition,

and the ripeness
of the apple
is its downfall.[1]

Our Work: the Minor and Major Vanities of It

The book of Ecclesiastes is a God-inspired look into what Mary
Oliver called "the great, black packet of time . . . [and] of ambition."
It examines how "the ripeness of the apple is its downfall." That
is, it shows us the futility of our work in this world, even our most
fruitful work. Like an apple that ripens only to fall to the ground
and decay, so our work eventually comes to nothing. That is what
"the Preacher, the son of David, king in Jerusalem" (1:1) saw many
years ago,[2] and that is what we will see now in our exploration of
Ecclesiastes 1:1–11.

We begin with verses 2–3. Here we find the opening cry and question: "Vanity of vanities . . . vanity of vanities! All is vanity. What does man gain by all the toil at which he toils under the sun?" Here, as Solomon speaks of life "under the sun" (i.e., earthly life apart from God), we quickly realize it is an overcast day. Darkness looms on the distant horizon, a precursor to an ominous storm— one that will inevitably envelope us. From 1:2 until 12:8 we will ride out this storm, for as the book opens so it ends, striking us with its sober superlative: "Vanity of vanities, vanity of vanities! All is vanity." And between these bookends, like relentless lightning bolts striking a house of hay, the word "vanity" (*hevel*) will come down upon us thirty-eight times, setting aflame all we have sought to accomplish. Outside of God, every human endeavor is like smoke that vanishes into the engulfing air.[3] This explains the nature of Solomon's question. In 1:3 (cf. 3:9; 5:16), he asks pessimistically, "What does man gain by all the toil at which he toils under the sun?" The answer: nothing! All our toil vanishes into the great, black packet of time.

Nothing New

In 1:4–11, like an overly critical building inspector, Solomon shows us what's wrong with our work. Later in Ecclesiastes he will point out what I call "minor problems"—that our willingness to work often comes from impure motives such as envy (4:4); that our work, if profitable, often leads to sleepless nights (5:12; cf. 2:23); and that all the wealth from our work must be bequeathed to someone who doesn't deserve it and who may foolishly squander it (2:18–19). The two major problems in our construct, however, he addresses in 1:4–11.

The first major problem is that our work adds *nothing new* to this world.

What has been is what will be, and what has been done is what will be done, and there is nothing new under the sun. Is there a thing of which it is said, "See, this is new"? It has been already in the ages before us. (vv. 9–10)

We might balk at this strongly pessimistic view. In fact, we might instead boast of how "new and improved" everything is. This is the information age! The day of discovery! The time of technology! However, I don't think we would balk or boast if we had our perspective appropriately shaped by a proper understanding of these two important insights.

First, the Wisdom Literature of the Bible most often deals with general realities. The book of Job is different, as are Psalm 73 and other wisdom texts. Such texts speak of the exceptions to the rule. But in general, the wicked are punished and the righteous prosper. In general, sloth leads to poverty and adultery to discord. Thus, in general, most of our work is not new.

Think of it this way. Many people today still labor with their hands, doing work very similar to what was done thousands of years ago. There is not much difference between the guy who dug ditches in Jerusalem in 942 BC and the guy who digs them today for Shanghai's sewer and sanitation department. And those who don't work with their hands, even if they are part of the new division of a new company selling a new product that was newly invented, what they actually do isn't all that new: an owner is still an owner, a manufacturer is still a manufacturer, and a salesman is still a salesman. The Apple salesman who sells the latest MacBook is just like the Spanish merchant 550 years ago who sold the newest silk from the Far East. The newest is relative to the age in which we live. But when viewed against the backdrop of human history, the novelty fades.

Solomon describes this unoriginality and repetitiveness of our activities in verses 4–8:

A generation goes, and a generation comes, but the earth remains forever. The sun rises, and the sun goes down, and hastens to the place where it rises. The wind blows to the south and goes around to the north; around and around goes the wind, and on its circuits the wind returns. All streams run to the sea, but the sea is not full; to the place where the streams flow, there they flow again. All things are full of weariness; a man cannot utter it; the eye is not satisfied with seeing, nor the ear filled with hearing.

Here Solomon illustrates the weariness of our work with the sun, the wind, and the sea. These hard-working forces all seem to be quite busy doing something *new* each and every day. But a closer look will show their motion-filled monotony.

First we have the sun. The sun rises and sets—over and over and over again, same old, same old. It never gets anywhere. It never does anything new. Then we have the wind. One day the wind blows south, and then the next day that same wind blows north. What a lot of hot air! What a lot of commotion for so little consequence. It appears that this wind is getting somewhere, when in reality it is just moving in an endless circle. Finally, we have the sea. How is it that the Mississippi River can flow into the Gulf of Mexico and then into the Atlantic Ocean, but that ocean never overflows or gets any deeper? The mighty Mississippi works exhaustively, pushing its waters south every second of every day. But what does it accomplish? What can we see? To the visible eye, it accomplishes nothing.[4] It doesn't affect the ocean's water level. Amazing, isn't it? It is especially amazing in Solomon's context, as he is perhaps thinking of the Dead Sea. The Jordan River incessantly empties into the Dead Sea (from which no river flows out) and yet this sea is "not full" (v. 7a).[5]

Do you see what he's saying? The work of the sun, wind, and waters is like our work upon the earth. We think we are making such a difference, but the irony (the sad reality of the curse) is that the earth remains and we die: "A generation goes, and a generation comes, but the earth remains forever" (v. 4).[6]

Nothing Remembered

The first major problem with our work is that there is nothing significantly or substantially new. The second major problem is that our work won't be remembered. Nothing new, *nothing remembered*. Look at the last verse of our text: "There is no *remembrance* of former things, nor will there be any *remembrance* of later things yet to be among those who come after" (v. 11).

Again we are dealing with generalizations. Every generation will likely remember the work of David, Isaiah, and Paul as well as that of Aristotle, Shakespeare, and Mozart. But what about other famous people—will they be remembered? For example, what about Elvis Presley, Mohammad Ali, John F. Kennedy, and Walt Disney? These men made a recent list of the top ten most famous people of all time. Or consider John Lennon who said that he and his band were "more popular than Jesus"? In 1966, at the height of the Beatles' popularity, Lennon made this prediction:

> Christianity will go. . . . It will vanish and shrink. I needn't argue with that; I'm right and I will be proved right. We're more popular than Jesus now; I don't know which will go first—rock and roll or Christianity.[7]

Well, John, I can tell you which will go first. "Imagine there's no Beatles, it's easy if you try." Just ask the children today to name "the Fab Four." Just name them. With two of these superstars still alive and touring—coming to a city near you—there should be no excuse if our six-year-olds, or twelve-year-olds, or eighteen-year-olds don't know the names of the Beatles. But they probably don't. Or, if they do, just wait a few years—maybe fifteen or fifty or 150—and soon the memory of even the Beatles will be as dead and buried as George and John. The black-and-white silhouettes of these four extraordinarily famous men will soon be but relics in a time capsule buried deep in the Liverpool soil.

Do you think I'm exaggerating? Maybe I am. Maybe I'm not. Let's test your own memory. Can you name any of the rulers of the Aztec Empire? Can you name one of the winners of the 40-yard dash for the first three Olympics? Can you name Europe's most popular musician of the late fourteenth century? Can you name even one of the actors from Shakespeare's guild, who starred in the original *Romeo and Juliet*? Okay. Maybe these are too obscure or too historically removed. Here's an easy one: can you name five pre-1960s vice presidents of the United States?[8]

All of these questions have answers, but most of us (all of us?) have no idea what the answers are. Men and women, many so mighty and glorious in their days, are now mere ashes lying lifeless and unremembered in the ground or scattered upon the endless sea.

Don't be fooled into believing that today's celebrities will forever enjoy popular acclaim, for the fate awaiting the famous is the same fate awaiting the forgotten. Ninety-nine percent of our celebrities— our politicians, our sports heroes, our rock stars, and our actors— will soon be forgotten as well. Today's celebrities are tomorrow's obituaries, and their names are as disposable as the morning paper in which their life stories will be printed.[9]

And if that is what becomes of our celebrities, what becomes of us?

A few years ago I went back to my high school to play in an alumni basketball game. I was the star back in the day. I was the leading scorer of the conference and its MVP. (Yeah, I broke a few school records—woot woot and toot toot.) Yet, when I returned to play in this game (a mere fifteen years after my graduation) almost nobody recognized my face or my name. The alumni team I was on, which had players mostly ten years older or younger than I, didn't know me. I was so frustrated by it that I wanted to pull out the record book, point to my name, and say, "Hey, that's me." But then I looked at the record book and saw that my name was relegated to the bottom of a few long lists. Someone had broken every glorious record I once held. How tragic! I worked so hard back then, only to be forgotten now. What a waste. What vanity. My fame was as short (and embarrassing) as an air ball.

Have you ever had that kind of realistic look in the mirror? I know it's not a pleasant thing to do or see, for we all want to be remembered. And I know that it's this "need" that makes us call our friends and relatives when our name or our picture makes the paper. It is this need that attracts us to Facebook, Twitter, MySpace, and other Internet sites, where our face and our story and even our deepest thoughts can be shared. It is even this need, so twisted and distorted, that makes people do the most banal things on the most banal reality TV shows. And in part it is also what makes a deranged teenager walk into his school and open fire on his own classmates—the need to be remembered.

But what does it all matter? That is what Solomon is getting us to think about. There is one problem with our need to be known and remembered. That problem is death.[10] "Ask not for whom the bell tolls, it tolls for thee." Death stands, almost boastingly, at the end of the corridor of our lives. And death doesn't play favorites. No, death makes a mockery of us all. Death takes all our solid labors and vaporizes them.

Just think about it. Think seriously, soberly, and realistically about it. What good is work? What good is ambition? What good is fame? We must admit that the history of the world appears to be a mass of men and women living, working, and dying—punching in and punching out of this life. Each weekday, as the sun peeks its head over the horizon, we peek our heads over the bed sheets, hit the alarm, wash and feed our bodies, and then spend the remainder of our day working. But working for what? Will we be remembered?

Naked a man comes from his mother's womb, and as he comes, so he departs. He takes nothing from his labor that he can carry in his hand. . . . As a man comes, so he departs, and what does he gain, since he toils for the wind? (5:15–16 NIV)

As the hourglass of human history is turned over, all our accomplishments are slowly buried by the sands of time. All our work, toil, and labors—they're nothing new, nothing that will be remembered.[11] Ah, the tragedy of time and death. Time and death. Time and death. Time. And. Death.

Our Work: Labor in the Lord Is Not in Vain

What are we to do with time and death? What are we to do about the tick and tock of time over our heads and the trapdoor of death beneath our feet? Shall we try to escape? Give up? Party? Those are three widespread ways people deal with this meaninglessness of which Solomon writes: escapism, nihilism, and hedonism.

The Escapist

I have an open invitation to watch Notre Dame Football at a neighbor's house. I enjoy college football, the Irish, and my neighbor and his friends. But I was struck the first time I attended (I'm unfortunately dulled to it now) by the fact that six sensible, well educated, reasonably successful men could gather together and spend a whole afternoon watching and talking only about the game and the games—as we switched from channel to channel, from football to baseball to golf. The most interesting and probing question anyone asked all afternoon was about Wake Forest's team name, Demon Deacons. "Is the school religiously affiliated?" someone asked. That was the deepest question of the day. The answer—via cell-phone technology—came quickly: "Yes, Baptist." The word *Baptist* was the closest we got to talking about the meaning of life.

Perhaps I should have taken that opportunity to grab the remote, hit MUTE, stand up, and ask, "So, guys what kind of work do you do? And does it ever bother you that it won't last forever?" I had no such courage. But can you imagine if I had? Such unorthodox behavior might have started a good conversation or, more likely, a barrage of secret text messages: "Who *is* this guy?" "Please don't invite him again." "Oh, and pass the chips."

Some people, normal "good" people (your neighbors and mine), deal with the bleak reality that Ecclesiastes addresses through *escapism*—not escapism through drugs or alcohol or sex (although some do that), but escapism through watching the game, going to work, playing with the kids, loving the wife, taking the family vacation, and then watching the game, watching the game, watching the game, watching the game. Escapism.

The Nihilist

Others are more philosophical about life. They have attempted a stare-down with time and death, and lost; as such, they have come to the end of themselves.[12] The esteemed Russian novelist Leo Tolstoy was one such person. Despite having written two of the world's greatest works, *War and Peace* and *Anna Karenina,* he considered his life to be a meaningless, regrettable failure. In his book *A Confession*, he wrote,

> My question—that which at the age of fifty brought me to the verge of suicide—was the simplest of questions, lying in the soul of every man . . . a question without an answer to which one cannot live. It was: "What will come of what I am doing today or tomorrow? What will come of my whole life? Why should I live, why wish for anything, or do anything?" It can also be expressed thus: Is there any meaning in my life that the inevitable death awaiting me does not destroy?[13]

That is precisely what Ecclesiastes is getting at, isn't it?

Listen also to Jean-Paul Sartre, the French existentialist philosopher. He was also a novelist and far more depressing than Tolstoy. We might call him nihilistic (*nihil* in Latin means "nothing," as in *ex nihilo*, "out of nothing"). Nihilism teaches that life has no objective meaning or intrinsic value. It's the soil from which postmodern thinking has grown. In his novel *La Nausee* ("Nausea"—an uplifting title indeed!), Sartre writes:

> It was true, I had always realized it—I hadn't any "right" to exist at all. I had appeared by chance, I existed like a stone, a plant, a microbe. I could feel nothing to myself but an inconsequential buzzing. I was thinking . . . that here we are eating and drinking, to preserve our precious existence, and that there's nothing, nothing, absolutely no reason for existing.[14]

Those are depressing, hopeless answers but realistic ones. Why live if life is meaningless? Why bask in the summer sunlight if you're just a leaf that will soon fall from a tree, only to be raked up and burned?

The Hedonist

I know that most people don't come to the nihilist position. That's why the philosophy department will always be smaller than the business/economics department. And that's why, instead of becoming nihilistic, most people become hedonistic. That is, they live for pleasure as the ultimate pursuit. "Let us eat and drink, for tomorrow we die" (Isa. 22:13; 1 Cor. 15:32)—that's their slogan. We know we're dying, so let's live life for all it's got. Peggy Lee's famous refrain still resounds today:

> Is that all there is? Is that all there is?
> If that's all there is, my friends, then let's keep dancing.
> Let's break out the booze and have a ball, if that's all there is.

Just pick up an issue of *People* magazine, as I did the other day while waiting for an oil change, and you will see this lifestyle in living color. Or take an hour this week and read Voltaire (another French philosopher). Read his short and witty novel *Candide,* which I did after the oil change. In this book, Candide is a man who lives in an allegedly "best of all worlds," and yet he experiences one senseless and random suffering after another until finally he abandons the view of his upbringing and embraces hedonism. He decides that since "we can't know the whys and wherefores of what happens in this world," we should just do our "very best to enjoy it while [we] can."[15]

Gospel Glasses

Escapism, nihilism, and hedonism—those are the three prevalent answers our world offers to Ecclesiastes' questions. Yet, thankfully, Ecclesiastes directs us to a vastly different resolution. Although our text does conclude that the answer to the question, "What do we gain from all the toil which we toil under the sun?" is "Nothing," it does not offer this same bleak conclusion to the question, "In light of such vanity—that time and death makes all human work, wisdom, possession, and pleasures 'vain'—how then should we live this temporary life under the sun?" In fact, the answer is not "Nothing." Rather, the answer is "something," something very wonderful. In the words of Jesus it is this: "Seek first the kingdom of God . . . and all these things will be added" (Matt. 6:33). In the words of Solomon it is this: abandon human wisdom, embrace divine wisdom, and then receive all the good things of this life as a gift from God.

This answer is found throughout Ecclesiastes, and most poignantly in its final verses (12:13–14).[16] At this point in the sermon, however, I want to leap from that final coda toward the Gospels, to the person and work of our Lord Jesus Christ.[17] For I want us to view Ecclesiastes 1:4–11 as we should every Old Testament text: with Christian eyes. In other words, I want us to put on gospel glasses and look at this text again so that we might see clearly how what we have in Christ transforms a world shrouded in hopeless blackness into a garden of beautiful and brilliant light, or, to change the metaphor, how it changes a buried seed into a budding flower.

So, why work? Let's put on our gospel glasses to see what we can and should see. First, we see that Jesus's work mattered. Our work—nothing new, nothing remembered. Jesus's work—oh, it was and is *new*, and it certainly has been and will be remembered. Second, the work that we do as enabled by and through him therefore matters too. I'll put it this way: life under the sun (s-u-n) is brief and bleak, but life through the Son (s-o-n) is eternal and joyful.

The Work of Jesus

First, we have the work of Jesus. Here I am not referring to our Lord's work with Joseph as a carpenter (Mark 6:3), although that work mattered, too, because it was all part of his humanity. I am referring to Jesus's work of redemption, which entails not only his death and resurrection but also every deed recorded for us in the Gospels: his obedience to and fulfillment of the law, his proclamation of the gospel of the kingdom, and his miracles. I am referring to every time he was about his Father's business (Luke 2:49).[18]

In John's Gospel the apostle especially emphasizes the work of Jesus. In John 4:34, Jesus says, "My food is to do the will of him who sent me and to accomplish his work." In 5:36, he speaks of the works his Father has given him to accomplish, the very works he is doing. In 9:4, after healing the man blind from birth, he speaks of working "the works of him who sent me" (cf. 10:32ff; 17:4). And when upon the cross he cried out, "It is finished" (19:30), his work of atonement was indeed finished. He had accomplished all the work that the Father had sent him to do.

If we are viewing Ecclesiastes 1:1–11 through our gospel glasses, we first see the significance of Jesus's work. His work is *new*. Through our Lord's life, death, and resurrection, for the first and only time the fundamental problem of humanity's sin has been fixed. Jesus has done what no one before or after him could accomplish: he has reconciled sinners to God (Eph. 2:16). Jesus's work is also *remembered*. At the Last Supper, Jesus established the new covenant, and through our perpetual celebration of his death in the sacrament of Communion we remember his work. Jesus's work is *new* and *remembered*; very few people can claim that. More precisely, many people can claim that, but very few can prove it. It continues to be proven two thousand years after the fact. We prove it every Sunday as we gather together in his name, singing and speaking of him and of what he has done.

A New Workforce

When we come to believe in Jesus—partaking of the new covenant that gives new birth, new life, and a new commandment—we enter into a new workforce.[19] Now what we do (even the smallest, seemingly insignificant act)—if done in faith, for the sake of the gospel, and for the glory of God—matters. Our labor is not in vain.[20] "Vanity of vanities. . . . All is vanity." True, unless we work "as to the Lord," as Paul puts it (Eph. 5:22; 6:7).

Let me illustrate. Don't you just love all the seemingly insignificant details we find in the Gospels? I think about that thief on the cross who saw his sin for what it was, repented, and came to faith in Christ—all while hanging next to Jesus. While dying he was brought to life, while suffocating he breathed in the Holy Spirit. In his profession of faith he said to Jesus, "Jesus, *remember* me when you come into your kingdom." With kingly confidence, Jesus replied, "Truly, I say to you, today you will be with me in Paradise" (Luke 23:42–43). In other words, "Remember you? Of course I'll remember you." Now, you would think that Jesus would have had other more important things to do as he died and went into glory than to remember this criminal. But as Paul writes in 1 Corinthians 8:3, "If anyone loves God, he is known by God." Isn't that extraordinary? Don't take that verse for granted. "If anyone loves God, he is *known* by God."[21]

It is not as though God doesn't know everything and everyone equally. But he especially knows—in a unique, fatherly way—what's going on in the lives of those who believe, who call out to him as sons and daughters through Christ, "Abba! Father!" (see Gal. 4:6–9).[22] And because he knows us, he knows our work. In Philippians 2:12, Paul echoes the Wisdom Literature by instructing believers to "work out your own salvation with fear and trembling." This kind of work is known to God and thus meaningful because, as

Paul goes on to say, it is ultimately God's own work through us: "For it is God who works in you both to will and to work for his good pleasure" (v. 13).

Think of what Jesus said in Matthew 25 about the righteous—those who cared for the hungry, the thirsty, the stranger, the naked, the sick, and the imprisoned. He said, "Truly, I say to you, as you did it to one of the least of these my brothers, you did it to me" (v. 40). Or think of the example in Matthew 26 of what kind of work matters. Do you remember the woman who came to Jesus as he was reclining at table and poured upon his head an alabaster flask of expensive ointment (the equivalent to whole year's wages)? The disciples were indignant. "What a waste!" they said. But Jesus said (and this is just marvelous!):

> Why do you trouble the woman? For she has done a beautiful thing to me. . . . In pouring this ointment on my body, she has done it to prepare me for burial. Truly, I say to you, wherever this gospel is proclaimed in the whole world, *what she has done* will also be told *in memory of her.* (vv. 10–13)

That little act of sacrificial love made it into the Bible, and to this day preachers like me are still writing about her and what she did. Jesus was right! That is one of those Bible prophecies I find most fascinating. It is fulfilled in your reading. She is still being discussed. Her work for Jesus mattered, and so does ours.

In Luke 12, Jesus told the parable of the rich fool. This parable is about a man who worked solely for himself, and as soon as a big barn was built to hold all his stuff, his life was demanded of him (vv. 16–21). He died a fool. After that parable Jesus warned his disciples about working for self and wealth and instead instructed them to "seek his kingdom" (v. 31). That's what lasts. That's what is remembered. That's what is of eternal value. And that's what I'm trying to teach. Your work—all your toil under the sun—is meaningless if not done for God and the building of his kingdom.

Paul gives an analogy in 1 Corinthians 3:9–14. God is building a kingdom. Jesus is the foundation. We are called to build upon that foundation. If we work for ourselves and our own glory, it is like building our own foundation with wood or hay or straw. It will not last. But if we build for the sake of our God, it's like building a medieval cathedral: our names might be forgotten by man, but our names and our work will be remembered by God.[23]

Our work under the sun: nothing new, nothing remembered. But our work in and through the Son: something very new. It is significant, substantial, and something that will indeed be remembered and even rewarded.

An Eternal Orchard

Perhaps you have dreamt of accomplishment, fed ambition, and traded nights of sleep for tomorrow's success. Yet perhaps you have discovered, as Solomon did, how as the seasons change and the leaves twist and tumble to the ground, so our work under the sun will vanish into that great, black packet of time.

But also I hope you have seen, through these gospel glasses, how through Christ your work can be substantial and lasting. Jesus brings life out of death. He takes decaying apples that have fallen to the ground and births from them a vast and beautiful and everlasting orchard, one full of fruit and life and joy.

4

REPINING RESTLESSNESS

Ecclesiastes 12:13–14

The end of the matter; all has been heard. Fear God and keep his commandments, for this is the whole duty of man. For God will bring every deed into judgment, with every secret thing, whether good or evil.

—Ecclesiastes 12:13–14

Can any praise be worthy of the Lord's majesty? How magnificent his strength! How inscrutable his wisdom! Man is one of your creatures, Lord, and his instinct is to praise you. He bears about him the mark of death, the sign of his own sin, to remind him that you thwart the proud. But still, since he is part of your creation, he wishes to praise you. The thought of you stirs him so deeply that he cannot be content unless he praises you, because you made us for yourself and our hearts find no peace until they rest in you.[1]

Above is the famous opening prayer of Augustine's *Confessions*, his autobiography of sorts, wherein he confesses to God and his readers how his restless heart found rest in Christ. He confesses how, after three decades of drinking the desiccāte dregs of sexual immorality and sipping from this world's parched philosophies, he quenched his impoverished soul with the living waters of Jesus Christ. He confesses how he gave up feasting on nature's appetites—drunkenness, lust, anger, and jealousy (Rom. 13:13)—and came instead to feed upon the Bread of Life (John 6:35, 48).

In this chapter, as we come to our second sermon on Ecclesiastes, we come to what I'll call Solomon's *Confessions*.[2] Here "the Preacher" not only confesses his failings but also his findings.[3] He confesses God's remedy for what the poet George Herbert called "our repining restlessness" (our God-given yearning for ultimate rest).[4]

The Dark Descent

In Dante's *Divine Comedy*, Dante is taken on a guided tour of hell and purgatory before he finally comes to heaven, where he experiences "the beatific vision" (an eternal and direct perception of God). Similarly, here in Ecclesiastes, Solomon takes us on a guided tour of his secular life before he invites us to *see* his new vision of God and his new life of blessedness under God's dominion.[5] However, unlike Dante's journey, which took him *up* the seven ledges of purgatory and the nine spheres of heaven, our journey through Ecclesiastes will take us *down* three large steps to three different levels of self-perception. Here we will find ourselves not steadily ascending to a beatific vision but slowly descending to a dark vision—a realistic look at this unsightly, unsaved world.

The Vanity of Worldly Work

The first level down is the work of our hands. You will recall from the last chapter how Solomon taught us—as it relates to our work—that there is nothing new and nothing to be remembered.[6] In Ecclesiastes 1:7, he compared our work to a mighty river that empties into the ocean. Although that river is always "working," it accomplishes little. Just as the water level of the ocean does not rise although millions of gallons pour into it each day, so the significance of our work is never seen—"A generation goes, and a generation comes, but the earth remains forever" (v. 4).

Nothing new, but also nothing remembered. Like the sun in the noon sky, our work now shines, but soon it will set. It will, as the poet Mary Oliver has put it, "vanish into the great, black packet of time."[7] "There is no remembrance of former things," is how Solomon says it, "nor will there be any remembrance of later things yet to be among those who come after" (v. 11). Even the famous will be forgotten.

The Vanity of Worldly Wisdom

The second level down is that of worldly wisdom. To those who believe that knowledge is power and wisdom alone is eternal—that labor of the mind (not hands!) is the answer to our restlessness—Solomon takes them to the Wonderland of Wisdom. At first this place seems ideal. Solomon himself lived here for a while. Yet the more he filled his head, the more the hole in his heart grew. He found wisdom without reference to God limiting and limitless. It was like climbing a wide hundred-step ladder to the roof of a tall tower where at the top you find another hundred-step ladder, not as wide, and then another, slimmer still, and another and another *ad infinitum*.

Such a climb reminds me of a recent best-selling book, *The Know-It-All: One Man's Humble Quest to Become the Smartest Man in the World*. This book records A. J. Jacobs's thoughts after reading the entire *Encyclopedia Britannica* (all 44 million words of it). Most of Jacobs's reflections are humorous, as he discovers funny people, ideas, and events he never knew existed in the world. Yet his conclusion is anything but humorous. In his last observation he says something very telling and very Solomonic: "I know firsthand the oceanic volume of information in the world. [And] I know that I know very little of that ocean."[8]

This man's discovery is but one of the discoveries Solomon made. Throughout Ecclesiastes Solomon laments the limitations and the longevity of human wisdom. What we can "know" (2:14; 3:12, 14; 9:5; 11:9) is often eclipsed by what we "can't know" (3:21; 6:12; 7:24; 8:17; 9:1, 12). We can acquire an infinitude of information yet still not have answers to life's most difficult questions, especially those of injustice: "What is crooked cannot be made straight, and what is lacking cannot be counted" (1:15; cf. 3:16; 4:1–3; 5:8; 7:15–18; 8:14; 9:11). We can learn all sorts of facts but never really contribute much to the advancement of civilization; there is "nothing new under the sun" (1:9). We can learn all this and all that, but ultimately death still has the last laugh: "Then I said in my heart, 'What happens to the fool will happen to me also.' . . . How the wise dies just like the fool!" (2:15–16).

Wisdom is surely better than folly, wealth, strength, and political power. Solomon will admit and teach that (2:13; 4:13; 9:16). Yet the wisdom of this world is as temporal as it is foolish. The idiotic talk-show host with his idiocy and the cerebral scholar with his scholarship both shall die, and both shall quickly or eventually be forgotten. "For of the wise as of the fool there is no enduring remembrance" (2:16). Yes, that tick and tock of time hangs over their heads, and that trapdoor of death lies beneath their feet.

When my wife and I were first married, we lived in Hyde Park three blocks from the University of Chicago, a university which is ranked as one of the best schools in the world. Needless to say, we lived in a highly intellectual environment. Even our neighbor downstairs in our three-flat, who taught salsa dancing, had a PhD in mathematics.

During this time, I worked at Ex Libris Theological Books, a small bookstore that was the local intellectual hub for theological banter. Many notable scholars from Chicago and around the world came through its doors on a daily basis. The owner (who knew everything about books and publishing) was an eccentric man who loved to put these celebrated scholars in their place with his biting sarcasm. One of his favorite putdowns went like this. First, he would ask Mr. or Mrs. Renowned Scholar, "So how's that book you've been working on?" If the scholar would say, "Oh, it just came out last week," or something like that, the owner would reply (and this was his favorite joke), "So is it out of print yet?"

The joke is this: few books, especially scholarly ones, stay in print very long. But the theological point is this: your work is soon to be "out of print," no longer relevant or interesting. People have stopped buying the book. Your wisdom is out of date. Its time of significance has expired.[9]

These scholars would always laugh, but it is really no laughing matter. For you can have worldly wisdom—have the best mind, be the most learned, understand how and why things work—but you can't understand everything, and you can't expect to be remembered for long. Your book will soon be out of print. Your significance will be as lasting as that beautiful bouquet of flowers a loved one will place by your gravestone on the day of your burial. Wisdom—human wisdom—is vanity.

The Vanity of Worldly Pleasures

Neither the first level on Solomon's journey (work) nor the second (wisdom) lead to the place of rest. And so, we journey further down. Down. Down. Down. Next and finally we come to the Place of Pleasure, or if you *desire*—the House of Hedonism.

If both human toil and human wisdom are meaningless, Solomon then reasoned that the purpose of life must be found in the pursuit of pleasure (especially pleasure brought by possessions). He embraced the philosophy and lifestyle that dominates most contemporary college campuses. He joined the fraternity of cheap thrills. He thought life to be a perpetual beer commercial, a continual happy hour without any hangovers. "I thought in my heart," Solomon said, "'Come now, I will test you with pleasure to find out what is good.' . . . [So] I denied myself nothing my eyes desired; I refused my heart no pleasure. . . . [Yet when] I considered all that my hands had done, . . . all was vanity and a striving after wind. . . ." (2:1, 10 NIV; 2:11)

Believing he had struck gold, he took his shovel and began to dig for this hidden treasure, only to find in the end that he had buried himself in his pursuit. Solomon here admits he tried cheering himself with laughter, alcohol, houses, gardens, servants, money, music, and a harem, but still he found himself empty both of meaning and true happiness.[10] Furthermore, what he discovered in his overindulgence was the God-ordained bitter aftertaste, those unexpected, unavoidable, and awful consequences of sin. Solomon lost his kingdom, and those who have followed upon his well-worn path (the path most traveled) have often lost much more—their very souls. For hell is a place filled with ordinary people who loved the fleeting pleasures of this world more than the eternal pleasures of God.

Work, wisdom, pleasure—vanity! Put these things first—make them your pursuit and/or your god—and just see how restful you are. Vanity of vanities! It's all vanity.

Depress You into Dependence

Without a doubt, Ecclesiastes is a dark book, and Solomon has taken us to a very dark place. I know that such darkness—this realistic look at our worldly work, wisdom, and pleasures—can be very depressing. In fact, on several occasions when I have read through Ecclesiastes I have become depressed. I don't get depressed easily or often, and rarely do I get depressed by simply reading the Bible. Yet I gladly accepted this melancholy, because I reasoned that it was a crucial part of our author's intention. It was the way I was supposed to *feel* after reading and thinking about such things.

Our culture, like every culture of which I'm aware, finds no value in depression. We despise it so much that we have taken nearly every medical precaution and treatment available to eliminate it. More and more our world resembles the imaginary world described in Aldous Huxley's famous novel *Brave New World*. In that "world" the government required all its citizens to consume the drug Soma, which made everyone happy and assured peace and prosperity. Yet it provided these benefits at the expense of genuine existence. Human beings sacrificed their humanity.

Ecclesiastes describes not a brave new world but a frightening old world still under the curse of Genesis 3. As such, this book gives no Duloxetine for the disenchanted.[11] It provides no Prozac for the pain. It offers no Soma for the sad soul. Rather, God's Word here prescribes a seemingly distasteful but effective elixir for the real soul. If you are a fallen human living in this fallen world, Ecclesiastes was written to depress you. It was written to depress you into dependence on our joyous God and his blessed will for your life.

This book is God's reminder that if you are attempting to live the "meaningful" secular life—"a life without absolutes, a life lived out of values without reference to God, a life that expects lasting satisfaction from earthbound things"[12]—you are attempting to grasp the unattainable. You are in fact chasing after the wind. You are like a foolish child trying to catch the winds of a hurricane within the strands of a butterfly net.[13]

The best remedy for our depression caused by this realistic observation of the world is not to pop pill after pill but rather to digest once and for all the goodness of God and his Word. The ultimate remedy to meaninglessness and the depression caused by a godless life is God.[14] The Lord alone is what fills the void in human hearts.

And, this end is precisely what we find at the end of Ecclesiastes.

The End of Ecclesiastes

Unlike Dante's *Inferno*, where at its entrance we read, "Abandon all hope ye who enter here," the exit of Ecclesiastes reads, "Abandon all hopelessness." That is, leave the idea that there is no cure to the dis-ease of our disease, no answer to our repining restlessness. Here is the answer! Here is the cure!

> [This is] the end of the matter; all has been heard. Fear God and keep [or "obey"] his commandments, for this is the whole duty of man. (12:13)

The fundamental reason we have been created is to be in relationship with our creator (v. 1), a relationship that reverently acknowledges him as king and seeks in humble submission to heed all his commands (cf. Matt. 28:18–20). That is the answer. That is the end of the matter.[15]

Life on Your Own Terms
The other day I was listening to a classical music station when the host of the program read an advertisement for a retirement home that has as its slogan, "Life on Your Own Terms." I had to laugh as I heard this slogan, because you would think that if anyone would know the vanity of attempting to live life on one's own terms, it would be those who have most experienced what life has to offer.

From reading Ecclesiastes, I believe Solomon would have reacted just as I did. He would have laughed, if not cried, at such foolishness. Solomon had lived "Life on His Own Terms" and found that such living was not a genuine retirement from restlessness. The real retirement from restlessness came only when he began to live "Life on God's Terms," the terms talked about in 12:13.[16]

Fear and Obey—Is There No Other Way?
Perhaps the terms *fear* and *obey* were not the terms you either expected or wanted to read. As Americans we tend to find the words *free* (instead of *fear*) and *independence* (instead of *obedience*) much easier to swallow. The words *fear* and *obey* sound so constricting. After all, we live and breathe and move and have our being in a made-to-order, drive-thru culture. We like things done our way and done fast: fat to skinny, dumb to smart, sad to happy, godless to godly, all with the snap of a finger, the push of a button, the dial of a phone—God in our hearts, fast and easy!

But the Word of God corrects our consumer Christianity and spoiled spirituality. The words *fear* and *obey* are the words God gives us here. Thus they are the precise words he wants us to reflect upon and heed. Fearing God and obeying his commands *is* God's solution, and as such it is the only solution that truly satisfies.[17]

To fear God (i.e., Yahweh)[18] is the central concept of the Wisdom Literature of the Bible.[19] It refers simply to an attitude of submission to, respect for, dependence on, and worship of the Lord (see Eccles. 5:1–7).[20] To fear God embodies faith and hope in God, as well as a genuine love for God. And when one, by the gift of God, possesses the fear of God, sin loses its sweetness and strength, and obedience to the Word of God follows naturally because it becomes the delight of the soul.[21] In the language of the Westminster Shorter Catechism, this "new obedience" (Q. 87) to "the word of God" (Q. 2) for the glory of God (Q. 1) flows from faith in Christ, wherein we "rest upon him alone for salvation" (Q. 86).[22] Therefore, the fear of God and obedience to his revelation are (in both Old and New Testaments) the two inseparable components of genuine faith—"the obedience of faith" (Rom. 1:5; 16:26).[23] For this reason some scholars use the terms *fear* and *faith* interchangeably;[24] and others go so far as to say, "Solomon . . . has anticipated perhaps the deepest mystery of the gospel: The just shall live by faith (Hab. 2:3; Rom. 1:16–17; Gal. 3:11; Heb. 10:38)."[25]

First Motivation: Joy

If you are struggling to embrace the terms *fear* and *obedience* as the answer to our emptiness, God graciously provides two motivations. First, there is the motivation of joy.

The Myth of Sisyphus is the legendary Greek tale of King Sisyphus. This king was condemned to roll a large rock up a mountain, watch it tumble back down, and bring that boulder back up again—for eternity. With this myth in mind, the philosopher Albert Camus wrote an essay entitled "The Myth of Sisyphus" (1942) wherein he argued for what he called "the philosophy of the absurd." Similar to Ecclesiastes, he wrote of "man's futile search for meaning . . . in the face of an unintelligible world devoid of God and eternity." But unlike Ecclesiastes, he argued that our response to this reality should be absurdity. He used the fate of King Sisyphus to illustrate what he means: yes, our lives are like his—we push the rock up and watch it roll down, only to do it again and again and again. But imagine the struggle itself; imagine that being "enough to fill a man's heart." In other words (in Camus's words), "imagine Sisyphus happy."[26]

Well, I don't know about you, but I can't imagine Sisyphus happy. The solution is not turning that frown upside down each time you see that rock roll back down. No, the solution is not revolution against reality but an embrace of the ultimate reality. It is not a rebellion against God but a relationship with him. I'll put it this way: there is no straight line to happiness;[27] one has to go through—and stay with—God to get there.[28]

Here's how it works. If we try to take the straight line from self to happiness, "all the things that we call the 'goods' of life—health, riches, possessions, position, sensual pleasures, honors, and prestige—slip through our hands."[29] But if we go through God (not making idols of creation but living in dependence upon the creator),[30] then whatever we receive from God is seen as a gift that brings joy.[31] Seven times in Ecclesiastes we find a refrain that reflects this "sacramental" philosophy (2:10, 24–26; 3:12–13; 5:17–19; 8:15; 9:7–9;[32] 11:7–10).[33] This philosophy is stated most clearly in 2:24–26a:

> There is nothing better for a person than that he should eat and drink and find enjoyment in his toil. This also, I saw, is from the hand of God, for apart from him who can eat or who can have enjoyment? For to the one who pleases him *God has given* wisdom and knowledge and joy.

Like dark curtains closed across a stage at the start of a play, Ecclesiastes intentionally waits for certain key points in the drama to open the dark drapery and shine the soft light of what life looks like under the reign of God.[34] This stark comparison brings out the beauty of life *under the sun* when directed *by the Son*. When one devotes one's life to the Lord, the mundane march through this passing world becomes a dance of eternal significance. However, it is not as though this world stops being cursed or becomes a substitute for the world to come.[35] We remain in this fallen world eating, drinking, and working,[36] but we do so to the glory of God and to the satisfaction of our souls.[37]

This is the way God works. He delights in irony. He loves to turn the values of this world on their head, that is, right side up. Those who labor only for the mouth will not find satisfaction, but those who hunger and thirst after righteousness, as Jesus said, will be filled (Matt. 5:6).[38]

Second Motivation: Judgment

So one reason to fear and obey is the positive motivation of joy.[39] But if that is not enough to persuade you to abandon the godless life, God graciously extends another motivation: judgment.[40] This is what we find in Ecclesiastes 12:14. After the decree to fear God and keep his commandments we read, "For God will bring every deed into judgment, with every secret thing, whether good or evil."

This verse can be read one of two ways, depending on your relationship with the Lord or lack thereof. If you have yet to realize that God is in charge of this exceedingly complex universe and therefore you are not,[41] then the door to the kingdom of God and a meaningful life remains closed. Your self-made keys simply won't fit the lock no matter how hard and long you try. And so, to you, this final verse serves as a final warning.

The weight of the warning falls on two words: "every" and "secret." Every secret deed is recorded and will be assessed by God. Think of it this way: the day you were born God hit the RECORD button, and the day you die, he'll hit STOP and REWIND and then PLAY. Each and every word, action, and thought—the good, the bad, and the ugly—will be judged by him (cf. 11:9c–12:7). The point is this: if you won't let joy draw you to a saving relationship with God through faith, then let this promise of judgment—this goad—get you. Let this pointed rod that a shepherd would use to move his sheep move you through the narrow gate that leads to life (Matt. 7:13–14). Let this final verse be not a sentence of condemnation but rather a gracious invitation.[42]

However, if you have come to God in faith or fear (whichever term you like best), and if you are willing to live happily under his reign, then this last verse serves as a reminder of the comfort that will come when God balances the scales of justice on the last day—vindicating the righteous and condemning the wicked. The comforting thought is this (and I paraphrase Eccles. 12:13–14):

> Listen, we've come to the end of our journey. After seeing that our work, wisdom, and earth-bound pleasures will eventually float into the air and disappear like smoke, don't you think it's best we bow the knee to our creator—fear him, trust him, worship him, and enjoy him? This is what it means to be truly human. And while injustice abounds—bad things happen to good people and good things happen to bad people—there is no reason to worry. Have faith *now* in the *future*. Believe that the Lord will make everything right. God will straighten the crooked rod. And then he will use that rod to bring every deed into judgment, whether good or evil.

You see, the end of Ecclesiastes brings eschatological hope for those who walk by faith and not by sight.[43] There is no need for despair or pessimism. God will win. The judge of all will do right. Christ will crush the Serpent's head. So be not dismayed. Get off the ash heap. Stand up straight. Walk forward in faith. And count it all joy as you do so.

"Woe to You. . . . Come to Me"

Ecclesiastes compares the words of the wise to "nails firmly fixed" (12:11). With that image, I imagine the book of Ecclesiastes, and especially these last two verses, like two nails firmly fixed to an ancient synagogue's stone wall. There these truths have hung for thousands of years.

I imagine then an apostle of the new covenant—let's say, Matthew—coming along to this wall. And instead of removing these old nails, he has a better idea. He paints a picture, frames it, and then hangs it upon them. Oh, it fits perfectly and looks just right with the limestone. It was as if those two nails were made to hold it.

Like part of a medieval church mosaic, Matthew's painting has two scenes. In the first scene Jesus is depicted as the powerful judge who denounces those who heard his words of wisdom and saw his mighty deeds yet rejected him. "Woe to you," he thunders. "I tell you that it will be more tolerable on the day of judgment for the land of Sodom than for you" (Matt. 11:20–24). Jesus himself will bring "every deed"—every sin of commission and omission—"into judgment."[44]

The second scene, which is directly next to the first, is quite different. Jesus's fist is no longer clenched, and he has discarded his judicial robes. Now as savior he opens wide his arms to any and all who would run to him like "little children" (v. 25):

Come to me, all who labor and are heavy laden, and I will give you rest. Take my yoke upon you, and learn from me, for I am gentle and lowly in heart, and you will find rest for your souls. (vv. 28–29)[45]

You see, when this picture of Matthew 11:20–30 rests upon the nails of Ecclesiastes 12:13–14, we are to see Jesus, the holy judge and loving savior. And we are to embrace him—the very embodiment of divine wisdom (Col. 2:3) and meaningful life (John 10:10). For only in doing so shall we find rest for our restless souls.[46]

5

THE DEVIL'S QUESTION

Job 1:1–12

And the Lord said to Satan, "Have you considered my servant
Job, that there is none like him on the earth, a blameless and
upright man, who fears God and turns away from evil?" Then
Satan answered the Lord and said, "Does Job fear God for no
reason? Have you not put a hedge around him and his house
and all that he has, on every side? You have blessed the work
of his hands, and his possessions have increased in the land.
But stretch out your hand and touch all that he has, and he will
curse you to your face." And the Lord said to Satan, "Behold,
all that he has is in your hand. Only against him do not stretch
out your hand."

—Job 1:8–12

On September 24, 1757, Aaron Burr, the son-in-law of Jonathan
Edwards, unexpectedly died. He was forty-two years old. It
was two days before his public commencement as the first
president of the College of New Jersey (now Princeton University).

During this tragic time his wife, Esther, wrote this letter to a close family friend:

> Your most kind letter of condolence gave me inexpressible delight, and at the same time set open afresh all the avenues of grief, and again probed the deep wound death has given me. My loss—Shall I attempt to say how great my loss is—God only can know—And to him alone would I carry my complaint. . . . Had not God supported me by these two considerations; first, by showing the right he has to his own creatures, to dispose of them when and in what manner he pleases; and secondly, by enabling me to [someday] follow [my husband] beyond the grave, into the eternal world, and there to view him in unspeakable glory and happiness, . . . I should not, long before this, have been sunk among the dead, and been covered with the clouds of the valley. God has wise ends in all that he does. This thing did not come upon me by chance; and I rejoice that I am in the hands of such a God.[1]

Less than eight months after Burr's death, Jonathan Edwards, Esther's father, also died. On April 3, 1758, Sarah Edwards, Jonathan's wife, wrote this to Esther:

> My dear child, what shall I say? A holy and good God has covered us with a dark cloud. O that we may kiss the rod, and lay our hands on our mouths! The Lord has done it. He has made me adore his goodness, that we had him so long. But my God lives; and he has my heart. O what a legacy my husband, and your father, has left us! We are all given to God; and there I am, and love to be.[2]

I wonder what you think of God in times of sorrow, sickness, and suffering. Have you ever thought of God the way that these two widows wrote of him? Do you believe that God has "the right to his own creatures, to dispose of them when and in what manner he pleases"? Do you believe that "God has wise ends in all that he does"? And do you "kiss the rod," even rejoicing in such tragic times that you are "in the hands of such a God"?

In this chapter and the next we come to the book of Job, the story of the kindness and severity of God, and of the sweetness and bitterness of his providence in the life of his servant Job. We come to a book that will teach us that God's love for us is bigger and broader than sentimentality and sympathy and that his will for our lives is vaster and grander than our personal happiness or success. We come to a book that will renew our vows, so to speak, reminding us that we are to be faithful to God—"for better or for worse, for richer or for poorer, in sickness and in health"—that we are to love God, to cherish him as he does us, whether he gives or takes away.

The First Test

This story starts like a summer sunrise, warm and bright with the grace of God:

> There was a man in the land of Uz whose name was Job, and that man was blameless and upright, one who feared God and turned away from evil. There were born to him seven sons and three daughters. He possessed 7,000 sheep, 3,000 camels, 500 yoke of oxen, and 500 female donkeys, and very many servants, so that this man was the greatest of all the people of the east. (Job 1:1–3)

Thousands of years ago atop the world's stage stood the figure of Job—healthy, wealthy, and wise. And yet the earth would soon spin and cool beneath his feet, and the warmth of the eastern star would fade. For into the life of this blessed man came the shadow of the Almighty. It was God who would put Job to the test.[3] That's what we read about in verses 6–12. Set within that cosmic chamber-room, these verses speak of God's initiation and invitation: "Have you considered my servant Job," the Lord says to Satan, "that there is none like him on earth?" (v. 8). Oh, yes, Satan has considered Job. And here's what he thinks of Job's piety: it's fake. Cheap. Spoiled. Shallow. Satan thinks Job's faith is but a refined form of selfishness,[4] so he replies:

Does Job fear God for no reason? Have you not put a hedge around him and his house and all that he has, on every side? You have blessed the work of his hands, and his possessions have increased in the land. But stretch out your hand and touch all that he has, and he will curse you to your face. (vv. 9–11)

Does Job fear God for no reason? That's the Devil's question.[5] He questions the depth, sincerity, and resilience of Job's faith. Take away all the blessings, Satan reasons, and you will find Job's faith to be superficial. Take away his children and wealth, and Job will surely curse God to his face.

Satan doubts Job. But God has confidence in his servant, or at least confidence in his gift—God's own gift of preserving faith. It is perhaps too far a stretch to say that God wants to show off Job's faith in order to glorify his own gift. But it's only a small stretch, for this scene is reminiscent of Jesus's words of confidence to Simon Peter: "Simon, Simon, behold, Satan demanded to have you, that he might sift you like wheat, but I have prayed for you that your faith may not fail" (Luke 22:31–32a). Satan is real. His power is real. But God is in control. God has confidence. God has enough control and confidence to loosen the Devil's chain. "Behold," the Lord says, "all that he has is in your hand. Only against him do not stretch out your hand" (Job 1:12). In other words, "Go ahead, take away all the material blessings, and let's see what happens."[6]

All this was carried out (vv. 13–19). In one day, through human savagery (the Sabeans and Chaldeans) and natural disasters (fire and wind), Satan destroyed all of Job's "perfect" possessions, including his ten beloved children.[7]

This is the first of three tests Job will undergo,[8] and we all know how well he fared with the first. Verses 20–21 are as famous as any in the Bible. Job's immediate reflex was that of both genuine sorrow and genuine praise:

Then Job arose and tore his robe and shaved his head and fell on the ground and worshiped. And he said, "Naked I came from my mother's womb, and naked shall I return. The LORD gave, and the LORD has taken away; blessed be the name of the LORD."

Don't be desensitized because of your familiarity with the story of Job to think that it didn't hurt him to lose all his possessions. Don't think it didn't hurt to lose all his children. Can you imagine? We know from the prologue that Job was no deadbeat dad. Through provisions and prayer he cared daily for the bodies and souls of his children (v. 5). So can you imagine what it must have been like to bury all ten in one day?

In 2009, during one of the worst economic recessions in American history, there were many sad stories of how people responded to economic loss.[9] One such story was that of a Los Angeles man who lost his senses nearly as quickly as he lost his job. Distraught because he could not find work, he took his anguish out on his family. In his upscale San Fernando Valley home, he senselessly shot to death his mother-in-law, wife, and three sons before killing himself.

Such stories shock us. But we are sympathetically shocked, for we know that when a man loses everything he has worked for, despair usually sets in. And what becomes of despair is hard to predict. You might think Job's reaction here was rather stoic. But it wasn't at all. It was passionate and compassionate. He tore his robe and shaved his head, which was an outward symbol of his inward sorrow. It was as if his heart had been torn in two and his head severed from his body. Through the ripping of his robe and the shearing of his scalp, he wept over his unimaginable loss.

Despite this great hardship, Job's immediate response was not to take it out on himself, others, or God (he didn't question or curse his creator) but, rather, in sorrow and humility and faith to prostrate himself upon the earth and worship its sovereign sustainer. There is nothing quite like this in the whole Bible or in the whole world—this extraordinary response to the sovereign will of God—other than our Lord Jesus Christ in the garden of Gethsemane.

Verse 22 understatedly summarizes God's perspective on Job's response to the first test: "In all this Job did not sin or charge God with wrong." The Lord was well pleased with Job's faith.

The Second Test

The Lord, however, was not finished with his severe mercy. Job 2 records the second test. Again, God says to Satan:

> Have you considered my servant Job, that there is none like him on the earth, a blameless and upright man, who fears God and turns away from evil? He still holds fast his integrity, although you incited me against him to destroy him without reason. (v. 3)

Despite Job's initial victory, Satan's response to God's second invitation displays that he was still unconvinced of the vitality of Job's faith. The loss of wealth. The loss of children. The loss of assets and legacy. Big deal. Give me the green light to turn Job's body black and blue—and red—then you'll see Job turn yellow. Then you'll see him pause in his praise. "Skin for skin!" Satan says. Give me Job's body. The reason?—oh, it's as natural as the sweetness of ice cream on the tongue and the sting of frostbite on the toes.

> All that a man has he will give for his life. But stretch out your hand and touch his bone and his flesh, and he will curse you to your face. (vv. 4–5)

The light turns green. God consents. So Satan attacks, striking "Job with loathsome sores from the sole of his foot to the crown of his head" (v. 7). Black. Blue. Red.

Yellow?

Sorry, Satan. No yellow.

Satan's strategy was ingenious—there is nothing that makes us more self-focused than bodily affliction—yet again unsuccessful.

Satan's silver bullet went in Job but didn't kill his faith. Even Mrs. Job's best shot missed the artery. Yes, Job stood not untouched—oh, he was touched head to toe—but unmoved. He would not curse God. He would not sin with his lips. Instead, he would open wide his mouth, his heart, and his hands to accept whatever God would give, both good and evil (v. 10b).[10]

The Third Test

With the arrival of Eliphaz the Temanite, Bildad the Shuhite, and Zophar the Naamathite,[11] who came "to show him sympathy and comfort" (v. 11), we might think the testing is over. Job has made it. Breathe in, breathe out—our protagonist has persevered. But alas, there is one final test, perhaps the toughest. Satan slithers away, while Job's closest companions cozy up.

God has taken everything from Job except his wife and best friends.[12] His wife, who surely grieved with Job both at the loss of their children as well as at her husband's health and wealth, didn't long endure with her husband's faithful attitude. Her heart was bitter, her tongue biting. She was less subtle than Eve but as straightforwardly tempting as Satan—"Curse God" (cf. 1:11; 2:9). Not "Stay strong," or "Good for you," or "You're my hero!" But, "Curse God."

Don't underestimate how tempting such a suggestion was. A man often feels most helpless when his helpmate helps not. But Job ate not from the fruit she offered. He snubbed this *diabolic adjutrix* ("devil's advocate," Augustine) and *organum satani* ("tool of Satan," Calvin).[13] Curse God? No ma'am.

But what about his friends? How would Job fare with them? He has rejected this "foolish" woman (2:10b), but will he reject these "wise" men? He has endured the pointed arrows of the divine warrior, and his own wife's slap in the face, but how will he fare with the repeated stabs in the back from his "friends" (2:11; 16:20; 19:21; 32:3; 35:4; 42:10), his "close friends" (19:14), his "intimate friends" (19:19)? Will he endure the full armory of their rebukes, accusations, scorn, and mockery?[14]

With the noblest of intentions, Job's good friends come to visit him in his time of sorrow, but in the end they are no good to him, bringing only sorrow upon sorrow. You know the story of chapters 3–37: their initial seven-day silence reaps a whirlwind of reckless words. Seeking "victory before truth," they condemn Job without ever refuting his claims.[15] Bildad, for example, mocks Job's admission of innocence with his rhetorical questions:[16]

> Is it for your piety that [God] rebukes you and brings charges against you? Is not your wickedness great? Are not your sins endless? (22:4–5 NIV)

Even Elihu, who offers a splendid defense for the justice of God, offers no defense for just Job.[17] He says:

> Oh, that Job might be tested to the utmost for answering like a wicked man! To his sin he adds rebellion; scornfully he claps his hands among us and multiplies his words against God. (34:36–37 NIV)

Job gives his best defense to his friends' false accusations. He says, for example, "Your maxims are proverbs of ashes; your defenses are defenses of clay" (13:12 NIV). Or again, "Miserable comforters are you all! Will your long-winded speeches never end? What ails you that you keep on arguing?" (16:2–3 NIV). But beneath Job's clever tongue lies the poison of his betrayal.[18] It is neither sticks nor stones that hurt Job's bones, but *words*. It is words that crush his inner spirit. He decries to his friends, "How long will you torment me and crush me with words?" (19:2 NIV). He bemoans to God, "All my intimate friends detest me; those I love have turned against me" (19:19 NIV).[19]

Have you ever had a friend not believe you? Turn against you? Attack you? This last test is no least test. It's the test failed every day by the Christian businessman at that annual conference when his "buddies" plead for one more round or by the Christian student sick of her schoolmates' thoughts and taunts. "Fool!"

Job remained resilient through false accusation after false accusation from true friends! That's not easy to do. Job didn't ace the test, but he passed it. He grumbled. He complained. He protested.[20] But he didn't give in, and he didn't give up. He feared the Lord. He trusted God—God's sovereign, just, and merciful providence.[21] His talk might have been excessive but not incredulous.[22]

So, three tests and three passing grades. Take away my possessions. Take away my family. Take away my health. Take away my friends and their respect. Take it all away, and yet I will praise God.

Three Roots

I realize that what Job did is easier said than done. And I realize that as much as Job is an extreme example of trials (your trials will most likely never be as tough as his), so he is an extreme example of faith (your faith may never be as strong as his). His faith was so deeply rooted that it was not as easy for Satan to sift him as he thought. So I realize that I'm no Job and that you're no Job. I realize that the roots of some of our faith are barely below the topsoil. But I also realize that the substance of Job's strength should be and can be ours. So what I will do in the rest of this chapter is expose Job's roots, that is, show you the under-the-surface theological foundations that made him (and can make us) hold up under duress.

Know That Suffering Can Be Good

The first root of Job's faith was his knowledge that suffering can be good. Since the fall of mankind, death and disease and sickness and suffering have entered our world. We live on a cursed planet with cursed people. As we have seen, Ecclesiastes is a poetic exploration of this reality. So while suffering is linked with evil, it also can be linked with good. Sometimes suffering can be good because it is for our good.

Job understood this. That is why, when the commodities of his comfortable life were snatched away, he didn't view it as something purely evil. He didn't say, "What's the Devil up to?" or "Why has this great evil come upon me?" In fact, nowhere in his reactions and replies do we have the remotest suggestion that Job saw suffering as abnormal or immoral (or satanic).

As we learned in Proverbs and Ecclesiastes, Job realized that both material and spiritual prosperity are divine gifts, and as divine gifts they can be freely given and freely taken away. He must have known that peace, prosperity, self-security, and happiness can become perils that threaten to hinder or prohibit one from undertaking and continuing the arduous journey of faith.[23] He must have believed that suffering possesses the strange but beautiful power of liberating one's soul from the seduction of safety and the love of temporal, perishable goods. In these ways, he anticipates the Christian necessity of cross bearing (Luke 9:23)—of persecution for righteousness' sake (Matt. 5:10), learning obedience from hardships (Heb. 5:8), and sharing in the sufferings of Christ (Phil. 1:29; cf. 3:10).[24]

Trust in God's Providence

Job didn't view suffering as an evil, as something necessarily negative. And neither should we. That's the first root. The second root is trust in God's providence.

In a more Christianized Western world, it used to be you could use the words *providence* and *God* interchangeably.[25] In those days people took for granted the reality that God rules every aspect of the universe, every event of history, and every detail of our personal lives; that God even numbers the very hairs on our heads, as Jesus said. But since the Enlightenment and the rise of the scientific worldview, it seems now that only American insurance companies recognize something of God's continuing activity in the world. Allstate and State Farm still call unpreventable destructive occurrences of the natural world, such as earthquakes and hurricanes, "acts of God." To them, at least on paper, God can be credited (or "blamed") as being the architect and builder of both personal calamities and national catastrophes.

Most people today hold a progressive view of providence like that advocated by H. G. Wells in his 1919 novel, *Undying Fire*. The protagonist in this story is a Job-like figure. In fact, his name is Job Huss. This Job is an atheistic evolutionist, and as such he sees no benevolence, wisdom, or justice in the random ways of this world. He refuses to recognize faith in the ultimate providence of God as a valid or respectable answer to cosmic and human cruelty. Rather, Job Huss believes that only the "undying fire"—the subjective spirit of God in the heart of man—can bring any meaning or significance to earthly affliction.

To him, if there is a God, he is silent in the midst of suffering. His eyes are closed. His hands are tied. He has fallen asleep, or perhaps rolled over and died. All that is left is you and me and our human love for each other—that undying fire. That's what remains to warm ourselves in this bitter cold cosmos.

Well, the biblical Job didn't think this way. Call him prehistorical. Call him unscientific. Call him naïve. Or call him correct! For why is it more historical, scientific, and sophisticated to reason that if God is all-loving, then the existence of suffering tells us that he must not be all-powerful; and if God is all-powerful and yet such affliction exists, well then he must not be all-loving? People say that today, don't they? And then they think they are so clever. They smugly wash their hands of God and Christianity and Jesus and religion. God-problem solved. Case closed. Debate won.

There are, however, at least two flaws in such logic. First, such a view refuses to fathom that human misery can in any way contain elements of divine love. Yet this is the message of our faith. At the very center of the gospel is God's omnipotent love incarnate, a love that is pierced through the wood of an old rugged cross. A love that suffers, a love that dies! Second, such a view assumes that if suffering appears to be pointless to me, then it must be pointless.[26] Sometimes we are so arrogant and ignorant. While we know from experience (as we look retrospectively to times of suffering in our lives and see the benefits of such times), we still assume that if our finite "minds can't plumb the depths of the universe for good answers to suffering, well, then, there can't be any!"[27]

Alvin Plantinga, the esteemed philosopher from Notre Dame, illustrates this flawed attitude by speaking of the existence of an extremely small insect called a no-see-um. A no-see-um—that's the bug's name! Tim Keller summarizes Plantinga's argument:

> If you look into your pup tent for a St. Bernard [those huge dogs], and you don't see one, it is reasonable to conclude there is no St. Bernard in your tent. But if you look into your pup tent for a "no-see-um" . . . and you don't see any, it is not reasonable to assume they aren't there. Because, after all, no one can see 'em.

Keller concludes, "Many assume that if there were good reasons for the existence of evil [or suffering], they would be accessible to our minds, more like St. Bernards than like no-see-ums, but why should that be the case?"[28] Yes! Why should that be the case?

Job had no idea what was going on in the heavens. He wasn't privy to the chamber-room conversation. And yet he gave God the benefit of the doubt. He knew who was the potter and who was the clay, and as the clay he didn't say to the potter, "Do you know what you're doing?" Rather, he was able to be cracked and battered about because he trusted that he was still in God's hands. He trusted in the purposeful *providence* of God.[29]

Do you trust God like that? Well, you should. See-em or no-see-um, you should see *him*, see him at work in every infinite action of the universe, even our dog-sized dilemmas.

Believe in the Resurrection

Know that suffering can be good. That's the first root. Trust in God's providence. That's the second. The third root is to believe in the resurrection. Believe that this life is not all there is. We live. We die. And then there is the resurrection.

This conviction is not apparent from these first two chapters. It is not apparent that Job believed in life after death, in a day in which all wrongs would be judged and made right.[30] Yet as Job speaks with his friends, it becomes apparent that he believes in a bodily resurrection. This is nowhere more evident than in 19:25–26, where he answers his friends' false accusations, "For I know that my Redeemer lives,[31] and at the last he will stand upon the earth.[32] And after my skin has been thus destroyed [after this body is turned to ashes], yet in my flesh I shall see God." Job held the belief that there would be a resurrection and that in that day there also would be retribution.[33]

If we would look toward the afterlife and live in light of the resurrection like Job did, then our troubles would be far more tolerable. The apparent tyrannies of providence would be more palatable, for we would remember that God still "has time," so to speak, to remedy any and all injustices of history.[34] By looking forward to a future vindication and the joy that will accompany it, we can affirm Paul's words in Romans 8:18: "For I consider that the sufferings of this present time are not worth comparing with the glory that is to be revealed to us" (cf. Heb. 11–12).[35]

His Question, Our Answer

When Jesus walked this earth, he called everyone, as he still calls them, to put him and his kingdom above possessions, family, friends, and reputation, and to accept, if necessary, suffering, persecution, and the loss of home, job, or money or even life.

How would you answer the Devil's question? Would you follow the Lord, trust in him, love him, and fear him no matter what? In times of sorrow, sickness, and suffering would you, as Sarah Edwards put it, "kiss the rod," rejoicing that you are "in the hands of such a God"?

6

MY SERVANT

Job 42:1–17

"I had heard of you by the hearing of the ear, but now my eye sees you; therefore I despise myself, and repent in dust and ashes." After the LORD had spoken these words to Job, the LORD said to Eliphaz the Temanite: "My anger burns against you and against your two friends, for you have not spoken of me what is right, as my servant Job has. Now therefore take seven bulls and seven rams and go to my servant Job and offer up a burnt offering for yourselves. And my servant Job shall pray for you, for I will accept his prayer not to deal with you according to your folly. For you have not spoken of me what is right, as my servant Job has."

—Job 42:5–8

used to think the book of Job was the Bible's answer to the philosophical question of the origins of evil and the problem of pain. But then I read it. That is, I carefully read through each and every sentence, realizing forty-two chapters later that the question—"Why suffering?"—was more my question than God's.[1] In other words, I realized that the book of Job answers questions related to the issues of life's incomprehensive cruelties,[2] but it does not specifically address the question of *why*.[3]

God's Questions

Most churches today design their sermon series to focus on *our* questions:

How can I mend my broken marriage?

What are seven keys to financial success?

Why does a good God allow good people to suffer so badly?

Interestingly, God's Word answers these questions but only indirectly. Our crucial questions, so it seems, are not as crucial to God. It is not that they are unimportant, but, rather, it is that they are less important. They are less important than the questions he raises in his revelation.

In the book of Job our Lord asks and answers three key questions through three different casts of characters. First, there is the Devil's question, which we talked about in the last chapter. In Job 1:9 Satan says, "Does Job fear God for no reason?" In broader terms: is it possible to love God not only in times of plenty but also in times of want? Is it possible, that is, to love God no matter what? Job, through three tough tests—the loss of his possessions and children, the loss of his health, and the loss of his friends and their respect—answers in the affirmative. Yes, it is possible. In fact, it is necessary.

The other two important questions center on the topics of the righteousness of man and the righteousness of God. "Do the righteous ever suffer?" That's the question Job's friends are dealing with. "Is God righteous in all he does, even when he allows or *ordains* suffering?" That's the question Job is struggling with. Those are the two remaining questions. Those are God's questions, questions that he wants us to know the answers to, and thus to which we will now turn.

Do the Righteous Ever Suffer?

The answer to the question, "Do the righteous suffer?" or "Do those who have faith in the Lord and live in obedience to his Word ever suffer even if they haven't sinned?" is an easy one: yes, of course. Job is righteous. Thrice it is said of him (twice from the mouth of the Lord), "There is none like him on the earth, a blameless and upright man, who fears God and turns away from evil" (1:1, 8; 2:3). Job is righteous, and yet he suffers.

This is evident to us. However, this was not so evident to Eliphaz, Bildad, and Zophar. You have to remember that as readers we have a satellite view of this whole situation. They had only the street view. Unlike us, they have not overheard the supernatural secrets, the cosmic chamber-room conversations and contracts. They don't know, as we do, if Job is telling the truth. So I sometimes think of them as being in a similar position to doubting Thomas. Thomas wasn't there in the upper room to see and hear and touch Jesus. He wouldn't believe until he could see and hear and touch. But when he did, he believed. Likewise, these men won't believe what Job has to say until they have heard from God himself.

The Wisdom of Fools

I say all that to say this: before we remove the speck (or log) from their eyes, I want us first to look around that log. That is, I want us to see that some of what they saw and did was commendable.

Perhaps most commendable is their initial sympathy and patience, shown when they first arrived on the scene. The Jewish sage Jesus son of Sirach wrote, "There are friends who are such when it suits them, but they will not stand by you in time of trouble" (Sir. 6:8). Not so Job's friends. These men put their lives on hold and journeyed to Job in order "to show him sympathy and comfort" (Job 2:11). Then, for seven days and seven nights they sat silently on the ground with him. Think about that. Would you take a week off work just to console a friend?

And not only did they begin well; they also finished well. In 42:9, we are told that after these three wise men realized their folly, they "went and did what the LORD had told them," which was to make a large and expensive offering *to* God *through* Job.

In my house, our family motto for obedience is this: you are to obey all the way, right away, and with a happy heart. Now, we don't know if these three had happy hearts, but we do know that they obeyed all the way and right away. And when you consider how difficult this must have been—not only to accept that they had been completely wrong, but also that they had to be reconciled to God through the very man they once mistreated and maligned—we must appreciate their courage and commitment to God to obey all that he asked of them.

Between this fine finish and that beautiful beginning, we have their words of counsel. It is, of course, these words that get them into trouble. Yet before we go there, I want us to see that there are nuggets of gold within this heap of rubble (their speeches in chapters 4, 5, 8, 11, 15, 18, 20, 22, 25).

If you read their counsel carefully, you should notice two things. First, both in their calm dialogue and in their heated debate, they honestly sought what they thought was best for Job, namely, to have him examine his attitude and actions to see if he had sinned against God. In other words, they had good intentions. Second, their words are beautifully spoken and *in most contexts* true.[4] This is why the words of Eliphaz in 5:13 are quoted by Paul in 1 Corinthians 3:19,[5] and also why his words of counsel are alluded to in six other places in the New Testament. Isn't that fascinating? Even the New Testament authors, under the inspiration of the Holy Spirit, understood that there was some wisdom to these fools.[6]

That's the bright side. That's looking around the log. Now here is the dark side—that deep brown tree sticking straight out of their retinas. What they are not to be commended for, as chapter 42 makes clear, is the way they spoke about Job and especially *about God*.

Twice the Lord says to them, "You have not spoken *of me* what is right" (see vv. 7–8).

Recently I did an interesting exercise in exegetical observation. I went through all the words of Job's friends looking for what they said about God. From this study I learned that in the proper context all of what they said about God is right and true. They spoke about how God is to be feared. They also spoke of his incomprehensible nature, manifold wisdom, great works, love toward the righteous, justice toward the wicked, and corrective discipline toward his people. Therefore, their problem wasn't precisely what they said about God; rather, it was what they said about God in the context of Job's sufferings, his *innocent* sufferings.[7] To them, the scales of divine justice were easy to weigh. Their logic looked like this:

> If a man suffers, God is punishing him for his sin.
> Job is suffering.
> Therefore, Job must have sinned.

The supreme irony is that the teachings of these three trained theologians are untrue, even though they are theoretically and theologically "true."[8] That is, the irony of their orthodoxy is that it doesn't rightly apply to Job's specific situation.[9] In many instances their counsel—which was in line with the "basic universal principle in biblical wisdom"—would be appropriate and correct.[10] I wouldn't mind having them around today to address our nation and the present economic crisis. We could use some tough talk about "what you sow you will also reap" (see Gal. 6:7–9; cf. 2 Tim. 4:14; Prov. 12:14b). Our greedy-for-gain CEOs, greedy-for-votes politicians, and greedy-for-possessions people could use some of the zings from Zophar to set them straight. Some cause-effect editorials, blog posts, and sermons would do us all some good.

Do you get what I'm saying? They are dead right: sin always (always!) has consequences, various sufferings of sorts—it might be physical suffering or perhaps a slow but sure searing of the conscience (Rom. 1:24; 1 Tim. 4:2). But they are dead wrong that suffering always (always!) is traced back to sin.[11]

In this way, they are similar to those in Jesus's day who asked if the blind man was blind because of his sin or his parents' sin. Before our Lord healed the blind man, Jesus answered this popular false perception: "It was not that this man sinned, or his parents, but that the works of God might be displayed in him" (John 9:3). In the case of Job, like that of the blind man, the works of God were on display. God was showing Job, his friends, and us that even a righteous man could indeed suffer.[12]

Is God Just If and When the Righteous Suffer?

So, the answer to the first question—"Do the righteous sometimes suffer?"—is yes. This leads naturally to the second question: "Is God just in all he does, even when the righteous suffer?" Good question. A question still heard on the train, in the coffee shop, at the neighborhood park, and in the back pew.

In 1959, Archibald MacLeish won the Pulitzer Prize for his play *J.B.*, which is a modern parody of the book of Job. J.B. is a millionaire who is faithful to God. In this way he is like Job. He is also like Job in that, as the story unfolds, he loses everything. Yet, unlike Job, he turns not to God for answers but rather to his wife. Since God doesn't care or exist anymore (the skies are made of "stone"), J.B. takes solace in what he can see and touch—human love. MacLeish writes:

> It's all the light now.
> Blow on the coal of the human heart.
> The candles in churches are out.
> The lights have gone out in the sky.
> Blow on the coal of the heart
> And we'll see by and by.[13]

The vast difference between *J.B.* and Job is that the biblical story does not depict a closed and cold universe but a universe in which God intimately acts and ultimately speaks.

Job underwent the same doubts that many of us have today, that God is apathetic to our needs and deaf to our cries.[14] But the remedy given in the Bible is not to dismiss God, to close the church's doors, or to have one's wife fan the flickering coal of the human heart. Rather, the remedy is to wait for God to extinguish the embers of pride in one's heart by the breath of his divine voice.

The Repentance of the Righteous

From chapter 3 through chapter 31, Job has begged God to appear to him, hear his case, and vindicate him. In chapters 38–41, God does indeed appear, but he will not hear Job's case. Rather, he will present his own. He will put Job on trial and he will cross-examine his creature about creation—about the detailed knowledge of how the world works.[15] The Lord (in a rare speech in the Wisdom Literature) interrogates Job, bringing in the material universe to testify. God says:

> Where were you when I laid the foundation of the earth? Who determined its measurements? Surely, Job, you know! Do you have a good grasp as to how the stars hang in the sky or why the sea doesn't spill over upon the land? Can you, Job, send forth the storehouses of snow, the torrents of rain, the bolts of lightning, the crash of thunder? Do you give the horse its might, the wild donkey its freedom, the eagle its sight, and the ostrich its stupidity? Have you entered into the springs of the sea, or walked the recesses of the deep? Have you comprehended the expanse of the earth? Tell me, Job, if you understand all this.[16]

In God's two speeches (chapters 38–41), he doesn't insist that Job simply and stupidly "blow on his human heart." Rather, he encourages him merely to open his human eyes. Open your eyes! "Stop and consider the wondrous works of God" (37:14).[17] For these wondrous works attest to God's abundant righteousness (37:23; cf. Rom. 1:18–20). The existence, maintenance, and operation of the earth, stars, waters, and animals confirm his just rule, as well as "testify against human arrogance, ignorance, and ingratitude."[18]

God calls creation to the witness chair, and creation's valid testimony renders Job, his friends, and all humanity morally inexcusable and intellectually incapable of criticizing God's character.[19] God's control, constraint, and care—clearly portrayed in nature every second of every day—ought to silence all accusations against his goodness. Is God good? Yes. See the stars. Can God handle death and the Devil?[20] Yes. Look at Leviathan. Behold Behemoth!

When the dust of God's opening and closing arguments settles, Job realizes that the only appropriate response to his ignorance and presumption is repentance: to repent in dust and ashes.[21] This is what we find in Job 42:1–6. Here is what I call "the repentance of the righteous."[22] "I have uttered," Job admits, "what I did not understand, things too wonderful for me. . . . I had heard of you by the hearing of the ear, but now my eye sees you" (vv. 3–5). He sees now, as William Blake memorably phrased it, "with, not through, the eye."[23]

Throughout the drama, Job didn't question God's power but rather his seeming indifference.[24] But now Job submits to God by acknowledging that the Lord *is* lovingly involved in the operations of an exceedingly complex universe.[25] *What* Job now comprehends is that God and his mysterious providence are too wonderful to comprehend and that human perceptions of justice are not the scales upon which the righteousness of God is weighed.[26] *What* he finally grasps (this "repentance" is indeed a change of mind) is that "God has an inescapable purpose in whatever he does,"[27] even if that inescapable purpose is never revealed to the creature it affects. *What* Job finally saw clearly is that he could *not* see clearly (cf. 1 Cor. 13:12).

And to his credit, Job doesn't suffer from our obsession with the question *why*, or from our obsession with having his felt or real needs met. God doesn't offer Job healing, and he certainly doesn't offer him a restored self-esteem. There is no therapeutic babble from the tongue of God. There is no healing here from the hand of God. And the beauty is that Job is not concerned about those things anymore. Job doesn't want anything but God.[28] That's what God offers, and that's what Job takes.

In the presence of the Lord, all Job's complaints now seem insignificant.[29] His intellectual problem remains unsolved but unimportant,[30] for in the midst of extreme pain, Job is spiritually cured by the revelation of God. And that is enough to heat the coal of his human heart on the coldest, darkest night of his soul.[31]

Two Questions, One Gospel

The book of Job asks three questions—God's questions. In this chapter we have answered the second and third questions.

> *Question:* Do the righteous suffer? *Answer:* Yes
> *Question:* Is God righteous when the righteous suffer? *Answer:* Yes

These are not only two important questions and answers but also intersecting ones. That is, these two questions and answers come together ultimately and intentionally in the gospel. For the book of Job was written to teach us about God and our relationship with him (that's Wisdom Literature), but also about his Son, our Lord Jesus Christ, and our relationship with him (that's also Wisdom Literature).

After the resurrection, Jesus appeared to two disciples who were on their way from Jerusalem to Emmaus. Jesus walked up to them, and they proceeded to tell him (because they did not recognize him) all that had happened in Jerusalem, namely that this man Jesus had been crucified. After that, quite surprisingly, our Lord sharply rebuked them: "O foolish ones, and slow of heart to believe all that the prophets have spoken!" (Luke 24:25). Why was Jesus so hard on them? How could they possibly have known that the Christ would come to suffer and die? Well, being devout Jews, they should have known their Bible better. They should have discerned what was written about the Messiah in all that "the prophets have spoken," and, as Jesus would later say, "everything written about *me* in the Law of Moses and the Prophets and the Psalms" (Luke 24:44), or "the Writings" which include the Psalms and the Song of Songs, and Proverbs and Ecclesiastes and, oh yes, the book of Job.[32]

What Does Job Have to Do with Jesus?

What then does the book of Job have to teach us about Jesus?[33] First, this book gives us the big picture of the gospel. Think back to what's going on in Job 42:7–9. Reread it:

> After the LORD had spoken these words to Job, the LORD said to Eliphaz the Temanite: "My anger burns against you and against your two friends, for you have not spoken of me what is right, as my servant Job has. Now therefore take seven bulls and seven rams and go to my servant Job and offer up a burnt offering for yourselves. And my servant Job shall pray for you, for I will accept his prayer not to deal with you according to your folly. For you have not spoken of me what is right, as my servant Job has." So Eliphaz the Temanite and Bildad the Shuhite and Zophar the Naamathite went and did what the LORD had told them, and the LORD accepted Job's prayer.

What's going on here? Here's my summary:

- Man has sinned against God. While Job's friends thought themselves to be in the right, they were very much in the wrong.
- God is angry at sin and rightfully so. It is an assault on his name and glory.
- In his mercy, God deals with these sinners not according to their folly.[34] It is through a blood sacrifice and an innocent man's mediation that their sins are forgiven.[35]

Does that scenario sound familiar to you? Sure! It's the big picture of the gospel of God.[36] It sure reads like a traditional gospel tract.

So the book of Job gives us the big picture of the gospel. But more than that, it also gives us some of the detailed work of the man and the message of the gospel. What does Job have to do with Jesus? That's the question we are attempting to answer now. Well, here's the story of Job. Tell me if you've heard this before:

- There was a righteous man.
- This man, by God's set purpose, was handed over to satanic-inflicted sufferings.[37]
- This man in his suffering was mocked and mistreated.
- This man prayed for his enemies, for those who persecuted him.
- This man, after a costly, perfect, substitutionary, blood sacrifice,[38] became a priestly mediator between God and sinners.[39]
- This man was fully and publicly vindicated by God.[40]
- This man, in the end, was exalted, receiving honor and glory and power and wealth, even (seemingly) to a greater extent than that which he first had.[41]

Sound familiar? Yeah!

Now, don't get me wrong, Job is not Jesus. Job was a sinner (as he admits he is, and that all men are),[42] and he is to blame for certain aspects of his weak-sighted perception of God.[43] Yet, it is difficult to deny that the story of Job (a story written many hundreds of years before the incarnation) prepares us in an extraordinary way for the story of Jesus—of what to expect in the Messiah.[44] To put it plainly: the narrative of Job prepares us mentally and spiritually for the master or meta-narrative of Jesus.[45] To put it boldly: the primary purpose of the book of Job is to prepare us for Jesus![46]

"My Servant"

I'm not done. In case we missed these two pictures of the gospel, there is perhaps one final connection between Job and Jesus, and that is the title "my servant." Twice in the prologue (1:8; 2:3) and four times in the epilogue (42:7–8) God refers to Job as "my servant."

I know that the term "my servant" can refer to a master-slave relationship. For example, Sarah used "my servant" in reference to Hagar (Gen. 16:5). I also know it can be used of a person who has served God loyally—as it is used of the "good and faithful servant" in Jesus's parable (Matt. 25:21), and also of Job in Job 1:8, 2:3. Yet, two facts persuade me that its usage in Job 42:7–8 has a viable christological connection.

First, for what I would imagine was a common expression in the ancient Near East, it is used sparingly in the Old Testament.[47] And when used, it is used almost exclusively as a title for key figures in salvation—especially Jacob/Israel, Moses, and David.[48] Moreover and most noteworthy, it is used in Isaiah 42–53 in reference to the Servant.[49] According to the Gospels, this Servant—the suffering servant—is our Lord Jesus Christ (see esp. Matt. 12:18; 27:26–35).[50]

Second, especially considering the New Testament understanding of the Isaianic "servant" texts, as relating to Jesus's mediatorial sacrifice for our sins, I find the fourfold repetition in the one and only atonement section in the book of Job (42:7–8) too thematically similar to be coincidental. To be clear, I am not proposing that Job's sufferings were vicarious. But I am stating that both Job and Jesus, as God's servants, suffered and interceded through blood sacrifice. In other words, the words—"My servant Job . . . go to my servant Job. . . . And my servant Job shall pray for you, for I will accept his prayer. . . . My servant Job"—are intended to make us think of the cross of Christ.[51]

So, you see, Job's friends were not too far removed from those who cried out to our suffering Savior, "If you are the Son of God, come down from the cross" (Matt. 27:40). The last picture they could imagine was a suffering servant. How could a suffering servant demonstrate the blessing of God? How could a suffering servant bring peace between God and man? How could a suffering servant defeat Satan and his schemes? How could a suffering servant be perfectly innocent and yet God be perfectly just?

Jesus once said to the Pharisees, "You search the Scriptures because you think that in them you have eternal life; and it is they [the Scriptures] that bear witness about me, yet you refuse to come to me that you may have life" (John 5:39–40). I think Jesus was so distraught by his disciples' lack of faith and so upset at the Pharisees' oppression of the truth because they were the ones who knew the Scriptures and therefore should have known better.[52] They should have seen the writing on the wall. They should have understood, as the prophet Isaiah so clearly foretold and as Job so perfectly illustrates, that it is quite possible that an innocent man could suffer and yet God—in it and through it—show forth his justice.

Trust Him

Two questions, one answer—that answer is Jesus. That answer is the gospel of our Lord Jesus Christ! Job's journey and Jesus's life show us that God can and does triumph over evil ultimately, and thus we can trust him. We can trust him as we look at creation. We can trust him as we look at the history of salvation. We can trust him as we look at his written revelation. We can trust that he will glorify what is stronger than hate and evil and suffering and death, and that he will do so through his Son, our Lord Jesus Christ, to whom all glory and honor and praise and adoration is forever due.

7

HOW SHALL WISDOM
BE PREACHED?

And behold, something greater than Solomon is here.

—Luke 11:31b

As we come now to our final chapter, on hermeneutics (and homiletics), it is important that whatever we learn, we keep the proper Wisdom Literature demeanor: that God remain large and we remain small. Sadly there is much truth in the saying in that old preaching manual: "The dust of vainglory often clings to the feet of preachers."[1] So here we come to what I'll call "The Humble Art of Preaching Great Sermons on the Wisdom Literature." I want our sermons on these texts to be prayed through, written, and delivered with humility, but I also want them to be great. And the only way they can be great is if our great Savior is lifted up—if Jesus is preached, and preached properly.

Here I am tempted to share some tips on living well, writing well, or speaking well, as important and as necessary as those topics are to good preaching, and especially to this genre. However, in this chapter I focus instead on how to take a wisdom text and show forth Christ, that is, how to relate verses and/or passages we find in Proverbs, Ecclesiastes, and Job to "the gospel of God" (Rom. 1:1).

I think of it this way: having *shown* you how to preach Christ from Proverbs, Ecclesiastes, and Job (with my sample sermons on the beginning and end of each book), I will now *tell* you how. Said visually, I have shown you the finished canvas—a mosaic of six paintings—but now I tell you what colors to use, how to mix them, and the when and whys of moving the brush.

We start where the New Testament starts, with gospel ethics.

Tip 1: Gospel Ethics

Most experienced preachers have some idea of how to preach Christ from the Law and the Prophets and even the Psalms (especially the messianic psalms). But when it comes to the Wisdom Literature, even those most experienced among us don't know where to start. We don't know where to start because there are few articles, books, or chapters in books written on this topic,[2] and also because Proverbs, Ecclesiastes, and Job are rarely quoted and/or alluded to in the New Testament. When dealing with New Testament quotations from these books, it isn't as easy as saying: if Peter, Paul, or James use the wisdom text on which you're preaching, see what they say *about Christ* and then teach what they taught.

Besides the lack of apostolic hermeneutical help, a further difficulty is that the seven (yes, only seven) New Testament quotations of the wisdom texts are not used to shed light on some new revelation, or to highlight some messianic fulfillment. Rather, they are used to support New Testament theology and ethics (see Table 7.1).[3] Only one citation, "like a dog that returns to his vomit,"[4] does not combine the attributes and/or actions of God with human morality or immorality. Yet note that even this text in context implies God as judge.

This apostolic use of the Wisdom Literature, with its reinforcement of Old Testament theology and ethics,[5] is just as important as "this

Table 7.1: New Testament Quotations of Proverbs and Job[6]

Proverbs 3:11–12 LXX: "My son, despise not the chastening of the Lord; nor faint when thou art rebuked of him: for whom the Lord loves, he rebukes, and scourges every son whom he receives."	**Hebrews 12:5–6**: "And have you forgotten the exhortation that addresses you as sons? '*My son, do not regard lightly the discipline of the Lord, nor be weary when reproved by him. For the Lord disciplines the one he loves, and chastises every son whom he receives.*'"
Proverbs 3:34 LXX: "The Lord resists the proud; but he gives grace to the humble."	**James 4:6**: "But he gives more grace. Therefore it says, '*God opposes the proud, but gives grace to the humble.*'" **1 Peter 5:5**: "Likewise, you who are younger, be subject to the elders. Clothe yourselves, all of you, with humility toward one another, for '*God opposes the proud but gives grace to the humble.*'"
Proverbs 11:31 LXX: "If the righteous is repaid on earth, how much more the wicked and the sinner!"	**1 Peter 4:17–18**: "For it is time for judgment to begin at the household of God; and if it begins with us, what will be the outcome for those who do not obey the gospel of God? And '*If the righteous is scarcely saved, what will become of the ungodly and the sinner?*'"
Proverbs 25:21–22a LXX: "If thine enemy hunger, feed him; if he thirst, give him drink; for so doing thou shalt heap coals of fire upon his head."	**Romans 12:16–21**: "Live in harmony with one another. Do not be haughty, but associate with the lowly. Never be wise in your own sight. Repay no one evil for evil, but give thought to do what is honorable in the sight of all. If possible, so far as it depends on you, live peaceably with all. Beloved, never avenge yourselves, but leave it to the wrath of God, for it is written, 'Vengeance is mine, I will repay, says the Lord.' To the contrary, '*if your enemy is hungry, feed him; if he is thirsty, give him something to drink; for by so doing you will heap burning coals on his head.*' Do not be overcome by evil, but overcome evil with good."
Proverbs 26:11a: "Like a dog that returns to his vomit."	**2 Peter 2:17–22**: "These are waterless springs and mists driven by a storm. For them the gloom of utter darkness has been reserved. For, speaking loud boasts of folly, they entice by sensual passions of the flesh those who are barely escaping from those who live in error. They promise them freedom, but they themselves are slaves of corruption. For whatever overcomes a person, to that he is enslaved. For if, after they have escaped the defilements of the world through the knowledge of our Lord and Savior Jesus Christ, they are again entangled in them and overcome, the last state has become worse for them than the first. For it would have been better for them never to have known the way of righteousness than after knowing it to turn back from the holy commandment delivered to them. What the true proverb says has happened to them: '*The dog returns to its own vomit,* and the sow, after washing herself, returns to wallow in the mire.'"

121

Job 5:13a: "He catches the wise in their own craftiness."	➡	**1 Corinthians 3:18–21a**: "Let no one deceive himself. If anyone among you thinks that he is wise in this age, let him become a fool that he may become wise. For the wisdom of this world is folly with God. For it is written, *'He catches the wise in their craftiness,'* and again, 'The Lord knows the thoughts of the wise, that they are futile.' So let no one boast in men."
Job 41:11a: "Who has first given to me, that I should repay him?"	➡	**Romans 11:34–36**—"'For who has known the mind of the Lord, or who has been his counselor?' 'Or *who has given a gift to him that he might be repaid?'* For from him and through him and to him are all things. To him be glory forever. Amen."

is that" christological fulfillment schemes (i.e., predictive prophecy).[7] It is as important because it highlights theological continuity and consistency between the Old and the New Testaments regarding the person of God, *and* because it highlights the importance of Christian morality—humility,[8] love,[9] perseverance,[10] holiness,[11] and so on. Yet, as important as I now recognize this apostolic hermeneutic to be, I must admit my initial alarm: this might kill the whole project! I thought to myself, "How am I supposed to write a book on how to preach Christ from the Wisdom Literature when *God, not Christ; morality, not the Messiah;* and *judgment, not justification* are the foci of all the quotations?"

Thankfully, two thoughts kept me on course. The first thought was that of submission. The idea is this: if this is how the apostles handled the Wisdom Literature, then I must submit to their interpretive principles.[12] The second thought involved a corrective to popular (or "narrow") Christ-centered preaching. I refer not only to sermons that focus on God's love to the neglect of his other attributes,[13] but also to sermons that use the cross not as a bridge to personal holiness but as a free ticket to unequivocal acceptance or licentiousness.[14] Put differently, I refer to sermons that use "Christ and him crucified" only as a means to get us off the hook (as we dangle above the eternal fires of hell) and not also as a goad to godliness (to encourage us to live for the kingdom of heaven).[15]

So let's be clear. Christ-centered sermons should call us to holiness in light of Christ's incarnation (2 Pet. 1:1–12, 17) and his second coming (3:11–12). Christ-centered sermons should promote the Great Commission's commission—"teaching them to observe all that I have commanded you" (Matt. 28:20a). Christ-centered sermons should make us wise in salvation through faith in Christ *and* train us in godliness (see 2 Tim. 3:16). Moreover, Christ-centered sermons should include Paul's confession of the work of the cross—"[Jesus] gave himself for us to redeem us from all lawlessness and to purify for himself a people . . . zealous for good works" (Titus 2:14; cf. Acts 3:26); the author of Hebrews' firm exhortations toward endurance in light of Jesus's high priesthood (e.g., 4:14); and our Lord Jesus's final words of warning (not consolation) in the Sermon on the Mount (Matt. 7:21–27).

Christ-centered sermons can and should have an ethical edge to them; our messages should carry a moral weight.[16] As we walk under the cross from Proverbs to Philippians, Ecclesiastes to Ephesians, or Job to James, we must not dull this edge or lessen this weight. Our Christ-centered sermons on the Wisdom Literature must impress upon us, on the one hand, the greatness of God and, on the other hand, our response of obedient gratitude to grace,[17] for as Paul says: the purpose of being "filled with . . . all spiritual wisdom" is so we might "walk in a manner worthy of the Lord" (Col. 1:9–10).[18]

This requires that we keep in mind various broader issues that are closely related to the gospel in the New Testament—(1) faith: the proper response to the gospel, and (2) ethics: life under the gospel.[19] In my sermons (see chapters 1–6), these broader issues and this often neglected apostolic hermeneutic is modeled. For now allow me to review briefly how I handled two texts in light of this first tip.

In my sermon on Ecclesiastes 1:1–11 ("Why Work?"), I first showed how our work "under the sun"—without reference to the Lord—is not new and will not be remembered. Second, I showed how Christ's work—the work "of the Son"—is new and will always be remembered. Third, I showed how our work in and through the Son, for the glory of God, is something that will indeed be remembered (and even rewarded). In this sermon, instead of drawing a straight line from Old Testament ethics to today, we went *through* the life of Christ and Paul's teaching on the person of Christ to get there. In this way, I sought to show more clearly how living only for the Lord can make our work meaningful.

I did something very similar in my sermon on Proverbs 31:10–31. There I drew the line from the servanthood of the godly wife to the servanthood of Christ, arguing that if we wish to be praised by God and man, the path to greatness is that of humble service.[20]

Tip 2: Gospel Types

My second tip is to explore any possible correspondence between a person, event, institution, or word in a wisdom text and Jesus's person and work. This is called "typology." Typology involves structural analogy, i.e., what happened to this person in history is similar to what happened to that person later.[21] For example, Jesus compares his cross (John 3:14–15) to when Moses lifts up the serpent in the wilderness (Num. 21:4–9); and Paul warns the Corinthian church of their need for perseverance by comparing their potential failure to Israel's failure after the crossing of the Red Sea (1 Cor. 10:1–13).[22]

Regarding the Wisdom Literature, my sermon on Job 42 provides a good example of some of the varieties of typology. In the section at the end of the sermon ("What Does Job Have to Do with Jesus?"), I highlighted three connections. First I showed how the overall story of Job is similar to the big picture of the gospel.[23] I compared Job 42:7–8 to a gospel tract.

- Man has sinned against God. While Job's friends thought themselves to be in the right, they were very much in the wrong.
- God is angry at sin, and rightfully so. It is an assault on his name and glory.
- In his mercy, God deals with these sinners not according to their folly. It is through a blood sacrifice and an innocent man's mediation that their sins are forgiven.

Second, after highlighting the larger storyline similarities, I showed some of the striking similarities between Job's story and Jesus's story, arguing that the narrative of Job prepares us mentally and spiritually for the meta-narrative of Jesus.

- There was a righteous man.
- This man, by God's set purpose, was handed over to satanic-inflicted sufferings.
- This man, in his suffering, was mocked and mistreated.
- This man prayed for his enemies—for those who persecuted him.
- This man, after a costly, substitutionary, blood sacrifice, became a priestly mediator between God and sinners.
- This man was fully and publically vindicated by God.
- This man, in the end, was exalted, receiving honor and glory and power and wealth, even (seemingly) to a greater extent than what he first had.

Third, I showed the possible linguistic/theological connection between Job (Job 42:7–8) and Jesus (Matt. 12:18) with the Isaianic title "my servant." I argued that what Isaiah foretold and Job illustrated, Jesus embodied. In Christ and him crucified, we see how an innocent man could suffer and yet God—in it and through it—show forth his justice. On this point, I concluded:

> Job's friends were not too far removed from those who cried out to our suffering Savior, "If you are the Son of God, come down from the cross" (Matt. 27:40). The last picture they could imagine was a suffering servant. How could a suffering servant demonstrate the blessing of God? How could a suffering servant bring peace between God and man? How could a suffering servant defeat Satan and his schemes? How could a suffering servant be perfectly innocent and yet God perfectly just?

The type of typological understanding demonstrated in the three examples above does require careful reading and cautious application. While we do recognize that Christ is the antitype of both Israel's wisdom teacher and student (i.e., the perfectly wise son of Proverbs), that like the narratives of salvation history each and every wisdom text finds its "goal and fulfillment in Christ,"[24] and that Jesus is the very embodiment of the "wisdom of God" and his cross the very demonstration of it (1 Cor. 1:24, 18), we still seek not to speculate or allegorize.[25]

Every servant or rock or king in the Wisdom Literature is not Jesus,[26] just as every godly character in the Bible—e.g., Joseph in Genesis—is not a type of Christ (or at least a perfect type).[27] The key to using this tip effectively is developing apostolic sensibilities— taste buds for typology. Such "taste" is only developed through an understanding of the content of Scripture as a whole and a grasp of how Jesus and the apostolic church handled the Old Testament. Goldsworthy explains:

> This is not to suggest some oversimplified and reductionist scheme. It is simply to say that no text in either Testament exists without some connection to Christ. We may not always be able to pin it down. We certainly may never exhaust the exegetical potential of a given text. But that the connection is there is a matter determined by the word of Christ and his apostles. Scholarly reserve and humility is one thing; loss of nerve in the implications of the New Testament's teaching is another.[28]

So, for example, when we read Jesus's statement in Matthew 12:42, "The queen of the South will rise up at the judgment with this generation and condemn it, for she came from the ends of the earth to hear the wisdom of Solomon, and behold, something greater than Solomon is here," we can, with exegetical integrity, apply valuable typological principles. (1) Jesus can be connected with Solomon in all his wisdom. This helps us in a general way in handling books such as Proverbs, Ecclesiastes,[29] and even the Song of Solomon.[30] (2) Jesus can also be connected with the theme of judgment. This helps us apply many of the abundant "judgment texts" in the Wisdom Literature.[31] The skill, however, is seeing connections that are neither stated nor obvious, for example, grasping how the central themes of restlessness and divine judgment in Ecclesiastes find a thematic fulfillment in Jesus, and that those thematic fulfillments can be found together in at least one New Testament text, Matthew 11:20–30.[32]

Again, this is not an easy skill to develop. It takes time, hard work, spiritual illumination, and thus prayer. But it is the kind of skill that is necessary if we are to honor God and to preach Christ in the colors that only the Wisdom Literature adds to the picture of his radiance.

Tip 3: Gospel Teaching

The second tip sometimes blurs into the third. The major difference between the two is that tip 3 deals solely with thematic connections, usually from but not limited to the teachings of Jesus. The idea is this: if we can't get to Christ through a fulfillment scheme or a typological connection,[33] perhaps there is something Jesus taught that can (a) summarize, and/or (b) shed further light on a wisdom text.[34] This tip is related to the notion that Jesus is the supreme Wisdom Teacher, in both person and method.[35]

So, let's say you're preaching on Proverbs 1:8–19, which ends, "Such are the ways of everyone who is greedy for unjust gain; it takes away the life of its possessors," or a topical sermon on money in Proverbs. My tip here is simply to see what Jesus has to say about money and include it. The parable of the rich fool (Luke 12:13–21) would fit perfectly, or a verse such as, "You cannot serve God and money" (Luke 16:13), would work as well.

Or, let's say you're preaching on a section from "The Third Test," as I've labeled Job 3–37, the ridicule of Job's friends. What would be a good connection between "the steadfastness of Job" in this final test and the necessity of Christian perseverance? Well, there are a number of places you could go, including James 5:11— where this phrase is from—or various verses in Hebrews. You also could go (to make a more direct connection with the teaching of Jesus) to the seven letters to the seven churches in Revelation 1:10–3:22, where Jesus—"the Alpha and the Omega" (1:8), the one who is "alive forevermore" (1:18)—speaks to the church then and now of patient endurance (2:2), conquering (2:11), holding fast to his name (2:13), keeping his works until the end (2:26), and so on.

Yes, this all takes imagination but not innovation. It takes a biblically informed imagination. I'm not making up texts or connections between them. I'm simply making correct connections, Lord willing, between one theme and two (or more) texts.[36]

Let me illustrate this idea further. A good place to start is with linguistic connections. These can be found in any Bible with cross references. I used my daily-reading Bible and the Nestle-Aland Greek New Testament.[37] First, I wrote out all possible allusions—phrases, clauses, sentences, or formulas—from these two sources. Second, I sifted through the possible connections, choosing only the ones I thought had theological (not just linguistic) correspondence. Then, I selected from those theological texts all the christological ones,[38] notably those related to Jesus's teaching. Finally, I made a nice little table. This table (Table 7.2) is now a resource for present and future preaching on these texts.

Beyond linguistic connections,[39] we can also make thematic ones. With such thematic connections, here's what I did. It reminds me of working on a Microsoft Word document while running an antivirus scan in the background. I read through Proverbs, Ecclesiastes, and Job with my mind "running in the background" looking not for viruses but for New Testament texts. (Okay, it's not the perfect analogy.) So, for example, when I read, "What does man gain by all the toil at which he toils under the sun?" (Eccles. 1:3), my mind searches and finds a phrase in the Gospels and then latches onto it: "For what does it profit a man to gain the whole world and forfeit his soul?" (Mark 8:36). I write it down. Then later I will decide if this connection is theologically viable.

Table 7.2: Linguistic Connections

WL Verse or Phrase		Connection with Christ's Teachings
Proverbs 3:12: "For the LORD reproves him whom he loves."	➡	**Revelation 3:19**: "Those whom I love, I reprove and discipline."
Proverbs 19:17: "Whoever is generous to the poor lends to the LORD, and he [the LORD] will repay him for his deed."	➡	**Matthew 25:40, 46**: "Truly, I say to you, as you did it to one of the least of these my brothers, you did it to me." Then, after Jesus judges the unrighteous, he speaks of the reward of the righteous: "but the righteous [will go] into eternal life." Cf. Matt. 10:42.
Proverbs 23:15 (cf. 27:11): "My son, if your heart is wise, my heart too will be glad."	➡	**Matthew 3:17**: "This is my beloved Son, with whom I am well pleased."
Proverbs 24:12: "Will he [God] not repay man according to his work?"	➡	**Matthew 16:27**: "Then he [Jesus at his coming] will repay each person [or "man"] according to what he has done." Cf. Luke 16:15; Rom. 2:6; 2 Tim. 4:14; 1 Pet. 1:17; Rev. 2:23; 20:12–13.
Proverbs 25:21: "If your enemy is hungry, give him bread to eat, and if he is thirsty, give him water to drink."	➡	**Matthew 5:44**: "Love your enemies."
Proverbs 29:3: "A companion of prostitutes squanders his [father's] wealth." Cf. 28:7b; 29:3.	➡	**Luke 15:13** (the parable of the prodigal son): "He squandered his property in reckless living."
Proverbs 29:23: "One's pride will bring him low, but he who is lowly in spirit will obtain honor."	➡	**Matthew 23:12**: "Whoever exalts himself will be humbled, and whoever humbles himself will be exalted."
Proverbs 30:4: "Who has ascended to heaven and come down . . . ? What is his name, and what is his son's name?"	➡	**John 3:13**: "No one has ascended into heaven except he who descended from heaven, the Son of Man."
Job 19:26–27: "And after my skin has been thus destroyed, yet in my flesh I shall see God, whom I shall see for myself, and my eyes shall behold, and not another."	➡	**Revelation 22:1, 3–4a**: "Then the angel showed me the river of the water of life, bright as crystal, flowing from the throne of God and of the Lamb. . . . No longer will there be anything accursed, but the throne of God and of the Lamb will be in it, and his servants will worship him. They will see his face."
Job 42:2: "I know that you can do all things."	➡	**Matthew 19:26**: "With God all things are possible."

Tables 7.3, 7.4, and 7.5 are rough drafts of a recent "scan" I did with Proverbs and Ecclesiastes. I assume I missed some connections and misread others. But that's fine. The idea here is simply (1) to build one's ability in connecting themes and texts, and (2) to have data to work with when it comes time to preach on that text. While this might technically fall under the "typology" category, here I avoid type/antitype (covered in tip 2), broadening my focus to (a) similar teachings, (b) opposite or contrastive teachings, and (c) progressive teachings.[40] For each category I have selected only five examples.

While there are hundreds of possible New Testament thematic connections—the elder qualification of managing one's own household in 1 Timothy 3:4 (cf. Titus 1:6) and a father's role in disciplining children in Proverbs 22:6;[41] keeping godly company in 2 Timothy 2:5a (see the context vv. 1–16) and avoiding ungodly companions in Proverbs 1:9–19;[42] the need for feminine modesty in 1 Timothy 2:9 and the embarrassment of immodesty in Proverbs 11:22; Paul's command to "rejoice in the Lord" throughout Philippians and the notion of "a joyful heart" in Proverbs 17:22—the focus in this section has been on making sound thematic connections from the Wisdom Literature to *the teachings of Jesus*. For, as I have hopefully demonstrated, Israel's wisest king, our Lord Jesus, has shed much light on Israel's wisdom.

Tip 4: Gospel Illustration

If our goal in preaching is to preach Christ (which it is), then if we are having a difficult time making any or many direct connections to Jesus, let's make some indirect ones.[43] My fourth tip is to select a story from the Gospels or any obvious Christ-centered text (Col. 1:15–20; Phil. 2:1–11; Rev. 5:9–10, et al.) as an illustration.

I'll give you an example, followed by some admonitions. Let's say you are preaching on Job 28:1–28, Proverbs 1:1–7, Ecclesiastes 12:13–14, or any other number of Wisdom Literature texts that speak of "the fear of the LORD." After you define that term, perhaps you want to illustrate it. If you particularly want to illustrate how

Table 7.3: Possible Thematic Connections—Similar[44]

WL Theme		Christ's Teachings (or Teachings on Christ)
Proverbs 4:23: "Keep your heart with all vigilance, for from it flow the springs of life."	⟹	Matthew 12:34: "You brood of vipers! How can you speak good, when you are evil? For out of the abundance of the heart the mouth speaks."
		Matthew 15:18–19: "But what comes out of the mouth proceeds from the heart, and this defiles a person. For out of the heart come evil thoughts, murder, adultery, sexual immorality, theft, false witness, slander."
Proverbs 10:3 (cf. 13:25): "The LORD does not let the righteous go hungry."	⟹	Matthew 6:25–33: Jesus teaches us not to "be anxious about . . . life . . . food . . . drink," but instead to worry, if you will, about the kingdom of God. Why? Because we can trust God to provide for the righteous.
Proverbs 20:11: "Even a child makes himself known by his acts, by whether his conduct is pure and upright."	⟹	Matthew 7:15–21: "Beware of false prophets. . . . You will recognize them by their fruits. Are grapes gathered from thornbushes, or figs from thistles? So, every healthy tree bears good fruit, but the diseased tree bears bad fruit. A healthy tree cannot bear bad fruit, nor can a diseased tree bear good fruit. Every tree that does not bear good fruit is cut down and thrown into the fire. Thus you will recognize them by their fruits. Not everyone who says to me, 'Lord, Lord,' will enter the kingdom of heaven, but the one who does the will of my Father who is in heaven." Cf. Matt. 12:33; 13:23; 25:31–46; John 15:2–8.
Proverbs 23:4 (cf. 15:16; 27:24; 30:9; Eccles. 5:8–20): "Do not toil to acquire wealth; be discerning enough to desist."	⟹	Matthew 6:19: "Do not lay up for yourselves treasures on earth, where moth and rust destroy and where thieves break in and steal."
		Luke 12:19–20: "'And I will say to my soul, Soul, you have ample goods laid up for many years; relax, eat, drink, be merry.' But God said to him, 'Fool! This night your soul is required of you, and the things you have prepared, whose will they be?'"
		Hebrews 13:5: "Keep your life free from love of money, and be content with what you have, for he [Jesus] has said, 'I will never leave you nor forsake you.'" (Cf. Josh. 1:5 and Matt. 28:20b; 1 Tim. 6:6–10).
Proverbs 25:27 (cf. 16:5; 29:23; Job 22:29): "It is not good to eat much honey, nor is it glorious to seek one's own glory."	⟹	Matthew 18:1–4: "At that time the disciples came to Jesus, saying, 'Who is the greatest in the kingdom of heaven?' And calling to him a child, he put him in the midst of them and said, 'Truly, I say to you, unless you turn and become like children, you will never enter the kingdom of heaven. Whoever humbles himself like this child is the greatest in the kingdom of heaven.'" Cf. Luke 14:11; 1 Pet. 5:6.

Table 7.4: Possible Thematic Connections—Opposite[45]

WL Theme		Christ's Teachings (or teachings on Christ)
Proverbs, especially, and the Wisdom Literature, in general, teaches, "The reward for humility and fear of the LORD is riches and honor and life." (Prov. 22:4; cf. 15:6; 16:31; 18:22, et al.)	➡	As much as Jesus is depicted as the Wise Teacher in the Gospels (Matthew especially), he nevertheless was poor (Matt. 8:20; cf. 2 Cor. 8:9), dishonored (Matt. 26:66–68; 27:26–30), and died young (Matt. 27:50; cf. Luke 3:23).
Proverbs 13:20 (cf. 23:20: "Whoever walks with the wise becomes wise, but the companion of fools will suffer harm."	➡	**Matthew 9:9–13:** Jesus is accused of eating with "sinners." In general, his "companions" or followers are a motley crew—former tax collectors, lepers, prostitutes, etc. As such, Jesus seems to transcend what is even wisdom for Christians today (2 Corinthians 6). His very presence makes all things pure. The leaven of sinners does not taint him.
Ecclesiastes especially is filled with verses that despair over injustice in the world (e.g., Eccl 1:15; 3:16–17).	➡	Jesus often spoke of himself as judge (e.g., Matt. 7:21–23). With Jesus as the coming judge (1 Cor. 4:4–5; 2 Tim. 4:1, 8; 1 Pet. 4:5; Rev. 6:10), believers today are to grieve over injustice but not despair.
The despair in Ecclesiastes (1:2; 12:8) is also due to God's curse on creation, which includes, most notably, the reality of death (2:16, 21; 3:18–21; 9:2–6, et. al.; cf. 1 Cor. 15:26, 54–55; Rev. 20:14).	➡	Through Christ's death and resurrection (1 Cor. 15), we know that death has lost its "sting," that we have "victory through our Lord Jesus Christ," that our "labor is not in vain," and that someday Jesus, as creator of all, will reconcile all to God (Col. 1:15–20), reversing completely the curses of the fall (Rom. 8:19–22). Thus, we can affirm with Paul, "to die is gain" (Phil. 1:21; cf. 2 Cor. 5:2), because, as Jesus said, "whoever believes in [him], though he die, yet shall he live" (John 11:25).
Ecclesiastes 7:20: "Surely there is not a righteous man on earth who does good and never sins."	➡	**Hebrews 4:15:** "For we do not have a high priest who is unable to sympathize with our weaknesses, but one [Jesus] who in every respect has been tempted as we are [see Matt. 4:1–11], yet without sin."

"the fear of the LORD" is not less than "faith in the Lord" (in New Testament terms), but also how this notion of "fear" broadens and deepens our concept of faith, how might you do so?

Here's what I did in my sermon on Proverbs 1:1–7. I pretended to search for just the right illustration. First, I walked through some of the Bible stories where humans encounter angels, highlighting

Table 7.5: Possible Thematic Connections—Progressive[47]

WL Theme	Christ's Teachings (or teachings on Christ)
Proverbs 9:1–6 (cf. 12:7): "Wisdom has built her house. . . . Leave your simple ways, and live, and walk in the way of insight."	**Matthew 7:24**: Jesus compares the one who embraces *his wisdom* (not just wisdom in general or the godly wisdom of the Wisdom Literature) to someone who builds a "house on the rock." So Jesus picks up on the "house" motif, which is many places in Proverbs, claiming his words equal wisdom!
Proverbs 14:21, 31: "Whoever despises his neighbor is a sinner, but blessed is he who is generous to the poor. . . . Whoever oppresses a poor man insults his Maker, but he who is generous to the needy honors him."	**Matthew 25:40**: Note how Jesus, as the "king" in the parable, takes on the "Maker" or God-role of Proverbs 14:31: "And the King will answer them, 'Truly, I say to you, as you did it to one of the least of these my brothers, you did it to me.'"
Proverbs 8:1–36: "Does not wisdom call? Does not understanding raise her voice? . . . Hear, for I will speak noble things, and from my lips will come what is right, for my mouth will utter truth; wickedness is an abomination to my lips. All the words of my mouth are righteous. . . . By me kings reign, and rulers decree what is just; by me princes rule, and nobles, all who govern justly. I love those who love me, and those who seek me diligently find me. . . . The LORD possessed me at the beginning of his work, the first of his acts of old. . . . Then [at creation] I was beside him, like a master workman, and I was daily his delight, rejoicing before him always, rejoicing in his inhabited world and delighting in the children of man. And now, O sons, listen to me: blessed are those who keep my ways. . . . For whoever finds me finds life and obtains favor from the LORD.'"	Tremper Longman makes the connection, and I have spliced together a number of his comments: "Jesus claims [in Matt. 11:19] that his behavior represents the behavior of Woman Wisdom herself" (107); "Paul is inviting a comparison: Wisdom was firstborn in Proverbs 8; Jesus is firstborn in Colossians. Wisdom is the agent of divine creation in Proverbs; Christ is the agent in Colossians. In Proverbs 8 we read: [cites vv. 15–16]. And in Colossians 1:16, Christ made 'kings, kingdoms, rulers, and authorities.' The message is clear: Jesus is Wisdom herself." (108); "Wisdom is not a pre-incarnate form of the second person of the Trinity [!] . . . the association between Jesus and Woman Wisdom in the New Testament is a powerful way of saying that Jesus is the embodiment of God's Wisdom" (110).[48] Cf. John 1:1–3; 17:5.

WL Theme		Christ's Teachings (or teachings on Christ)
Ecclesiastes 2:24–25: "There is nothing better for a person than that he should eat and drink and find enjoyment in his toil. This also, I saw, is from the hand of God, for apart from him who can eat or who can have enjoyment?"	➡	The positive refrain of Ecclesiastes, which involves the enjoyment of food and drink, comes to its richest fulfillment first in the earthly ministry of Jesus—his miracle at Cana (John 2:1–11), dining at Matthew's house (Matt. 9:10–15), the feeding of the 5,000 and 4,000 (Matt. 14:14–21; 15:32–38), the Last Supper (Mark 14:17–25), the post-resurrection breakfast on the beach (John 21:12)—and later in (the near future) the wedding supper of the Lamb (Rev. 19:9; cf. Matt. 8:11; Mark 14:25; Rev. 3:20), which we, in a sense, anticipate each time we celebrate the Lord's Supper, "proclaim[ing] the Lord's death *until he comes*" (1 Cor. 11:26; cf. Acts 2:46).
Ecclesiastes 5:1: "Guard your steps when you go to the house of God [i.e., the temple]. To draw near to listen is better than to offer the sacrifice of fools, for they do not know that they are doing evil."	➡	There are thematic relations between Jesus's teaching on the temple in his day as being a hide-out or "den of robbers" (Matt. 21:13). But the obvious theological progression here has to do with Jesus as the "replacement" of temple (Matt. 12:6; 24:2; 26:61; 27:40, 51; John 4:20–23) and the sacrificial system (Heb. 7:27); and the birth of the church, where God's presence dwells through his Spirit (Eph. 2:13–22).

how "fear" overtook Samson's father, our Lord's mother, and the women at Christ's tomb. Second, I used examples of human encounters with God from the Old Testament narratives, such as those of Moses, Isaiah, Daniel, and Job. Then, after those two steps—angelic encounters and divine theophanies—I took us to the best, fullest, and clearest pictures of the fear of God. This illustration focused on the incarnation, when men encountered God as man: the *Lord* Jesus Christ, in the flesh. And here is what I wrote:

> Although Jesus's humanity often veiled his divinity, we nevertheless have scenes in the Gospels where the brilliant light—the terrible majesty of God—shines through. What does it mean to fear the Lord?

Well, let's look to Jesus and at Jesus. Let's look at when the Lord became a man and dwelt among us.

Can you think of times in the Gospels when a person shows the fear of the Lord to our Lord, this attitude of submission and respect and dependence and worship? Think about the wise men. When the star of Bethlehem led them to the King of kings asleep in a lowly manger, what did they do? "When they saw the star" resting over the place where the child was, "they rejoiced exceedingly with great joy" (Matt. 2:10). But then, once they entered into the room and saw the child, what did they do? "They fell down and worshiped him" (v. 11). Or think of the various reactions to Jesus's miracles. After our Lord spoke to the dead son of a widow, "Young man, I say to you, arise," and the boy sat up and began to speak, how did the mother, the boy, the disciples, and the crowd react? "Fear," we are told, "seized them all" (Luke 7:14, 16).

Or think of the time when Jesus told Simon Peter and the others to put down their nets once again into the water after a fruitless night of fishing. Reluctantly but faithfully, Peter agreed. And then what happened? They caught so many fish that the "nets were breaking" (Luke 5:6). They filled two boats full of fish. Now, how would you respond to such a miracle? Leap for joy? Throw a party? Give Jesus a high-five? How did Peter respond? Look at this: "But when Simon Peter saw it [this miracle], he fell down at Jesus' knees, saying, 'Depart from me, for I am a sinful man, O Lord'" (v. 8).

Or think about the time when Jesus's frightened disciples woke him in the middle of a storm at sea, and he simply rebuked the wind and the waves with his word. He said, "Peace! Be still" (Mark 4:39), and the wind ceased and there was a great calm. Now, there was a great calm outside the boat, but inside there was a new fear, a greater fear—not a fear of drowning or of death, but of God. "And they were filled with *great fear* and said to one another, 'Who then is this, that even the wind and the sea obey him?'" (v. 41). Or think of when that very question was answered at the Transfiguration by God: "This is my beloved Son, with whom I am well pleased; listen to him" (Matt. 17:5). How did Peter, James, and John respond? "When the disciples heard this, they fell on their faces and were terrified" (v. 6).

While each of these Gospel narratives illustrates only part of what is meant by "fear of the Lord," each frame seen together fills in the full picture. Seen together we see fear and faith. Seen together we see Jesus's greatness, power, and holiness, along with our recognition of lack of greatness, power, and holiness. Seen together we see the attitude of submission and respect and dependence and worship. Seen together we see the fear of the Lord.

I hope this string of incarnation illustrations illustrates well this tip on gospel illustration. I'm not saying avoid illustrations from popular media or personal testimony or Old Testament narratives. Rather, I'm highlighting the importance of "getting to Jesus" (in a genre in which that is often difficult to do) by every appropriate means.[49]

From Illustrations to Admonitions

So, in your preaching (here are my admonitions), why not illustrate Job's extraordinary response to the sovereign will of God in Job 1–2 with Jesus in Gethsemane? Or why not relate the attitudes and actions of Job's friends with doubting Thomas, walking your congregation through that great drama of John 20:24–29?[50] Or why not make something of Job's non-Jewish status—being from the "east"—and how, like Abraham (Paul's argument in Galatians 4) or the Roman centurion (in Matthew 8; cf. 2:1–11; 15:21–28), he acts like an Israelite indeed?[51] Or why not take Proverbs 21:1—"The king's heart is a stream of water in the hand of the LORD; he turns it wherever he will"—and tie it to Jesus's words to Pontius Pilate, "You would have no authority over me at all unless it had been given you from above" (John 19:11a; cf. Acts 2:23)?

Or why not show how the proverbs on neighborly kindness (Prov. 3:28, 29) "take on flesh" in the parable of the Good Samaritan? Or, why not connect Solomon's self-indulgence in Ecclesiastes 2:1–11 with Herod's in Matthew 14:1–12, and then put forth Christ, as Matthew does in 14:13–21, as the good king, who brings ultimate satisfaction and joy to those who follow and serve him (cf. Matt.

25:23)? Or why not show how the whole story of Job, notably the epilogue, illustrates well Paul's teaching in Romans 8:17ff: "[We are] fellow heirs with Christ, provided we suffer with him in order that we may also be glorified with him. . . . And we know that for those who love God all things work together for good"? Or, why not take the admonition of Proverbs 26:5, "Answer a fool according to his folly, lest he be wise in his own eyes," and show how Jesus wisely answers the foolish Pharisees and Sadducees (see Matt. 16:1–4; 21:24–27; 22:23–33)?

Or why not take a verse such as, "There are those—how lofty are their eyes, how high their eyelids lift!" (Prov. 30:13), and compare it with Jesus's parable about the proud-praying Pharisee (Luke 18:10–14)? And instead of introducing your sermon on Ecclesiastes 5:1–7 with the "shameful" statistics on how many churches today allow coffee and donuts in the sanctuary, why not start with Jesus in the temple, throwing over a few tables (John 2:13–17)? Or, why not use the Lord's Prayer to summarize Wisdom Literature as a whole—the way Jesus teaches us to relate to God, others, and the world?[52] Do you see what I'm saying? Can you do what I'm saying? Sure you can!

Tip 5: Gospel Awe

The fifth and final tip is perhaps the most important. It's important because it is the necessary bridge from hermeneutics to homiletics. You can know, have, and use all the right tools in preaching Wisdom Literature but not get across the gravity (or gravitas!) of this genre. There is a certain necessary ethos to preaching the Wisdom Literature of the Bible. That's what I'm getting at in this final point.

When tempted to sin, I often repeat to myself two truths: holiness brings happiness, and purity brings power. The first motto is personal. With it I'm admonishing myself, "Remember, sin brings only temporary pleasure. In the end it leads to shame and guilt. It severs the joy of your salvation. But to follow in God's ways always brings true satisfaction and happiness. So choose holiness." The second motto is corporate; that is, it relates more directly to my congregation and their reception of the Sunday-morning sermon. The idea is this: I tell myself, "Your people can sense if you believe what you're preaching. They can sense if you're walking your talk. So, if you want this sermon to be powerful—filled with the power of the Spirit—then walk in the Spirit and give no foothold to the flesh." I share that to say this: there is usually a correlation between receptive ears and the preacher's godliness.[53] So, ethics, we might say, builds ethos, but so too does *awe*.

For the past two years, I have been preaching through the Gospel of Matthew, and by God's grace there has never been a week where—as I study and preach—I have not been taken aback by who Jesus is, what he does, and what he says. In each sermon, I honestly find myself in awe of him. You can't preach the Wisdom Literature without this "gospel awe." Each week as you open a text from Proverbs, Ecclesiastes, or Job, your answer to Jesus's question—Who do you say that I am?—will show. It will show in your vocabulary, your demeanor, your intonation—everything. And if you are not more in awe of Jesus than the queen of Sheba was of Solomon, then your congregation will never sense how the wisdom of the Son of David is so much greater than that of David's son.

APPENDIX A

PREACHING HEBREW POETRY

I am persuaded that without knowledge of literature pure theology cannot at all endure. . . . Certainly it is my desire that there shall be as many poets and rhetoricians as possible, because I see that by these studies, as by no other means, people are wonderfully fitted for the grasping of sacred truth and for handling it skillfully and happily. . . . Therefore I beg of you that at my request (if that has any weight) you will urge your young people to be diligent in the study of poetry and rhetoric.[1]

—Martin Luther

Take your Bible. Sit down. Close your eyes. Put your finger in the Bible, and quickly flip it open. Now, open your eyes. Look at the page. What do see?

A poem?

Half of you are nodding "yes."

Perhaps you turned to the Psalms, the Song of Songs, Proverbs, or Lamentations. These books are wholly poetic. Or perhaps you turned to Job, Ecclesiastes, or the prophets. These books are mainly poetic.[2] Or perhaps you are eyeing one of those songs that appear at the key points in salvation history, such as Exodus 15:1b–18, Deuteronomy 32:1–43, Judges 5:1b–31, 1 Samuel 2:1–10, 2 Samuel 22:2–51, Habakkuk 3:2–19, Luke 1:46–55, 68–79, Revelation 15:3–4,[3] or other poetic texts.[4] God's Word is filled with poetry! God likes poetry; so should you.

Characteristics of Biblical Poetry: Know What to Look For

God's prolific poetic artistry should prod us not only to value poetry but to understand how to read and preach it. As seminarians learn the fundamentals of Hebrew and Greek, so every preacher should be competent in the basics of biblical poetry. This skill is not optional. It's not optional because, as shown above, the Bible is filled with poems and poetic devices. Learn it or else!

Thankfully, during the last few centuries, and especially the past half century, scholarly research on this topic has been fruitful. We live in the land of milk and honey. Beginning with Bishop Robert Lowth's *De Sacra poesi Hebraeorum prelectiones* (1753),[5] today's preacher has at his fingertips, and hopefully in his library, many resources, including helpful introductions like those of Hassell Bullock and Leland Ryken,[6] as well as more advanced and detailed studies like those of Robert Alter, James L. Kugel, Wilfred G. E. Watson, and others.[7]

In this section I hope to summarize such scholarship as simply as possible, keeping in mind our goal: the preaching of poetry. The scholarship is abundant. It is like a large, cool pool of water. We should be thankful to God for that. But it is time we homileticians stop tipping our toes through the surface and jump right in.

What follows is my attempt to pull in any and all toe-tippers.

First, we will answer the question, "What poetic forms are employed, and how do I recognize them in the text?" and then, second, "What should we say about a Hebrew poem in an English prose sermon?" Put differently: (1) What is a Hebrew poem? and (2) How do I preach it?

One Fish, Two Fish, Red Fish, Blue Fish

To understand Hebrew poetry, you first must get Dr. Seuss out of your head, or Robert Burns, William Blake, or whatever American, Scottish, or English poet you prefer. That is, meter and rhyme, which characterize traditional English poetry, are not primary characteristics of Hebrew poetry.[8] As Douglas Stuart notes, this is likely because many Hebrew words have similar-sounding suffixes—the feminine *ah* (singular) or *oth* (plural) or the masculine plural *im*. So to rhyme Elohim with cherubim is, in Stuart's words, "too easy and would have been considered 'cheap.'"[9] Therefore, Hebrew poetry resembles Anglo-Saxon poetry (e.g., *Beowulf*) in that rhyme is ornamental, while alliteration, assonance, onomatopoeia, wordplay, and other poetic devices are the regular literary tools employed.[10] What poetic forms are employed, and how do I recognize them in the text?

Poetic Structure

PARALLELISM

"Art, ultimately, is organization."[11] That is the Hebrew poetic mindset. And the basic, most foundational, organizing form of their poetic art is parallelism,[12] what Andrew Hill calls, "a rhythm of thought."[13] There are various kinds of parallelisms. Lowth spoke of the three principal kinds, and I prefer his wording to newer (perhaps more accurate) ones.[14]

The first is *synonymous*. In a synonymous parallel, the second half-line is identical or similar to the first.[15] Below are two examples.[16] The words underlined, italicized, and in bold highlight the obvious similarities.

> But let <u>justice</u> *roll down* like **waters**,
> and <u>righteousness</u> like an *ever-flowing* **stream**. (Amos 5:24)

> <u>My soul</u> *magnifies* **the Lord**,
> and <u>my spirit</u> *rejoices* in **God my Savior**. (Luke 1:46–47)

The second is *antithetic*. In an antithetic parallel the second half-line is opposite the first. Below are two examples from Proverbs, as this book commonly uses this form. The words underlined, italicized, and in bold highlight the differences.[17]

> A <u>wise</u> son makes a *glad* **father,**
> but a <u>foolish</u> son is a *sorrow* to his **mother.** (Prov. 10:1b)

> <u>Whoever</u> goes about *slandering* **reveals secrets,**
> but <u>he who</u> is *trustworthy* in spirit **keeps a thing covered.**
> (Prov. 11:13)

The third is *synthetic*. In a synthetic parallel the second half-line imitates but also adds to the first. Here again Proverbs provides many good examples. Below I give examples from two popular proverbs.[18]

> Trust in the Lord with all your heart,
> and do not lean on your own understanding. (Prov. 3:5)

> Be not wise in your own eyes;
> fear the Lord, and turn away from evil. (Prov. 3:7)

Note the progression of thought in Proverbs 3:7. First we are exhorted not to be "wise in [our] own eyes." Then, the first part of the second half-line explains that thought by giving the alternative, "fear the Lord." Finally, the second part of the second half-line adds to that thought, explaining a central component of fearing God, namely, to "turn away from evil."

Beyond these three common types, there are also *chiasms*. The term *chiasm* derives its name from the Greek letter *chi*, because the basic form resembles the left half of that letter (X). The first example below is my own. When read left to right, top to bottom, the first theme (A) is repeated (A′) as the last, and the middle theme (B and B′) appears twice in succession. In more complex chiasms, the middle theme appears only once (not twice) at the center (e.g., the second example below, Prov. 31:10–31). Thus, chiasms found in biblical poetry can have a simple ABBA pattern or something more complex, ABCDEFGFEDCBA:

A. Simeon, my son, if you are wise in your own eyes

    B. My heart shall not be glad:

    B´. Yes, my soul shall not rejoice

A´. If you are proud in the sight of man.

A. The high value of an excellent wife (v. 10)

    B. Her husband's benefits (vv. 11–12)

        C. Her industrious work (vv. 13–19)

            D. Her doing kindness (v. 20)

                E. Fearless [of the present] (v. 21a)

                    F. Clothing her household and herself (vv. 21b–22)

                        G. Her husband's renowned respect (v. 23)

                    F´. Clothing herself and others (vv. 24–25a)

                E´. Fearless [of the future] (v. 25b)

            D´. Her teaching kindness (v. 26)

        C´. Her industrious work (v. 27)

    B´. Her husband's (and children's) praise (vv. 28–29)

A´. The high value of an excellent wife (vv. 30–31)

Chiasm Warning

      In Hebrew Poetry

           There is

              NOT

          A Chiasm

    In Every Hebrew Poem

Other structural forms include three-part praises,[19] five-part laments,[20] and acrostics.[21] As noted in chapter 2, Proverbs 31:10–31 is also an acrostic.

While these structural forms may seem complex, we should keep in mind that they are not as complex as many of the basic forms of Western poetry with which we are familiar (e.g., a Shakespearean sonnet or an ode).[22] In fact, they are quite simple. They are simple but beautiful. God delights, so it seems, in "the beauty of the simple,"[23] for most of the poems in our Bibles have simple structures, use simple images, and often convey simple (but important) theological truths, all quite beautifully.

REFRAINS AND REPETITIONS

Some biblical poems have a refrain, which is a phrase or sentence that is repeated at least twice. This should be easy to find, and once found, one may assume such repetition reveals the poem's theme. The most obvious example would be the refrain (repeated twenty-six times, at the end of each verse) in Psalm 136, "His steadfast love endures forever." Other examples include Psalms 42–43 (42:5–6a, 11; 43:5): "Why are you cast down, O my soul, and why are you in turmoil within me? Hope in God; for I shall again praise him, my salvation and my God," and the Song of Solomon (2:7; 3:5; 8:4): "I adjure you, O daughters of Jerusalem . . . that you not stir up or awaken love until it pleases." The Song of Solomon uses both a strict refrain (2:7; 3:5; 8:4)[24] and a variant refrain (2:16 is inverted in 6:3 and abbreviated in 7:11).[25]

Other poems have repeated words—key words—which function the same way as refrains. Martin Buber defines a key word as "a word or word-root that is meaningfully repeated within a text, or a sequence of texts or a complex of texts," and he then exhorts: "Those who attend to these repetitions will find a meaning of the text revealed and clarified, or at any rate made more emphatic."[26] Some examples are: "when?" in Psalm 13:1–2, "voice" in Psalm 29, "to raise" in Psalm 24, "to guard" in Psalm 121, "all" (seventeen times) in Psalm 145, and "vanity" (thirty-eight times) in Ecclesiastes.[27]

How Do I Find These Forms?

Once we know what to look for, next we need to know where to find them. Here's what I do. If you would like, follow my steps.

First, I start with the top and the tail, for where the poet starts and stops is often most significant. The top and the tail of a poem—if the same—will tell us to start moving inward, verse by verse, to see if there might be a chiasm. Also, key words are often found at the top and the tail (e.g., Pss. 103:1–2a/20–22; 118:1–4, 29; 139:1/23–24; cf. Eccles. 1:2/12:8).

Second, I stop, drop, and stare. I *stop* thinking about what preachers usually think about first—theological themes, helpful sermon illustrations, etc.—and I start thinking about possible poetic structures. Then I *drop* to my knees and pray for God's help.[28] (We all need the Spirit's illumination.) And then, I *stare* at the text. I look. I look again. And then I look one more time. The more we stop, drop, and stare, the more we will see.

Finally, I read good commentaries. In graduate school, my area of study was the history of biblical interpretation. I have continued in the last decade to grow in my knowledge of this academic discipline. In other words, I have read many commentaries or portions of commentaries from many different people from many different times and places. And without being a chronological snob or an overzealous patriot, I bravely and freely state: the commentaries written in the past fifty years (so many of them written by American evangelicals) are the best in the history of the church. Well, at least collectively; that is, take today's three best commentaries on Proverbs, for example, and you will find plenty of meat to chew and milk to drink. Few commentators of Calvin's caliber existed in the first sixteen hundred years of the church. But today the church is filled with them. Sure, not everyone is as theologically astute, pastorally sensitive, or relevant as Calvin, but today's best—bringing together these three strands—are indeed stronger and thus superior.

Now, I will warn you that the more academically elite the commentary, chances are the more unnecessary originality you will find. (Ah, the absurdity of novelty!) But the best commentators today have an erudite humility and a clarity that surpass so much of the best of biblical exegesis in the last nineteen hundred years. We can be thankful for the exegetical giants of the faith upon whose shoulders today's exegetes stand, but let's not forget the height of today's best is quite high indeed. And tomorrow's best, if they keep standing where they should, should be even higher.

So, preacher, you have no excuse not to step on these shoulders. Get your hands on such commentaries. Buy them. Pursue them on the university or seminary bookshelf. Check them out at your local library (interlibrary loan is heavenly). No excuses. Awake from your slumber. Seize the day.

Poetic Imagery

If the poetic forms discussed above can be likened to the frame of a painting, the poetic devices then are the painting itself. Devices such as metaphors, similes, alliteration, apostrophes, assonance, personifications, and hyperboles add color and texture to a poem. And, like the frame/painting combination, no matter how artistic the frame might be, it's the painting and not the frame that is the focus. Our job in preaching poetry is to recognize these images, sense them, understand them, and explain them.

While it would be beneficial if we understood (and remembered how to spell and pronounce) every possible poetic device—*epiphora* (repetition of final sounds or words), *paronomasia* (word play, including puns), or *figura etymologica* (variation on word roots, often including names)[29]—it is enough that we know the most common ones. Below are the ones that I rank the most necessary to understand:

- *Alliteration.* Alliteration is the occurrence of the same letter or sound at the beginning of adjacent or closely connected words.[30] Robert Burns's famous line "Round and round the rugged rocks" is a good example in English, as is the *kaph*-sound in Psalm 126:6 in Hebrew and the two sets of alliterations—"*hinneh, hakol, hevel*" and "*re'ut ruach*"—in Ecclesiastes 2:11. For other examples see Psalms 6:8 and 27:17.

- *Assonance.* Assonance is another alliterative technique that "employs the same or similar vowel (rather than consonant) sounds in accented positions."[31] Due to the repetition of the *e* and *ai* sounds, Bullock gives Ezekiel 27:27 as an example (cf. Gen. 49:17; Ex. 14:14; Deut. 3:2).
- *Apostrophe.* Apostrophe is the device that uses direct address to someone or something not present—"Lift up your heads, O gates"—speaking to it as though it were there.
- *Personification.* This convention treats as human something nonhuman. For example, in the Song of Deborah, the poet writes, "Asher [the tribe, not the person] sat still at the coast of the sea" (Judg. 5:17).
- *Metaphor* and *Simile.* Poets think and write in images. Metaphors and similes are images that make ideas concrete, precise, memorable, lively, and engaging. When you read the metaphor, their "tongues are sharp swords" (Ps. 57:4), it gets you to stop and think—to engage in the idea. Similes function similarly: "He is like a tree planted by streams of water" (Ps. 1:3). Similes use *like* or *as* to compare this with that. Metaphors assert with poetic license this *is* that, transferring meaning from one thing to another: "Your word is a lamp to my feet" (Ps. 119:105). The point of such pictures is for the reader to sense better the truth presented. It is fine to say, "My soul feels at peace and secure," but how much better to say, "I have calmed and quieted my soul, like a weaned child with its mother" (Ps. 131:2). It is romantic enough to tell your wife, "I enjoy kissing you," but imagine how she'd respond to the poetic description, "Your lips drip nectar, my bride; honey and milk are under your tongue" (Song 4:11a).

Although I have not spent much time on the topic of imagery, we should not underestimate its importance. Ryken argues convincingly that understanding and interpreting imagery—most notably metaphor and simile—is the most important task in explaining biblical poetry.[32] He concludes that the prime function of parallelism is artistic beauty and enjoyment,[33] while imagery is where the ideas come to life. If you understand the imagery, you will understand the ideas. See the frame. Grasp its form, its function, and even its beauty. But focus on the picture—the color, texture, and themes.

Preaching Poetry: What to Say about a Hebrew Poem in an English Prose Sermon

I agree with Stuart: "If the passage is poetic, analyze it accordingly."[34] So, yes, we should see any possible parallelisms, chiasms, key-word repetitions, and more subtle characteristics such as governing metaphors and changes in metaphors (e.g., in Psalm 23 the change from *shepherd* in vv. 1–4 to *host* in vv. 5–6).[35] However, not everything we see in a Hebrew poem should be preached in an English sermon. Below are my five suggestions for preaching an English prose sermon on a Hebrew poem.

1) Pick Poetic Portions Properly

How's that for an *a*bsolutely *a*wesome *a*lliteration! Concerning how to choose a pericope, Duane Garrett rightly advises: "Select a portion of the text that has structural integrity."[36] The example Garrett gives comes from Psalm 119. Due to that poem's length, he suggests preaching on one of the twenty-two sections, e.g., the *beth* verses (vv. 9–16), or at least one section at a time. When I preached Psalm 119, I did so in three sermons, dividing the poem thematically, based on images and key words: (1) knowing God's Word, (2) loving God's Word, and (3) obeying God's Word. I took verse 32 as the summary verse: "I will run in the way of your commandments when you enlarge my heart!" I think both methods can work—either selecting the poetic unit or taking your cue from the imagery and allowing that imagery to lead you to similar ideas found throughout the poem.

2) *Let the Form Inform*

Most biblical poems have structure. Your first task is to find such structure. Once you have found it, let it aid you in your sermon outline. For example, the twofold structure of Psalm 19 can be outlined with precisely the poet's structure:

Verses 1–6: Praise of God's revelation in creation
Verses 7–14: Praise of God's revelation in the law

However, a poem's structure does not necessarily make for a good sermon outline. When I preached Psalm 19, the poetic form *informed*, but the three theological themes *formed* my outline.

Verses 1–6: The heavens speak (general revelation)
Verses 7–11: The Scriptures speak (special revelation)
Verses 12–14: How we should listen (responding to the two voices)

Similarly, a sermon on Job 28 can be outlined based on the refrain (vv. 12 and 20), or it can be outlined based on theological key words (vv. 1–22 speak of man's pursuit of wisdom; then, in vv. 23–28, God with his wisdom enters and answers the refrain's dilemma, "Where shall wisdom be found?"). When I preached Job 28, this was my outline:

Verses 1–11: The wisdom of man
Verses 12–22: The inaccessibility of man's wisdom
Verses 23–28: The wisdom of God

So, the poetic form informs, but it does not necessarily give you a sermon outline. This is because, as Garrett well summarizes, "what works well in a poem may not work well in a speech."[37] So, yes, if the poem is a chiasm, you should preach the point of the chiasm as the thematic point,[38] but you don't need to have seven points for the seven parallels. *Capiche?*

3) DOA

Here DOA does not mean "dead on arrival" (although the idea is close to DOD, "dead on delivery") but rather "don't over-analyze." That is, don't over-analyze *in* your sermon. Yes, analyze the poetry in the study, but don't analyze every aspect of it from the pulpit. After all, this is a sermon. And sermons should be clear and interesting, and there are few things more ambiguous and boring than listening to lectures on poetry. Would you rather see Macbeth acted out on stage or hear an erudite academic talk about the thane of Glamis's (i.e., the Scottish general Macbeth) 146 lines? Would you rather hear my sermon series on the Song of Solomon or see my detailed notes on the imagery?

Matthew Arnold wrote, "The language of the Bible is fluid . . . and literary, not rigid, fixed, scientific."[39] He is right. The Bible is not a mind-numbing, high-minded scientific journal. It's living literature. Thus, we must show its liveliness. This means we should not "mechanically grind every poem," showing our congregations every structural form and poetic device.[40] Apply aesthetic minimalism to preaching poetry—"less is more" or "less is better."[41] Hide that ugly radiator in the floorboards. Strip the poem down to its most fundamental features, thus highlighting that beautiful simplicity. Always point out what is important (e.g., the acrostic structure of Psalm 119), but only point out what you think is most relevant to the point of the poem.

4) *Allow the Imagery to Embellish the Idea*

Ryken notes, "It is important for an audience that an explication [exposition or sermon] possess *a discernable strategy*. Jumping from one isolated detail to another, or from one part of a poem to another, is a sure path to an ineffective explication."[42] Each biblical poem or unit within a poem has a unifying idea or theme, which every line, and perhaps every word, embellishes. My discernable strategy is (a) to find this idea, and (b) to explain how the imagery adorns it. Sadly, our sermons often simply identify, emphasize, and explain the idea, while our commentaries often do the opposite: they give us plenty of information on the imagery but almost nothing on how such imagery fits into the idea. So put them together and there you have it. Perfection.

For example, in my sermon on Song of Solomon 1:5–2:7, "Black but Beautiful," I explained *the idea* of the beloved's transformation from negative self-perception to rapturous acceptance. And throughout the exposition I showed how each image enhanced the idea: she is ashamed of her looks because her skin has been blackened by the sun—"I am very dark . . . like the tents of Kedar" (1:5) / "Do not gaze at me because I am dark, because the sun has looked upon me" (1:6). However, the beloved overturns her self-objections with his loving affirmations, "as a lily among brambles, so is my love among the young women" (2:2).

5) Feel It

Perhaps the Song of Solomon is the perfect place to stay for this final point. If you preach the words, "Arise, my love, my beautiful one, and come away" (2:10), with the same intonation and affection as when you timidly turn to the passenger seat and ask your wife for driving directions, you've missed it. You must preach passion with passion, lament with lamentation, joy with joy, and so on. In other words, your heart should be so engaged that your tone is in tune with the lyrics. To preach, "As a deer pants for flowing streams, so pants my soul for you" (Ps. 42:1), without spiritual thirst in your voice is intolerable, and to preach, "My God, my God, why have you forsaken me?" (Ps. 22:1a), without anguish is unacceptable.

So while the question, how did this passage make you feel? is often a recipe for disaster in your average church Bible study, it is a very appropriate question for the preacher to ask himself, especially once all the details of the poetic structure and devices are in his head.

Feelings aren't everything, but they are something, something indispensable for the humble preacher of great Wisdom Literature sermons.

The Telos of Your Teaching: You have succeeded in preaching a biblical poem if a person leaves saying to himself or herself, "(a) that was a poem he preached on, (b) I felt its tone, (c) I now understand its images and theme, and thus, (d) I want to do what that text teaches me to do."

Six Helpful Resources

Alter, Robert. *The Art of Biblical Poetry.* New York: Basic Books, 1985.

Bullock, C. Hassel. *An Introduction to the Old Testament Poetic Books.* Chicago: Moody, 1988.

Garrett, Duane A. "Preaching from the Psalms and Proverbs." In *Preaching the Old Testament*, edited by Scott M. Gibson, 101–14. Grand Rapids, MI: Baker, 2006.

Klein, George L. "Preaching Poetry." In *Reclaiming the Prophetic Mantle*, edited by George L. Klein, 59–77. Nashville: Broadman, 1992.

Ryken, Leland. *Words of Delight: A Literary Introduction to the Bible.* 2nd ed., 157–289. Grand Rapids, MI: Baker, 1992.

Watson, Wilfred G. E. *Classical Hebrew Poetry: A Guide to Its Techniques.* Journal for the Study of the Old Testament 26. Sheffield: JSOT Press, 1984.

APPENDIX B

BOOK SUMMARIES AND SUGGESTED SERMON SERIES

The subtitle of this book is *Preaching Christ from the First and Last Chapters of Proverbs, Ecclesiastes, and Job.* This book, however, is not about how to preach only six chapters but how to preach all eighty-five chapters of the wisdom books. It is my hermeneutical hypothesis that if you understand the first and last chapter of each book, you will better understand the remaining chapters. The tops and tails, if you will, contain not only the key verses of each book—Proverbs 1:7, Ecclesiastes 12:13–14, and Job 42:8–9—but also the keys that unlock each treasure. Thus the six sermons serve not merely as example expositions but also as book summaries.

However, for the sake of easy reference, I include and conclude with three brief book summaries,[1] as well as with several suggested sermon series. Oddly enough, as I searched commentaries, introductions, and study Bibles for the best summaries, I found the summaries of the *ESV Children's Bible* to be the most succinct and accurate. How fitting for the Wisdom Literature! These summaries lacked only christological connections (which is sadly all too common).

Thus, I include my own two-sentence christological summary of each book as well.

Book Summaries

Proverbs

The book of Proverbs shows the blessings of seeking wisdom and the consequences of walking in foolishness. The first six verses of chapter 1 tell us that Proverbs was written to give wisdom. Wisdom is found in fearing God. The writers of Proverbs wanted the people of Israel to learn to treasure wisdom. The first nine chapters describe wisdom and show the rewards of walking in wisdom. Chapters 10–31 are full of practical instructions. Several people wrote the proverbs in this book. King Solomon wrote many of them. The proverbs were probably written between the tenth and sixth centuries BC.[2]

CHRISTOLOGICAL SUMMARY

For our own good and the glory of God, the book of Proverbs invites and instructs God's covenant people—especially young men—to embrace wisdom. Such wisdom comes through fearing God's beloved Son, the Lord Jesus Christ (Eph. 5:21), and walking in his wisdom.

Ecclesiastes

Ecclesiastes contains the thoughts of a wise old man called "the Preacher." He writes about the meaning of life. He had enjoyed many good things in life—good food, satisfying work, much pleasure, and a lot of money. These things may bring happiness for a short time but that kind of happiness doesn't last. In fact, death puts an end to things like pleasure and money. (God had told Adam and Eve about this, in Gen. 3:17–19.) People who fear the Lord are different. They can enjoy good things because they know that those good things are gifts from God. At the end of the book the preacher urges children to love God and obey him all their life. The preacher is called "the son of David, king in Jerusalem" (1:1). Many people think that Solomon wrote this book in the tenth century BC.[3]

CHRISTOLOGICAL SUMMARY

Ecclesiastes is about finding the goodness of God while living within the vanity of this world.[4] Such goodness or "wisdom" is found only through a relationship with Christ. This relationship involves trusting in Christ and heeding his commands, which brings rest, justice, and joy.

Job

The book of Job tells how God allowed a man to suffer even though he loved God. Satan claimed that Job loved God only because of the good things that God gave him. So God gave Satan permission to test Job's faith. Job lost almost everything—his property, his health, and even his children—but he still believed that God is good. In chapters 3–37 Job argues with his friends about the cause of his suffering. In chapters 38–41 God speaks to Job. These chapters show the greatness of God and man's inability to understand God's ways. Job responded in humble repentance, and God blessed Job. The author is unknown to us.[5]

CHRISTOLOGICAL SUMMARY

The book of Job prefigures the purposeful sufferings of Christ. That is, the story of God's servant Job prepares us for the story of Jesus, the suffering servant, who in his passion and death shows how innocent suffering can show forth the justice of God.

Suggested Sermon Series
Proverbs

Concerning the book of Proverbs, Tremper Longman writes, "The final editors of the book were not interested in putting it into the kind of order that would appeal to modern Western logic."[6] This is very true. And this truth makes this book difficult to preach. There are places where we can take a purely linear approach (1:1–9:18) and other places where a thematic approach is more fitting (most of 10:1–22:21).

However, there are editorial remarks within the inspired text itself that give us some structural guidance, headings such as "The proverbs of Solomon, son of David, king of Israel" (1:1), "The words of Agur son of Jakeh" (30:1), and so on. These headings, and other clues within the text, have led many scholars to view Proverbs as seven collections:

1) 1:1–9:18
2) 10:1–22:16
3) 22:17–24:22
4) 24:23–34
5) 25:1–29:27
6) 30:1–33
7) 31:1–31

Doing seven sermons on each collection would prove valuable. Also, preaching Proverbs 1:1–9:18 in ten to fifteen sermons would make for a very helpful and practical sermon series. I have attached (brave man that I am) my attempt to plot out a sermon series for the whole book. Let us pray.

THE PROVERBS OF SOLOMON

1:1–7	The Beginning of Wisdom
1:8–19	Walk Not in the Way of Sinners
1:20–4:27	The Benefits of Embracing Wisdom
1:20–33	Wisdom Shouts in the Streets
2:1–22	Why Listen to Wisdom
3:1–35	Trust in the Lord
4:1–27	Embrace Her (Wisdom)
5:1–23; 6:20–7:27; 9:13–18	Lady Folly
6:1–5	Go to Your Wronged Neighbor
6:6–11	Go to the Industrious Ant
6:12–19	Seven Abominations
8:1–9:6	Lady Wisdom
9:7–18	Correct a Scoffer

MORE PROVERBS OF SOLOMON

10:1–22:16	Contrasts ("but") and Consequences (do thematic sermons)

For 10:1–22:16, I suggest topical sermons on themes.[7] I would start with an overview sermon explaining the motive for embracing wisdom: live wisely in attitude and actions toward God and others and (usually) you will prosper. Two titles I have come up with for this overview sermon are "The *What* and *Why* of Wisdom" and "The Rewards of Righteousness, the Outcome of Unrighteousness."

Below are my sermon titles for the topics to tackle: money, parenting, business ethics, the tongue, work ethic, politics, companionship, and godly attitudes and emotions. You should give at least one sermon on each.

Company Kept
The Power of the Tongue
Neither Poverty nor Riches
A Wise Son
Train Up a Child
O Sluggard
Tempering Our Tempers
Haughtiness and Humility
God's Guidance
Fear the Lord *and the King*
When the Earth Trembles: Injustices
Business as Usual?

22:17–24:34	Do Not[8]
23:22–35	Woman and Wine[9]

THE PROVERBS OF SOLOMON VIA HEZEKIAH

25:1–7	Kingly Conduct
25:8–26:28	"Like" (A sermon on similitudes)
27:1–29:27	But the Righteous

THE PROVERBS OF AGUR

| 30:1–6 | Where to Find Wisdom: The Word |
| 30:7–33 | Two Things, Three Things, Four Things |

THE PROVERBS OF LEMUEL

| 31:1–9 | The Wise King |
| 31:10–31 | Wedding Wisdom[10] |

Ecclesiastes

If you desire to do a short series on Ecclesiastes, I suggest six sermons on these texts: 1:1–11; 2:1–11; 3:1–15; 5:1–7; 11:1–12:8; 12:13–14. If you want to tackle the whole text, I recommend a winter sermon series (post-Advent to Easter) consisting of sixteen texts. Preach them one after another until your people are begging for Easter.[11]

1:1–11	Why Work?
1:12–18	Much Wisdom, Much Grief
2:1–11	House of Hedonism
2:12–26	Madness and Meaning
3:1–15	Everything Beautiful in Its Time
3:16–4:16	Sights under the Sun
5:1–7	A Warning about Worship
5:8–6:12	Grievous Evils
6:1–12	Passing Shadows
7:1–13	Better Than
7:14–29	The Scheme of Things
8:1–9:10	The Limits of Man's Power, Justice, and Knowledge
9:11–10:20	Time and Chance
11:1–12:8	Rejoice, Remove, Remember
12:9–12	Many Words, One Shepherd
12:13–14	Repining Restlessness

Job

If you would like to do a short series on Job, I suggest the following six texts: 1:1–2:13; 19:23–29; 28:1–28; 38:1–11; 42:1–6; 42:7–17. I do not recommend a verse-by-verse exposition of the entire book. But, with its linear story line, this book can be preached in the linear fashion, beginning to end, section by section, as follows:

1:1–22	First Test
2:1–10	Second Test
2:11–31:40	Third Test[12]
3:1–26	Why Is Light Given to Him Who Suffers?
4:1–5:27	God Is Just; Are You, Job?
6:1–13	The Arrows of the Almighty
6:14–30	The Arrows of the Friends
7:1–21	The Arrows of Death
8:1–22	New Singer, Same Tune
9:1–10:22	You Can't Sue the Judge
11:1–20	Spread Out Your Hand to Him
12:1–25	The Lord's Hand Has Done This
13:1–12	Worthless Physicians
13:13–28	Hope for God's Vindication
14:1–22	Dirge of Death
15:1–35	Empty Words
16:1–17:16	Adversary and Advocate
18:1–21	Bad Things Happen to Bad People
19:1–22	Sticks and Stones
19:23–29	My Redeemer Lives
20:1–29	Broken Record
21:1–34	The Inexplicable Blessedness of the Wicked
22:1–30	Accusation and Exhortation
23:1–27:23	God Talk
28:1–28	Where Shall Wisdom Be Found?

29:1–30:31	But Now
31:1–40	If
31:1–33:39	Full of Words, Not Wisdom
34:1–37:24	Preparing the Way for the Lord
38:1–40:5	The Trial: God Calls His First Witnesses
40:6–42:6	The Trial: God Calls His Final Star Witnesses
42:7–17	The Sacrifice of My Servant

BIBLIOGRAPHY

Besides listing the commentaries in the many excellent evangelical commentary series—e.g., New International Commentary on the Old Testament, Tyndale Old Testament Commentaries, and New American Commentary—I have asterisked my top thirty Wisdom Literature books for the *pastor's* library.

The Book of Proverbs

Aitken, Kenneth T. *Proverbs*. Daily Study Bible. Philadelphia: Westminster John Knox, 1986.

Alden, R. L. *Proverbs: A Commentary on an Ancient Book of Timeless Advice*. Grand Rapids, MI: Baker, 1983.

Atkinson, David. *The Message of Proverbs: Wisdom for Life*. Bible Speaks Today. Downers Grove, IL: InterVarsity, 1996.

Bartholomew, C. G. *Reading Proverbs with Integrity*. Cambridge: Grove, 2001.

Bland, David. "A New Proposal for Preaching from Proverbs." *Preaching* 12 (1997): 28–30.

Boström, Lennart. *The God of the Sages: The Portrayal of God in the Book of Proverbs*. Coniectanea Biblica Old Testament Series 29. Stockholm: Almqvist & Wiksell, 1990.

Bridges, Charles. *Proverbs*. Crossway Classic Commentaries. Wheaton, IL: Crossway, 2001.

Chrysostom, St. John. *Commentary on the Sages*. Vol. 2, *Commentary on Proverbs; Commentary on Ecclesiastes*. Translated by Robert Charles Hill. Brookline, MA: Holy Cross Orthodox Press, 2006.

Clifford, R. J. *Proverbs*. Old Testament Library. Louisville: Westminster, 1999.

Cohen, Aelred. *Proverbs*. London: Soncino, 1967.

Collins, J. J. *Proverbs and Ecclesiastes*. Knox Preaching Guides. Atlanta: John Knox, 1980.

Davis, Ellen F. *Proverbs, Ecclesiastes, and the Song of Songs*. Louisville: Westminster, 2000.

Delitzsch, F. *Proverbs, Ecclesiastes, Song of Solomon*. Commentary on the Old Testament. Reprint, Peabody, MA: Hendrickson, 2006.

Estes, Daniel J. *Hear, My Son: Teaching and Learning in Proverbs 1–9*. New Studies in Biblical Theology. Downers Grove, IL: IVP Academic, 1997.

Farmer, Kathleen A. *Who Knows What Is Good? A Commentary on the Books of Proverbs and Ecclesiastes*. International Theological Commentary. Grand Rapids, MI: Eerdmans, 1991.

Fox, Michael V. *Proverbs 1–9*. Anchor Bible. New York: Doubleday, 2000.

Garrett, Duane A. *Proverbs, Ecclesiastes, and Song of Songs*. New American Commentary. Nashville: Broadman, 1993.

Goldingay, John. "Proverbs." In *New Bible Commentary*. 4th ed. Edited by G. J. Wenham, J. A. Motyer, D. A. Carson, and R. T. France. Downers Grove, IL: IVP Academic, 1994.

Goldsworthy, Graeme. *The Tree of Life: Reading Proverbs Today*. Sydney: Anglican Information Office, 1993.

Harrison, R. K. "Proverbs." In *Evangelical Commentary on the Bible*. Edited by Walter A. Elwell, 399–431. Grand Rapids, MI: Baker, 1989.

Hawkins, Tom R. "The Wife of Noble Character in Proverbs 31:10–31." *Bibliotheca Sacra* 153 (1996): 12–23.

Hubbard, David A. *Proverbs*. Communicator's Commentary. Dallas: Word, 1989.

Jones, John N. "'Think of the Lilies' and Prov 6:6–11." *Harvard Theological Review* 88 (1995): 172–77.

Kidner, Derek. *Proverbs*. Tyndale Old Testament Commentaries. Edited by D. J. Wiseman. Downers Grove, IL: 1964.

Kitchen, John A. *Proverbs*. A Mentor Commentary. Ross-Shire, Scotland: Christian Focus, 2006.

Koptak, Paul E. *Proverbs*. NIV Application Commentary. Grand Rapids, MI: Zondervan, 2003.

*Longman III, Tremper. *How to Read Proverbs*. Downers Grove, IL: Inter-Varsity, 2002.

_____. *Proverbs*. Baker Commentary on the Old Testament Wisdom and Psalms. Grand Rapids, MI: Baker Academic, 2006.

McCreesh, Thomas. "Wisdom as Wife: Proverbs 31:10–31." *Revue Biblique* 92 (1985): 25–46.

McKane, William. *Proverbs*. Old Testament Library. Philadelphia: Westminster John Knox, 1970.

Murphy, Roland. *Proverbs*. Word Biblical Commentary. Nashville: Nelson, 1998.

Perdue, Leo G. *Proverbs*. Interpretation. Louisville: Westminster, 2000.

_____. "Proverbs and Ecclesiastes." In *Chalice Introduction to the Old Testament*. Edited by Marti J. Steussy, 209–21. St. Louis: Chalice, 2003.

Ross, Allen P. "Proverbs." In *Expositor's Bible Commentary*. Edited by Frank E. Gaebelein, 883–1136. Grand Rapids, MI: Zondervan, 1991.

Schwab, George M. *The Book of Proverbs*. Cornerstone Biblical Commentary. Carol Stream, IL: Tyndale, 2009.

Targum of Proverbs. The Aramaic Bible 15. Collegeville, MN: Liturgical Press, 1991.

Tepox, Alfredo. "The Importance of Becoming Wise: Proverbs 1.1–7." *Bible Translator* 52 (2001): 216–22.

Toy, C. H. *The Book of Proverbs*. International Critical Commentary. Edinburgh: T&T Clark, 1899.

Waltke, Bruce K. "The Authority of Proverbs: An Exposition of Proverbs 1:2–6." *Presbyterion* 13 (1987): 65–78.

_____. *The Book of Proverbs*. New International Commentary on the Old Testament. 2 vols. Grand Rapids, MI: Eerdmans, 2004–2005.

_____. "The Book of Proverbs and Old Testament Theology." *Bibliotheca Sacra* 136 (1979): 302–17.

_____. "Does Proverbs Promise Too Much?" *Andrew University Seminary Studies* 34 (1966): 319–36.

Whybray, R. N. *The Book of Proverbs*. The Cambridge Bible Commentary on the New English Bible. Cambridge: Cambridge University Press, 1972.

———. *Proverbs*. New Century Bible Commentary. Grand Rapids, MI: Eerdmans, 1994.

Wright, J. Robert, ed. *Proverbs, Ecclesiastes, Song of Solomon*. Ancient Christian Commentary on Scripture. Downers Grove, IL: IVP Academic, 2005.

The Book of Ecclesiastes

Bartholomew, Craig G. *Ecclesiastes*. Baker Commentary on the Old Testament Wisdom and Psalms. Grand Rapids, MI: Baker Academic, 2009.

———. *Reading Ecclesiastes: Old Testament Exegesis and Hermeneutical Theory*. Rome: Pontificio Istituto Biblico, 1998.

Beza, Theodore. *Ecclesiastes, or the Preacher: Solomon's Sermon Made to the People*. Cambridge: John Legatt, 1593.

Bonaventura. *Commentary on Ecclesiastes*. Works of St Bonaventure 7. Translated by R. J. Karris and Campion Murray. St. Bonaventure, NY: Franciscan Institute Publications, 2005.

Bonhoeffer, Dietrich. *Ethics*. Translated by Neville Horton Smith. Edited by Eberhard Bethge. New York: Macmillan, 1955.

———. *Letters and Papers from Prison*. Translated by Reginald H. Fuller and Frank Clarke. Edited by Eberhard Bethge. New York: Macmillan, 1972.

Bozanich, R. "Donne and Ecclesiastes." *Proceedings of the Modern Language Association* 90 (1975): 270–76.

Brown, W. P. *Ecclesiastes*. Interpretation. Louisville: Westminster, 2000.

*Christianson, E. S. *Ecclesiastes through the Centuries*. Blackwell Bible Commentaries. Malden, MA: Blackwell, 2007.

Collins, J. J. *Proverbs and Ecclesiastes*. Knox Preaching Guides. Atlanta: John Knox, 1980.

Craigie, Peter C. "Biblical Wisdom in the Modern World: I. Proverbs." *Crux* 15 (1979): 7–9.

Crenshaw, J. L. *Ecclesiastes*. Old Testament Library. Philadelphia: Westminster John Knox, 1987.

Davis, Ellen F. *Proverbs, Ecclesiastes, and the Song of Songs*. Louisville: Westminster, 2000.

Delitzsch, F. *Proverbs, Ecclesiastes, Song of Solomon*. Commentary on the Old Testament. Reprint, Peabody, MA: Hendrickson, 2006.

Devine, J. Minos. *Ecclesiastes, or The Confessions of an Adventurous Soul*. London: Macmillan, 1916.

Eaton, Michael A. *Ecclesiastes*. Tyndale Old Testament Commentaries. Edited by D. J. Wiseman. Downers Grove, IL: IVP Academic, 1983.

_____. "Ecclesiastes." In *New Bible Commentary*. 4th ed. Edited by G. J. Wenham, J. A. Motyer, D. A. Carson, and R. T. France, 609–18. Downers Grove, IL: IVP Academic, 1994.

Ehlke, Roland Cap. *Ecclesiastes; Song of Songs*. People's Bible Commentary. St. Louis: Concordia, 1988.

Ellul, Jacques. *Reason for Being: A Meditation on Ecclesiastes*. Translated by Joyce Main Hanks. Grand Rapids, MI: Eerdmans, 1990.

Erasmus. *Ecclesiastes; or, the Preacher*. London: Rivington, Faulder, & Gardner, 1797.

Erasmus, Desiderius. *The Praise of Folly and Other Writings*. Edited by Robert Adams. New York: W. W. Norton, 1989.

Fox, Michael V. *Ecclesiastes*. JPS Bible Commentary. Philadelphia: Jewish Publication Society of America, 2004.

_____. *A Time to Tear Down and a Time to Build Up: A Rereading of Ecclesiastes*. Grand Rapids, MI: Eerdmans, 1999.

Fredericks, Daniel C. *Coping with Transience: Ecclesiastes and Brevity of Life*. The Bible Seminar 18. Sheffield: Sheffield Academic Press, 1993.

Fredericks, Daniel C. and Daniel J. Estes, *Ecclesiastes and the Song of Songs*. Apollos Old Testament Commentaries. Downers Grove, IL: IVP Academic, 2010.

Frydrych, T. *Living Under the Sun: An Examination of Proverbs and Qoheleth*. Leiden: Brill, 2002.

Ginsburg, Christian D. *The Song of Songs and Coheleth*. New York: Ktav, 1970.

Goldin, J. "The End of Ecclesiastes: Literal Exegesis and Its Transformation." In *Biblical Motifs: Origins and Transformations*. Edited by A. Altmann, 135–58. Cambridge, MA: Harvard, 1966.

Gregory of Nyssa. *Gregory of Nyssa: Homilies on Ecclesiastes*. Edited by S. G. Hall. Berlin: deGruyter, 1993.

Gregory Thaumaturgos. *Gregory Thaumaturgos's Paraphrase of Ecclesiastes*. Translation and notes by John Jarick. Society of Biblical Literature Septuagint and Cognate Studies 29. Atlanta: Scholars Press, 1990.

*Greidanus, Sidney. *Preaching Christ from Ecclesiastes: Foundations for Expository Sermons.* Grand Rapids, MI: Eerdmans, 2010.

Greissinger, James A. "The Worst Understood Book." *Methodist Review* 91 (1909): 734–41.

Hall, Stuart George, ed. *Gregory of Nyssa, Homilies on Ecclesiastes: An English Version with Supporting Studies, Proceeding of the Seventh International Colloquium on Gregory of Nyssa (St Andrews, 5–10 September 1990).* Berlin: de Gruyter, 1993.

Hengstenberg, Ernest W. *A Commentary on Ecclesiastes.* Eugene, OR: Wipf & Stock, 1998.

Horne, Milton P. *Proverbs, Ecclesiastes.* Smyth & Helwys Bible Commentary. Macon, GA: Smyth & Helwys, 2003.

Hubbard, David. *Ecclesiastes and Song of Songs.* Mastering the Old Testament. Dallas: Word, 1991.

Jarick, John. "Theodore of Mopsuestia and the Interpretation of Ecclesiastes." In *The Bible in Human Society: Essays in Honour of John Rogerson.* Edited by R. Carroll, David J. A. Clines, and Philip R. Davies. Journal for the Study of the Old Testament: Supplement Series 200, 306–16. Sheffield: Sheffield Academic Press, 1995.

Jerome. "Commentaries in Ecclesiasten." In *Patrologiae Latine.* Edited by J. P. Migne, 1063–173, vol. 23. Paris: Migne, 1863.

Johnston, Robert K. *Useless Beauty: Ecclesiastes through the Lens of Contemporary Film.* Grand Rapids, MI: Baker Academic, 2004.

Kaiser, Walter C. *Ecclesiastes: Total Life.* Everyman's Bible Commentary. Chicago: Moody, 1979.

Kallas, E. "Ecclesiastes: Traditum et Fides Evangelica. The Ecclesiastes Commentaries of Martin Luther, Philip Melanchthon, and Johannes Brenz Considered within the History of Interpretation." PhD diss., Graduate Theological Union, Berkeley, 1979.

Kempis, Thomas à. *The Following of Christ* [aka, *The Imitation of Christ*]. Edited by J. van Ginneken. New York: American Press, 1937.

Kidner, Derek. *The Message of Ecclesiastes: A Time to Mourn, and a Time to Dance.* Bible Speaks Today. Downers Grove, IL: IVP Academic, 1976.

Kushner, Harold. *When All You've Ever Wanted Isn't Enough: The Search for a Life That Matters.* New York: Summit, 1986.

Leithart, Peter J. *Solomon Among the Postmoderns.* Grand Rapids, MI: Brazos, 2008.

*Leupold, H. C. *Expositions of Ecclesiastes*. Grand Rapids, MI: Baker, 1952.

*Limburg, J. *Encountering Ecclesiastes: A Book for Our Time*. Grand Rapids, MI: Eerdmans, 2006.

Loader, J. A. *Ecclesiastes: A Practical Commentary*. Text and Interpretation. Grand Rapids, MI: Eerdmans, 1986.

Longman III, Tremper. *The Book of Ecclesiastes*. New International Commentary on the Old Testament. Grand Rapids, MI: Eerdmans, 1998.

_____. *Ecclesiastes*. Cornerstone Biblical Commentary. Carol Stream, IL: Tyndale, 2006.

Luther, Martin. *Ecclesiastes, Song of Solomon, Last Words of David: 2 Samuel 23:1–7*. Luther's Works, vol. 15. St. Louis: Concordia, 1972.

Meyers, Jeffery. *A Table in the Mist: Meditations on Ecclesiastes*. Through New Eyes Bible Commentary Series. Monroe, LA: Athanasius Press, 2006.

Moore, T. M. *Ecclesiastes: Ancient Wisdom When All Else Fails*. Downers Grove, IL: InterVarsity, 2001.

Murphy, Roland. *Ecclesiastes*. Word Biblical Commentary. Nashville: Nelson, 1992.

Parson, Greg W. "Guidelines for Understanding and Proclaiming the Book of Ecclesiastes." *Bibliotheca Sacra* 160 (2003): 159–73, 283–304.

Paulson, Gail Nord. "The Use of Qoheleth in Bonhoeffer's *Ethics*." *Word and World* 18 (1998): 307–13.

Perdue, Leo G. "Proverbs and Ecclesiastes." In *Chalice Introduction to the Old Testament*. Edited by Marti J. Steussy, 209–21. St. Louis: Chalice, 2003.

Perrin, Nicholas. "Messianism in the Narrative Frame of Ecclesiastes?" *Revue Biblique* 108 (2001): 51–57.

Provan, Iain. *Ecclesiastes/Song of Songs*. NIV Application Commentary. Grand Rapids, MI: Zondervan, 2001.

*Ryken, Philip Graham. *Ecclesiastes: Why Everything Matters*. Preaching the Word. Wheaton, IL: Crossway, 2010.

Schultz, Carl. "Ecclesiastes." In *Evangelical Commentary on the Bible*. Edited by Walter A. Elwell, 1137–1200. Grand Rapids, MI: Baker, 1989.

Seow, Choon-Leong. *Ecclesiastes*. Anchor Bible. New York: Doubleday, 1997.

*Webb, Barry G. *Five Festal Garments: Christian Reflections on the Song of Songs, Ruth, Lamentations, Ecclesiastes, and Esther*. New Studies in Biblical Theology. Downers Grove, IL: IVP Academic, 2000.

White, G. "Luther on Ecclesiastes and the Limits of Human Abililty." *Neue Zeitschrift für systematische Theologie und Religionsphilosophie* 29 (1987): 180–94.

Whybray, R. N. *Ecclesiastes.* Old Testament Guides. Sheffield: JSOT Press, 1989.

_____. "Ecclesiastes 1:5–7 and the Wonders of Nature." *Journal for the Study of the Old Testament* 41 (1981): 105–12.

_____. "Qoheleth, Preacher of Joy." *Journal for the Study of the Old Testament* 23 (1982): 87–98.

*Wilson, Douglas. *Joy at the End of the Tether: The Inscrutable Wisdom of Ecclesiastes.* Moscow, ID: Canon, 1999.

Wolters, Al. *The Song of the Valiant Woman: Studies in the Interpretation of Proverbs 31:10–31.* Carlisle, UK: Paternoster, 2001.

Wood, David. "Ecclesiastes: Millennium Gospel?" *Epworth Review* 26 (1999): 25–33.

Wright, Addison G. "Ecclesiastes (Qoheleth)." In *New Jerome Biblical Commentary.* Edited by Raymond E. Brown, Joseph A. Fitzmyer, and Roland E. Murphy, 489–98. Englewood Cliffs, NJ: Prentice-Hall, 1990.

Wright, J. Robert, ed. *Proverbs, Ecclesiastes, Song of Solomon.* Ancient Christian Commentary on Scripture. Downers Grove, IL: IVP Academic, 2005.

Zuck, Rob B., ed. *Reflecting with Solomon: Selected Studies in the Book of Ecclesiastes.* Grand Rapids, MI: Eerdmans, 1994.

The Book of Job

Alden, Robert L. *Job.* New American Commentary. Nashville: Broadman, 1993.

Anderson, Francis I. *Job.* Tyndale Old Testament Commentaries. Downers Grove, IL: IVP Academic, 1976.

Aquinas, Thomas. *The Literal Exposition of Job: A Scriptural Commentary Concerning Providence.* American Academy of Religion, Classics in Religious Studies. Translated by Anthony Damico. Atlanta: Scholars Press, 1989.

*Ash, Christopher. *Out of the Storm: Grappling with God in the Book of Job.* Vancouver: Regent College, 2004.

Atkinson, David. *The Message of Job.* Bible Speaks Today. Downers Grove, IL: IVP Academic, 1991.

Balentine, Samuel E. "My Servant Job Shall Pray for You." *Theology Today* 58 (2002): 502–18.

Blake, William. *Illustrations on the Book of Job.* New York: D. Appleton, 1903.

Calvin, John. *Sermons on Job, 1547.* Carlisle, PA: Banner of Truth, 1993.

Carson, D. A. *How Long, O Lord? Reflections on Suffering and Evil.* 2nd ed. Grand Rapids, MI: Baker Academic, 2006.

Clines, David J. A. "Job." In *New Bible Commentary.* 4th ed. Edited by G. J. Wenham, J. A. Motyer, D. A. Carson, and R. T. France, 459–84. Downers Grove, IL: IVP Academic, 1994.

_____. *Job 1–20.* Word Biblical Commentary, vol. 17. Dallas: Word, 1989.

_____. "Job and the Spirituality of the Reformation." In *The Bible, the Reformation, and the Church.* Edited by W. P. Stephens. Journal for the Study of the New Testament: Supplement Series 105, 49–72. Sheffield: Sheffield Academic Press, 1995.

_____. "'The Fear of the Lord Is Wisdom' (Job 28:28): A Semantic and Contextual Study." In *Job 28: Cognition in Context.* Edited by Ellen van Wolde, 57–92. Biblical Interpretation Series 64. Leiden: Brill, 2003.

Crenshaw, James L. "The Book of Job" (1992). In *Urgent Advice and Probing Questions: Collected Writings on Old Testament Wisdom,* 426–48. Macon, GA: Mercer, 1995.

Dhorme, Edouard. *A Commentary on the Book of Job.* Translated by H. Knight. London: Nelson, 1967.

Driver, S. R., and G. B. Gray. *A Critical and Exegetical Commentary on the Book of Job.* International Critical Commentary. Reprint, Edinburgh: T&T Clark, 1997.

Eaton, J. H. *Job.* T&T Clark Study Guides. Reprint, New York: T&T Clark, 2004.

Fyall, Robert S. *How Does God Treat His Friends?* Ross-Shire, Scotland: Christian Focus, 1995.

_____. *Now My Eyes Have Seen You: Images of Creation and Evil in the Book of Job.* New Studies in Biblical Theology. Downers Grove, IL: IVP Academic, 2002.

Gordis, Robert. *The Book of Job and Man: A Study of Job.* Chicago: University of Chicago Press, 1965.

*Green, J. H. *The Argument of the Book of Job Unfolded.* Reprint, Minneapolis: Klock, 1977.

Habel, Norman. *The Book of Job: A Commentary.* Old Testament Library. Philadelphia: Westminster, 1985.

Hartley, John E. *Book of Job.* New International Commentary on the Old Testament. Grand Rapids, MI: Eerdmans, 1988.

Hoffman, Y. A. *Blemished Perfection: The Book of Job in Context.* Journal for the Study of the Old Testament Supplement 213. Sheffield: Sheffield Academic Press, 1996.

*Jackson, David R. *Crying Out for Vindication: The Gospel According to Job.* The Gospel According to the Old Testament. Phillipsburg, NJ: P&R, 2007.

Jansen, J. Gerald. *Job.* Interpretation. Atlanta: John Knox, 1985.

Jung, C. G. *Answer to Job.* Bollingen Series 20. Translated by R. F. C. Hull. Princeton: Princeton University Press, 1991.

*Kline, Meredith. "Job." In *Wycliffe Bible Commentary.* Edited by Charles F. Pfeiffer and Everett F. Harrison. Chicago: Moody, 1962.

Konkel, August H. *Job.* Cornerstone Biblical Commentary. Carol Stream, IL: Tyndale, 2006.

Kuyper, Lester J. "The Repentance of Job." *Vetus Testamentum* 9 (1959): 91–94.

Lasine, Stuart. "Bird's-eye and Worm's-eye Views of Justice in the Book of Job." *Journal for the Study of the Old Testament* 42 (1988): 344.

MacKenzie, R. A. F., and Roland E. Murphy. "Job." In *New Jerome Biblical Commentary.* Edited by Raymond E. Brown, et al., 466–88. Englewood Cliffs, NJ: Prentice Hall, 1990.

Moore, R. D. "The Integrity of Job." *Catholic Biblical Quarterly* 45 (1983): 17–31.

Morgan, G. Campbell. *The Answers of Jesus to Job.* London; Edinburgh: Marshall, Morgan & Scott, 1900.

O'Connor, Daniel J. "Job's Final Word—'I am consoled . . .' (42:6b)." *Irish Theological Quarterly* 50 (1983): 181–97.

Perdue, Leo and W. C. Gilpin, eds. *The Voice from the Whirlwind: Interpreting the Book of Job.* Nashville: Abingdon, 1992.

Pope, Marvin H. *Job: Introduction, Translation and Notes.* Anchor Bible. Garden City, NY: Doubleday, 1973.

Porter, S. E. "The Message of the Book of Job: 42:7b as Key to Interpretation." *Evangelical Quarterly* 63 (1991): 291–304.

*Robinson, H. Wheeler. *The Cross in the Old Testament: The Cross of Job; The Cross of the Servant, and the Cross of Jeremiah.* London: SCM, 1955.

Rowley, H. H. *Job.* New Cambridge Bible Commentary, rev. ed. Reprinted, Grand Rapids, MI: Eerdmans, 1980.

Sasson, Victor. "The Literary and Theological Function of Job's Wife in the Book of Job." *Biblica* 79 (1998): 86–90.

*Schreiner, Susan E. *Where Shall Wisdom Be Found? Calvin's Exegesis of Job from Medieval and Modern Perspectives.* Chicago: University of Chicago Press, 1994.

Schultz, Carl. "Job." In *Evangelical Commentary on the Bible.* Edited by Walter A. Elwell, 337–66. Grand Rapids, MI: Baker, 1989.

Simonettie, Manlio, and Marco Conti, eds. *Job.* Ancient Christian Commentary on Scripture. Downers Grove, IL: IVP Academic, 2006.

Smick, Elmer B. "Job." In *Expositor's Bible Commentary.* Edited by Frank E. Gaebelein, 843–1060. Grand Rapids, MI: Zondervan, 1988.

Thomas, Derek. *Calvin's Teaching on Job: Proclaiming the Incomprehensible God.* Ross-Shire, Scotland: Mentor, 2004.

*_____. *The Storm Breaks: Job Simply Explained.* Welwyn Commentary Series. Reprinted, Webster, NY: Evangelical Press, 2005.

Westermann, C. *The Structure of the Book of Job.* Philadelphia: Fortress, 1981.

Whybray, R. N. *Job.* Readings: A New Biblical Commentary. Sheffield: Sheffield Academic Press, 1998.

Wolfers, David. *Deep Things Out of Darkness: The Book of Job.* Grand Rapids, MI: Eerdmans, 1995.

Zerafa, Peter P. *The Wisdom of God in the Book of Job.* Rome: Herder, 1978.

Zuck, Roy B. *Job.* Everyman's Bible Commentary. Chicago: Moody, 1978.

_____, ed. *Sitting with Job: Selected Studies on the Book of Job.* Grand Rapids, MI: Baker, 1992.

Zuckerman, Bruce. *Job the Silent: A Study of Historical Counterpoint.* Oxford: Oxford University Press, 1991.

Other Resources

Achtemeier, Elizabeth. *Preaching from the Old Testament.* Louisville: Westminster, 1989.

Adams, Jay E. *Preaching with Purpose: A Comprehensive Textbook on Biblical Preaching.* Grand Rapids, MI: Baker, 1982.

*Alter, Robert. *The Art of Biblical Poetry.* New York: Basic Books, 1985.

Barre, Michal L., ed. *Wisdom, You Are My Sister: Studies in Honor of Roland E. Murphy, O. Carm., on the Occasion of His Eightieth Birthday.* Catholic Biblical Quarterly Monograph Series 29. Washington DC: Catholic Biblical Association of America, 1997.

Barton, Stephen C., ed. *Where Shall Wisdom Be Found? Wisdom in the Bible, the Church and the Contemporary World.* Edinburgh: T&T Clark, 1999.

Beale, G. K. and D. A. Carson, eds. *Commentary on the New Testament Use of the Old Testament.* Grand Rapids, MI: Baker Academic, 2007.

Beardslee, W. A. "Uses of the Proverb in the Synoptic Gospels." *Interpretation* 24 (1970): 61–73.

Berlin, Adele. *The Dynamics of Biblical Parallelism.* Bloomington: Indiana University Press, 1985.

Blocher, Henri. "The Fear of the Lord as the 'Principle' of Wisdom." *Tyndale Bulletin* 28 (1977): 3–28.

Boadt, Lawrence. "St. Thomas Aquinas and the Biblical Wisdom Tradition." *The Thomist* 49 (1985): 575–611.

Brown, W. P. *Character in Crisis: A Fresh Approach to the Wisdom Literature of the Old Testament.* Grand Rapids, MI: Eerdmans, 1996.

*Bullock, C. Hassell. *An Introduction to the Old Testament Poetic Books.* Chicago: Moody, 1988.

Bultmann, Rudolf. "Logia (Jesus as Teacher of Wisdom)." *The History of the Synoptic Tradition.* Translated by John Marsh. New York: Harper & Row, 1963.

Bunyan, John. *The Fear of God.* Orlando: Soli Deo Gloria, 2006.

*Chapell, Bryan. *Christ-Centered Preaching: Redeeming the Expository Sermon.* 2nd ed. Grand Rapids, MI: Baker Academic, 2005.

Clements, R. E. *Wisdom in Theology.* Grand Rapids, MI: Eerdmans, 1992.

Clowney, Edmund P. *Preaching Christ in All of Scripture.* Wheaton, IL: Crossway, 2003.

_____. *The Unfolding Mystery: Discovering Christ in the Old Testament.* Reprint, Phillipsburg, NJ: P&R, 1991.

Conzelmann, Hans. "Wisdom in the NT." *Interpreter's Dictionary of the Bible.* Supplementary vol., 956–60. Nashville: Abingdon, 1976.

Davidson, Robert. *Wisdom and Worship.* London: SCM, 1990.

Day, J., R. P. Gordon, and H. G. M. Williamson, eds. *Wisdom and Ancient Israel.* Cambridge: Cambridge University Press, 1995.

Dillard, Raymond B., and Tremper Longman III. *An Introduction to the Old Testament.* Grand Rapids, MI: Zondervan, 1994.

Dumbrell, William J. *The Faith of Israel: A Theological Survey of the Old Testament,* 2nd ed. Grand Rapids, MI: Baker Academic, 2002.

Dunn, James D. G. *Christology in the Making.* Philadelphia: Westminster John Knox, 1980.

Efird, James M. *Biblical Books of Wisdom: A Study of Proverbs, Job, Ecclesiastes, and Other Wisdom Literature of the Bible.* Eugene, OR: Wipf & Stock, 2001.

*Estes, Daniel J. *Handbook on the Wisdom Books and Psalms: Job, Psalms, Proverbs, Ecclesiastes, Song of Songs.* Grand Rapids, MI: Baker Academic, 2005.

Fokkelman, J. P. *Reading Biblical Poetry: An Introductory Guide.* Louisville: Westminster, 2001.

Gammie, J. G., and L. G. Perdue, eds. *The Sage in Israel and the Ancient Near East.* Winona Lake, IN: Eisenbrauns, 1990.

Garrett, Duane A. "Preaching from the Psalms and Proverbs." In *Preaching the Old Testament.* Edited by Scott M. Gibson, 101–14. Grand Rapids, MI: Baker, 2006.

*_____. "Preaching Wisdom." In *Reclaiming the Prophetic Mantle: Preaching the Old Testament Faithfully.* Edited by George L. Klein. Nashville: Broadman, 1992.

Gibson, R. J., ed. *Interpreting God's Plan: Biblical Theology and the Pastor.* Explorations 11. Carlisle, UK: Paternoster, 1997.

Gibson, Scott M., ed. *Preaching the Old Testament.* Grand Rapids, MI: Baker, 2006.

Gillingham, S. E. *The Poems and Psalms of the Hebrew Bible.* Oxford: Oxford University Press, 1994.

Goldingay, J. E. "The 'Salvation History' Perspective and the 'Wisdom Perspective' within the Context of Biblical Theology." *Evangelical Quarterly* 51 (1979): 194–207.

Goldsworthy, Graeme. *Gospel and Kingdom: A Christian Interpretation of the Old Testament.* Exeter: Paternoster, 1983.

*_____. *Gospel and Wisdom: Israel's Wisdom Literature in the Christian Life.* Biblical Classics Library. London: Paternoster, 1995.

*_____. *Gospel-Centered Hermeneutics: Foundations and Principles of Evangelical Biblical Interpretation.* Downers Grove, IL: IVP Academic, 2006.

_____. *Preaching the Whole Bible as Christian Scripture: The Application of Biblical Theology to Expository Preaching.* Grand Rapids, MI: Eerdmans, 2000.

Greidanus, Sidney. *The Modern Preacher and the Ancient Text: Interpreting and Preaching Biblical Literature.* Grand Rapids, MI: Eerdmans, 1988.

*_____. *Preaching Christ from the Old Testament: A Contemporary Hermeneutical Method.* Grand Rapids, MI: Eerdmans, 1999.

Hill, R. Charles. *Wisdom's Many Faces.* Collegeville, MN: Liturgical Press, 1996.

Holbert, John C. *Preaching Job.* St. Louis: Chalice, 2002.

House, Paul R. *Old Testament Theology.* Downers Grove, IL: IVP Academic, 1998.

Hubbard, D. A. "The Wisdom Movement and Israel's Covenant Faith." *Tyndale Bulletin* 17 (1966): 3–33.

*Johnson, Dennis E. *Him We Proclaim: Preaching Christ from All the Scriptures.* Phillipsburg, NJ: P&R, 2007.

Kaiser Jr., Walter C. *The Majesty of God in the Old Testament: A Guide for Preaching and Teaching.* Grand Rapids, MI: Baker Academic, 2007.

_____. *The Messiah in the Old Testament.* Grand Rapids, MI: Zondervan, 1995.

*Kidner, Derek. *The Wisdom of Proverbs, Job and Ecclesiastes: An Introduction to Wisdom Literature.* Downers Grove, IL: IVP Academic, 1985.

Klein, George L. "Preaching Poetry." In *Reclaiming the Prophetic Mantle.* Edited by George L. Klein, 59–78. Nashville: Broadman, 1992.

Kugel, James L. *Great Poems of the Bible.* New York: Free Press, 1999.

_____. *The Idea of Biblical Poetry.* New Haven: Yale University Press, 1981.

LaSor, William Sanford, et al. *Old Testament Survey: The Message, Form, and Background of the Old Testament.* 2nd ed. Grand Rapids, MI: Eerdmans, 1996.

Long, Thomas G. *Preaching and the Literary Forms of the Bible.* Philadelphia: Fortress, 1989.

*Longman, Tremper, III, and Peter Enns, *Dictionary of the Old Testament: Wisdom, Poetry, and Writings*. The IVP Bible Dictionary Series. Downers Grove, IL: IVP Academic, 2008.

Lucas, Ernest C. *Exploring the Old Testament: A Guide to the Psalms and Wisdom Literature*. Downers Grove, IL: IVP Academic, 2003.

*McKenzie, Alyce M. *Hear and Be Wise: Becoming a Preacher and Teacher of Wisdom*. Nashville: Abingdon, 2004.

*Murphy, Roland E. *The Tree of Life: An Exploration of Biblical Wisdom Literature*. Anchor Bible Reference Library. New York: Doubleday, 1990.

O'Connor, Kathleen. *The Wisdom Literature*. Message of Biblical Spirituality 5. Wilmington, DE: Glazier, 1988.

O'Connor, M. *Hebrew Verse Structure*. Winona Lake, IN: Eisenbrauns, 1980.

Packer, J. I., and Sven K. Soderlund, eds. *The Way of Wisdom: Essays in Honor of Bruce K. Waltke*. Grand Rapids, MI: Zondervan, 2000.

Perdue, Leo G. *Wisdom and Creation*. Nashville: Abingdon, 1994.

_____. *Wisdom Literature: A Theological History*. Louisville: Westminster, 2007.

_____. "The Wisdom Sayings of Jesus." *Forum* 2 (1986): 3–35.

Perkins, Pheme. "Jesus: God's Wisdom." *Word and World* 7 (1987): 273–80.

_____. *Jesus as Teacher*. New York: Cambridge University Press, 1990.

Rad, Gerhard von. "The Joseph Narrative and Ancient Wisdom." In *The Problem of the Hexateuch and Other Essays*. New York: McGraw Hill, 1966.

_____. *Wisdom in Israel*. Translated by James D. Martin. Harrisburg, PA: Trinity Press International, 1972.

Ranston, Harry. *The Old Testament Wisdom Books and Their Teachings*. London: Epworth, 1930.

*Ryken, Leland. *Words of Delight: A Literary Introduction to the Bible*. 2nd ed. Grand Rapids, MI: Baker, 1992.

Ryken, Leland, and Tremper Longman III, eds. *A Complete Literary Guide to the Bible*. Grand Rapids, MI: Zondervan, 1993.

Scobie, Charles H. H. "The Place of Wisdom in Biblical Theology." *Biblical Theology Bulletin* 14 (1984): 43–48.

Scott, R. B. Y. *The Way of Wisdom in the Old Testament*. New York: Macmillan, 1971.

Stuart, Douglas K. *Old Testament Exegesis: A Handbook for Students and Pastors.* 2nd ed. Philadelphia: Westminster John Knox, 1984.

Suggs, M. Jack. *Wisdom, Christology, and Law in Matthew's Gospel.* Cambridge, MA: Harvard University Press, 1970.

Troxel, Roland L., Kelvin G. Friebel, and Dennis R. Magary, eds. *Seeking Out the Wisdom of the Ancients: Essays Offered to Honor Michael V. Fox on the Occasion of His Sixty-fifth Birthday.* Winona Lake, IN: Eisenbrauns, 2005.

Van Groningen, Gerard. *Messianic Revelation in the Old Testament.* Grand Rapids, MI: Baker, 1990.

Vos, Geerhardus. *Biblical Theology: Old and New Testaments.* Grand Rapids, MI: Eerdmans, 1975.

Waltke, Bruce K. "The Fear of the Lord: The Foundation for a Relationship with God." In *Alive to God: Studies in Spirituality Presented to James D. Houston.* Edited by J. I. Packer and Loren Wilkinson, 17–33. Downers Grove, IL: InterVarsity, 1992.

*_____. *An Old Testament Theology: An Exegetical, Canonical, and Thematic Approach.* Grand Rapids, MI: Zondervan, 2007.

Watson, Wilfred G. E. *Classical Hebrew Poetry: A Guide to Its Techniques.* Journal for the Study of the Old Testament Supplement Series 26. Sheffield: JSOT Press, 1984.

Westermann, Claus. *Roots of Wisdom.* Edinburgh: T&T Clark, 1995.

Wilken, Robert L., ed. *Aspects of Wisdom in Judaism and Early Christianity.* Notre Dame, IN: University of Notre Dame, 1975.

Williamson, H. G. M. *Wisdom in Ancient Israel.* Cambridge: Cambridge University Press, 1995.

Witherington III, Ben. *Jesus the Sage: The Pilgrimage of Wisdom.* Minneapolis: Fortress, 1994.

NOTES

Preface

1. Here I refer to John Knox's famous statement concerning John Calvin's Geneva: that it was "the most perfect school of Christ that ever was on earth since the days of the Apostles." Quote found in Philip Schaff, *A History of the Creeds of Christendom*, 6th ed., 3 vols. (Harper & Brothers, 1919), 1:460.

2. John Donne (1572–1631) was the dean of St. Paul's in London. Yet he is best known today as one of the great "metaphysical" poets. My thesis is entitled, *Walking on "the Ashes of God's Saints": John Donne's Interpretation of the Song of Songs and the Origenist Exegetical Tradition.*

3. It is telling that a recently published book on this topic (Scott M. Gibson, ed., *Preaching the Old Testament* [Grand Rapids, MI: Baker, 2006]) has chapters on preaching from Old Testament narrative, the law, the prophets, and Psalms and Proverbs (which is more on poetry than genre), but there is no chapter on preaching the Wisdom Literature. Even Sidney Greidanus's excellent and thorough book *Preaching Christ from the Old Testament: A Contemporary Hermeneutical Method* (Grand Rapids, MI: Eerdmans, 1999) has only a few short sections on Wisdom Literature (pp. 240, 265–66, 271, 276, 346). See also Greidanus, *The Modern Preacher and the Ancient Text: Interpreting and Preaching Biblical Literature* (Grand Rapids, MI: Eerdmans, 1988), which has only one paragraph on the genre (see the bottom of p. 115) and a few other passing remarks (see pp. 156, 189, 228, 311). Thankfully, Greidanus's recent book *Preaching Christ from Ecclesiastes: Foundations for Expository Sermons* (Grand Rapids, MI: Eerdmans, 2010) tackles this topic. Still, despite his attempt and mine, and perhaps others'

of which I am unaware, the gap is still large. So what Robert L. Wilken wrote thirty-five years ago summarizes well my findings on preaching the Wisdom Literature: "And even here the Wisdom Literature has long been a stepchild neglected in favor of the Pentateuch, the Psalms or the prophets. Wisdom was, in the phrase of R. B. Y. Scott, a 'foreign book' within the Hebrew Bible." See his "Introduction," in *Aspects of Wisdom in Judaism and Early Christianity*, ed. Robert L. Wilken (Notre Dame, IN: University of Notre Dame Press, 1975), *xv*.

4. I limit my study to the books of Proverbs, Ecclesiastes, and Job simply because these three books best embody the genre. As Ernest C. Lucas notes, "These three books account for the majority of occurrences of the root *hkm* [wise/wisdom/to be wise] in the Hebrew Bible," Proverbs (101 times), Ecclesiastes (53), and Job (28). *Exploring the Old Testament: A Guide to the Psalms and Wisdom Literature* (Downers Grove, IL: IVP Academic, 2003), 68. According to R. N. Whybray, other possible wisdom texts include: Genesis 2–3; 37–50; Deuteronomy 1–4; 32; 2 Samuel 9–20; 1 Kings 1–2; 1 Kings 3–11; Psalms 1, 19, 37, 49, 51, 73, 90, 92, 104, 107, 111, 119; Isaiah 1–39; Ezekiel 28; and the books of Jeremiah and Daniel. *The Intellectual Tradition of the Old Testament*, Beihefte zur Zeitschrift für die alttestamentliche Wissenschaft 135 (Berlin: de Gruyter, 1974).

5. I agree with William J. Dumbrell's assessment that the prologue and epilogue of Job provide the key to understanding the whole book. See *The Faith of Israel: A Theological Survey of the Old Testament*, 2nd ed. (Grand Rapids, MI: Baker Academic, 2002), 255. I add that the beginning and end of both Proverbs and Ecclesiastes provide the keys to unlocking the meaning of those books as well. In the layout of this book, I have chosen neither to follow the order of the Christian canon—Job, Proverbs, and Ecclesiastes—nor the Jewish canon—Proverbs, Job, and Ecclesiastes—purely for christological reasons: I think my Job 42 sermon ties together well many Wisdom Literature themes developed in the Proverbs and Ecclesiastes sermons, and it packs the best christological punch.

6. Peter F. Jensen writes: "The goal of 'preaching the whole Bible' is attained when we so preach Christ that every part of the Bible contributes its unique riches to his gospel." "Preaching the Whole Bible: Preaching and Biblical Theology," in *When God's Voice Is Heard: Essays on Preaching Presented to Dick Lucas*, ed. Christopher Green and David Jackman (Leicester: Inter-Varsity, 1995), 64. Moreover, what Barry G. Webb says of Ecclesiastes is true of all three wisdom books: "Our ultimate goal is to understand how Ecclesiastes relates to the New Testament gospel."

Five Festal Garments: Christian Reflections on the Song of Songs, Ruth, Lamentations, Ecclesiastes, and Esther, New Studies in Biblical Theology (Downers Grove, IL: IVP Academic, 2000), 83.

Introduction

1. I read *The Works of Jonathan Edwards*, ed. Edward Hickman, 2 vols., (repr., Carlisle, PA: Banner of Truth, 1992). These volumes are large books (7 by 10.5 inches) with very small lettering (8-point font). I estimated that if the text in this edition was printed in normal book format (12-point font), it would amount to about 7,568 pages.

2. Cf. "For this reason, because I have heard of your faith in the Lord Jesus and your love toward all the saints, I do not cease to give thanks for you, remembering you in my prayers, that the God of our Lord Jesus Christ, the Father of glory, *may give you a spirit of wisdom and of revelation in the knowledge of him*" (Eph. 1:15–17); "*If any of you lacks wisdom*, let him ask God, who gives generously to all without reproach, and it will be given him. But let him *ask in faith*" (James 1:5–6a).

3. "And the child grew and became strong, filled with wisdom. . . . And Jesus increased in wisdom and in stature and in favor with God and man" (Luke 2:40, 52); "They were astonished, and said, 'Where did this man get this wisdom?'" (Matt. 13:54).

4. "Prologue," in *Commentary on Isaiah*, ed. J. P. Migne, Patrologia latina 24, p. 17; cf. Corpus Christianorum, Series Latina 73, p. 1.

5. Martin Luther, quoted in David Jackman, "The Hermeneutical Distinctives of Expository Preaching," in *Preach the Word: Essays on Expository Preaching in Honor of R. Kent Hughes*, ed. Leland Ryken and Todd Wilson (Wheaton, IL: Crossway, 2007), 18. More broadly, Augustine famously summarizes this concept in this way: "The New Testament is in the Old concealed; the Old Testament is in the New revealed."

6. While the term "Psalms" could reference only the book of Psalms, the more natural reading linguistically is to understand Jesus speaking of the Hebrew Scriptures in full. In other words, it makes better sense to think Jesus is speaking of the whole Jewish canon, not only two parts and one other book. This is also a historically viable position, as we know this threefold division existed by this date (e.g., Philo, *De Vita Contemplativa* 25). Thus I agree with Leon Morris's summary: "The solemn division of Scripture into *the law of Moses and the prophets and the psalms* (the three divisions of the Hebrew Bible) indicates that there is no part of Scripture

that does not bear its witness to Jesus." *Luke*, Tyndale New Testament Commentaries (Grand Rapids, MI: Eerdmans, 1988), 373.

Chapter 1: Ship of Fools

1. C. Hassell Bullock's summary reflects well my view of authorship: "It is our opinion that 1:1–29:27 is Solomonic in authorship, although some allowance may be made for editorializing in the process of compilation and final edition of the book." *An Introduction to the Old Testament Poetic Books* (Chicago: Moody, 1988), 159.

2. Part of this wisdom included Solomon's ability to write proverbs (see especially v. 32): "And God gave Solomon wisdom and understanding beyond measure, and breadth of mind like the sand on the seashore, so that Solomon's wisdom surpassed the wisdom of all the people of the east and all the wisdom of Egypt. For he was wiser than all other men, wiser than Ethan the Ezrahite, and Heman, Calcol, and Darda, the sons of Mahol, and his fame was in all the surrounding nations. He also spoke *3,000 proverbs* and his songs were 1,005. He spoke of trees, from the cedar that is in Lebanon to the hyssop that grows out of the wall. He spoke also of beasts, and of birds, and of reptiles, and of fish. And people of all nations came to hear the wisdom of Solomon, and from all the kings of the earth, who had heard of his wisdom" (1 Kings 4:29–34).

3. See Duane A. Garrett, *Proverbs, Ecclesiastes, and Songs of Songs*, New American Commentary (Nashville: Broadman, 1993), 67–68.

4. In this chapter, our focus will be on 1:7.

5. According to Christine Roy Yoder, the word "beginning" can be interpreted "temporally as 'beginning or starting point' (cf. Gen 10:10, Jer 26:1)" . . . or "qualitatively, as 'first, best, or epitome' (Amos 6:6, Jer 2:3, Ezek 48:14). Either way (and the ambiguity may well be intentional), there is no wisdom without it." See "Forming 'Fearing of Yahweh': Repetition and Contradiction as Pedagogy in Proverbs," in *Seeking Out the Wisdom of the Ancients: Essays Offered to Honor Michael V. Fox on the Occasion of His Sixty-fifth Birthday*, ed. Ronald L. Troxel, Kelvin G. Friebel, and Dennis R. Magary (Winona Lake, IN: Eisenbrauns, 2005), 167–83. For the phrase "first controlling principle," see Derek Kidner, *Proverbs*, Tyndale Old Testament Commentaries (repr., Downers Grove, IL: IVP Academic, 1981), 59.

6. I take "knowledge" in verse 7a to be a synonymous parallel with "wisdom" in verse 7b (cf. Prov. 2:6, 10; 8:12; 9:10; 14:6; 30:3; 2 Chron. 1:10–12).

7. Roland E. Murphy writes: "The positioning of this verse (echoed in 9:10; 15:33; Job 28:28; Ps 111:10) is important. It is the seventh verse, following upon the introduction, and it is repeated in 9:10, at the end of the first collection. Fear of the Lord also appears in 31:30, as a kind of inclusion to the book." *The Tree of Life: An Exploration of Biblical Wisdom Literature*, Anchor Bible Reference Library (New York: Doubleday, 1990), 16. Also, the phrase "the fear of the LORD" (1:7; 2:5; 8:13; 9:10; 10:27; 14:26–27; 15:16, 33; 16:6; 19:23; 22:4; 23:17) and the imperative "fear the LORD" (3:7; 14:2; 24:21) are found in key places, used as inclusios to sections (1:7; 9:10) and the book itself (1:7; 31:30).

8. Bullock speaks of it as being "the undergirding notion of the wisdom-controlled life." It is the attitude that leads to a right knowledge of God (and self) and moral obedience to his ways. See, *An Introduction to the Old Testament Poetic Books*, 23–24. I also like what Derek Thomas says: "Fearing God is the very soul of godliness. It is the attribute, above all others, that reflects a right relationship of a sinner to Almighty God. It is the response of a sinner towards the greatness of God. Reverence, awe and submission are its chief components, as is the notion of being afraid when there is just cause for it. A person who fears God puts God first in every area of life. God is not thought of as an equal, still less an inferior, but an all-powerful, all-knowing, everywhere present God who may do with us as he wills." *The Storm Breaks: Job Simply Explained*, Welwyn Commentary Series (repr., Webster, NY: Evangelical Press, 2005), 21.

9. John Bunyan, *The Fear of God* (Orlando: Soli Deo Gloria, 2006), 4–5.

10. Henri Blocher argues that the fear of the Lord in the Wisdom Literature equals faith in Christ, in "The Fear of the Lord as the 'Principle' of Wisdom," *Tyndale Bulletin* 28 (1977), 25–28.

11. I once heard Sinclair Ferguson give a telling illustration of this reality in a sermon on James 3. He shared how his college alma mater, the University of Aberdeen (est. 1495), had as its original motto, *Initium Sapientiae Timor Domini* (The fear of the Lord is the beginning of wisdom). Ferguson regretfully shared how today that motto has been cut down to the nebulous/postmodern "The beginning of wisdom."

12. For the dialogue in this paragraph, see Luke 23:35–42.

13. Gerhard von Rad rightly notes that "the 'fool' was not simply an imbecile, but a man who resisted a truth." *Wisdom in Israel,* trans. James D. Martin (Harrisburg, PA: Trinity Press International, 1972), 298.

14. For perhaps the most famous example, see theologian Sebastian Brant's book *Stultifera Navis* (1494). *Navis* is Latin for "boat."

15. Such sins are often labeled "the seven deadly sins": pride, envy, greed, gluttony, sloth, lust, and anger.

16. I am indebted to Alyce M. McKenzie, *Hear and Be Wise: Becoming a Preacher and Teacher of Wisdom* (Nashville: Abingdon, 2004), 137–38, 141–42.

17. On the forms of Jesus's sayings in the Synoptics, see Rudolf Bultmann, "Logia (Jesus as Teacher of Wisdom)," *The History of the Synoptic Tradition*, trans. John Marsh (New York: Harper & Row, 1963), 69–108.

18. McKenzie, *Hear and Be Wise*, 77.

19. "He is, it turns out, both teacher and message, Wisdom-in-Person." Ellen F. Davis, *Proverbs, Ecclesiastes, and the Song of Songs* (Louisville: Westminster, 2000), 28. Origen thought the most appropriate title for Jesus is "Wisdom." See Robert L. Wilken, "Introduction," in *Aspects of Wisdom in Judaism and Early Christianity*, ed. Robert L. Wilken (Notre Dame, IN: University of Notre Dame Press, 1975), *xvii*.

20. Cf. M. Jack Suggs, *Wisdom, Christology, and Law in Matthew's Gospel* (Cambridge, MA: Harvard University Press, 1970), 130.

21. "The connections between Jesus and Sophia or Wisdom are explicitly drawn in the prologue to the Gospel of John, written near the end of the first century C.E. Jesus' preexistence and salvific role are expressed in concepts familiar to us from Wisdom reflection in Proverbs and the wisdom and apocalyptic reflection of the later intertestamental period. However, the assignation 'wisdom' or 'Sophia' is never used. Instead, Jesus is described in terms of the Son's relationship to the Father. The grammatically masculine metaphor *Logos* (Word) dominates the prologue." McKenzie, *Hear and Be Wise*, 34.

Chapter 2: Imperishable Beauty

1. "What are you doing, my son? What are you doing, son of my womb? What are you doing, son of my vows? Do not give your strength to women, your ways to those who destroy kings. It is not for kings, O Lemuel, it is not for kings to drink wine, or for rulers to take strong drink, lest they drink and forget what has been decreed and pervert the rights of all the afflicted. Give strong drink to the one who is perishing, and wine to those in bitter distress; let them drink and forget their poverty and remember their misery no more. Open your mouth for the mute, for the rights of all who are destitute. Open your mouth, judge righteously, defend the rights of the poor and needy" (31:1–9).

2. I am aware that 31:1–9 may not have been placed before 31:10–31 in the Septuagint (LXX). Yet I see what perhaps a later canonical editor/ compiler saw: a thematic connection between the two sections. On whether chapter 31 should be viewed as a "collection," see Bruce K. Waltke, *Book of Proverbs, Chapters 1–15*, New International Commentary on the Old Testament (Grand Rapids, MI: Eerdmans, 2005), 27–28.

3. On why "sons" should be taken to mean young men or adolescent males, see Duane A. Garrett, "Preaching from the Psalms and Proverbs," in *Preaching the Old Testament*, ed. Scott M. Gibson (Grand Rapids, MI: Baker, 2006), 106–7. See also Tremper Longman III, *Proverbs*, Baker Commentary on the Old Testament Wisdom and Psalms (Grand Rapids, MI: Baker Academic, 2006), 540, and *How to Read Proverbs* (Downers Grove, IL: InterVarsity, 2002), 24–25. This view is contra Hubbard, Dumbrell, Stuart, and others who take the term to refer to a broader, less literal relationship (e.g., between a wisdom teacher and his/her pupil). Yet, as Longman points out: "Note that the book only teaches men about proper relationships with women, not vice versa" (131). Also note the clear connection between "young man" and "son" in Proverbs 7:1, 7 and 24. Cf. the literal nature of the father-son instructions in Egyptian wisdom texts, such as "The Instruction of Amen-em-opet" and "The Instruction of King Amen-em-het" (c. 1995–1965 BC).

4. "Sons" is used four times and "daughters" only once. And "daughters" is used only as a poetic personification: "The leech has two daughters: Give and Give. Three things are never satisfied; four never say, 'Enough'" (Prov. 30:15). The language of Proverbs is indeed "male-dominated." C. Hassell Bullock, *An Introduction to the Old Testament Poetic Books* (Chicago: Moody, 1988), 177.

5. See also Sirach 21:3; 23:22–7; 24:1–34, and especially chaps. 25–26.

6. Kenneth T. Aitken divides his commentary thematically. He entitles the three sections: "Nagging Wives" (which covers 19:13; 27:15; 27:16; 21:9; 25:24; 21:19); "The Good Wife—I" (18:22; 12:4; 14:1; 19:14); and "The Good Wife—II" (31:10–31). *Proverbs*, Daily Study Bible (Philadelphia: Westminster, 1986), 152–58.

7. I like Gerhard von Rad's analogy of the "considerable care" that went into much of "the literal form and presentation" of Hebrew poetry being similar to the precision of a modern scientist. He adds (almost gushingly, if one can say that of a German higher critic), "Only the man who has allowed his senses to be dulled in his dealing with the materials or who does not know the real purpose of this poetic wisdom can be deceived as to the magnitude

of the intellectual achievement of our wisdom teachers." See *Wisdom in Israel*, trans. James D. Martin (Harrisburg, PA: Trinity Press International, 1972), 50. Having studied poetry—biblical and otherwise—I must add that the use of simple words and concepts combined with thoughtful and at times complex structures (acrostics, alliteration, and synonymous, antithetical, and synthetic parallelisms) make Hebrew poetry especially beautiful and timeless. I am not far from admitting what novelist Thomas Wolfe did of Ecclesiastes, that Proverbs 31:10–31 is "the greatest single piece of writing I have ever known." From *You Can't Go Home Again* (New York: Harper & Row, 1968), 732–33.

8. While Hebrew poetry often employs this acrostic technique simply to aid the memory, here it may also be an "expression of wholeness (i.e., 'from A to Z')." See David Atkinson, *Message of Proverbs*, Bible Speaks Today (Downers Grove, IL: IVP Academic, 1996), 166. Of additional interest, Roland E. Murphy writes of Proverbs 2, "[This chapter] is an astonishing literary composition. In Hebrew it is one long sentence: an alphabetizing poem, in twenty-two lines according to the letters of the Hebrew alphabet. The first three strophes (vv 1–4, 5–8, 9–11) begin with the first letter, *'aleph*, and contain an 'if-then' message. The strophes in part two (vv 12–15, 16–19, 20–22) all begin with *lamed*, the middle letter of the alphabet, and they stress how Wisdom 'saves' (vv 12, 16) those who follow her." *The Tree of Life: An Exploration of Biblical Wisdom Literature*, Anchor Bible Reference Library (New York: Doubleday, 1990), 16.

9. There are also chiasms that pivot around a central pair:

A
   B
      C
      C´
   B´
A´

10. On Proverbs 31:10–31 as a chiasm or chiasmus, see Duane A. Garrett, *Proverbs, Ecclesiastes, and Songs of Songs*, New American Commentary (Nashville: Broadman, 1993), 248; Bruce K. Waltke, *Book of Proverbs, Chapters 15–31*, 528; Paul E. Koptak, *Proverbs*, NIV Application Commentary (Grand Rapids, MI: Zondervan, 2003), 674, 676.

11. Roland Murphy, *Proverbs*, Word Biblical Commentary (Nashville: Nelson, 1998), 24.

12. Ibid.

13. Ibid. Koptak titles his section on Proverbs 31:10–31, "The Woman of Worth Brings Her Husband Good." *Proverbs*, 674.

14. While I wholeheartedly embrace Waltke's summary—"In conclusion, this valiant wife has been canonized as a role model *for all Israel* for all time. Wise daughters aspire to be like her, wise men seek to marry her (v. 10), and all wise people aim to incarnate the wisdom she embodies, each in his own sphere of activity"—for the reasons stated, I differ with his view that "one should avoid emphasizing one of these applications at the expense of another." *Book of Proverbs, Chapters 15–31*, 520. I will make application to all, but firstly and primarily to "sons."

15. As R. N. Whybray states: "It has been suggested that the poem is a handbook for brides; but everything is viewed from the man's point of view, and it is more likely that it is a handbook for prospective bridegrooms." *The Book of Proverbs*, Cambridge Bible Commentary on the New English Bible (Cambridge: Cambridge University Press, 1972), 184.

16. Luther, quoted without reference in Charles Bridges, *Proverbs*, Crossway Classic Commentaries (Wheaton, IL: Crossway, 2001), 281.

17. Garrett, *Proverbs, Ecclesiastes*, and *Song of Songs*, 249.

18. Ibid., 250.

19. Bridges, *Proverbs*, 282.

20. Murphy, *Proverbs*, 247.

21. "It [v. 23] tells us what is really the point of the whole text. Now it seems certain that the point here is *not* that the reason the woman is industrious, wise, and kind is because she is married to an important man. Rather; the man is highly regarded by his peers *because he has such a great wife*. In short, by placing the honored husband at the center of the poem, the text is telling the young man: 'If you want to succeed and be well thought of, marry this kind of woman!'" Garrett, "Preaching from the Psalms and Proverbs," 107–8.

22. Garrett, *Proverbs, Ecclesiastes, and Songs of Songs*, 251.

23. Ibid.

24. This would include Paul's command in 1 Corinthians 7:39 to marry "in the Lord," that is, to marry a God-fearing woman who practices true worship (see Eccles. 5:1–7) and true religion (James 1:27). Note the emphasis in this poem (Prov. 31:10–31) on the latter. There is no mention of the typical and expected religious practices, such as prayer, fasting, and formal/cultic worship.

25. Murphy, *Proverbs*, 249.

26. And, we might add: we should look upon the *hands*. Schwab notes "palms" occurs four times in 31:13–20. See George M. Schwab, *Book of Proverbs*, Cornerstone Biblical Commentary (Carol Stream, IL: Tyndale, 2009), 658.

27. In the Hebrew the phrase *eseht hayil*, "woman of valor" is used only of Ruth; and in the Hebrew canon the book of Ruth comes right after Proverbs 31.

28. Might we say she "feared the Lord"?

29. Speaking of the parson/pastor, George Herbert (1593–1633) writes, "If he be married, the choice of his wife was made rather by his ear than his eyes; his judgment, not his affection found out a fit wife for him, whose humble and liberal disposition he preferred before beauty, riches, or honour." From "The Country Parson, His Character, and Rule of Holy Life," in *The Complete English Works*, Everyman's Library (New York: Knopf, 1995), 209.

30. William J. Dumbrell notes: "Proverbs 31:10–31 draws together the major themes, motifs, and ideas of the book in a final summarizing statement about wisdom as an industrious, resourceful, and selfless wife." *The Faith of Israel: A Theological Survey of the Old Testament*, 2nd ed. (Grand Rapids, MI: Baker Academic, 2002), 272.

31. Garrett, *Proverbs, Ecclesiastes, and Songs of Songs*, 252. Cf. Kathleen O'Connor, *The Wisdom Literature*, Message of Biblical Spirituality 5 (Wilmington, DE: Glazier, 1988), 77.

32. Garrett, *Proverbs, Ecclesiastes, and Songs of Songs*, 252. Dumbrell adds, "Wisdom is thus presented throughout, not as a mysterious, lofty ideal for the initiated, but as a practical, faithful, lifelong companion for those who would choose her way." *The Faith of Israel*, 273.

33. "In sum, the woman so concerned for others now becomes the central concern and praise of others." Waltke, *Book of Proverbs, Chapters 15–31*, 533.

34. Martin Luther aptly summarizes: "Here [Phil. 2:1–4] we see clearly that the Apostle has prescribed this rule for the life of the Christians, namely, that we should devote all our works to the welfare of others, since each has such abundant riches in this faith that all his other works and his whole life are a surplus with which he can by voluntary benevolence serve and do good to his neighbor." "The Freedom of a Christian," in *Martin Luther's Basic Theological Writings*, Timothy F. Lull, ed. (Minneapolis: Fortress, 1989), 617–18.

Chapter 3: Why Work?

1. Mary Oliver, "The Orchard," in *Red Bird* (Boston: Beacon Press, 2008), 20–21.

2. The book title, "Ecclesiastes," is the Greco-Latin form of the Hebrew *qōhelet*. It might be that Ecclesiastes is a "royal autobiography," that is, "the person who calls himself Qoheleth [the Preacher] pretends to be Solomon in order to argue that if Solomon cannot find satisfaction and meaning in life in these areas, no one can." Tremper Longman III, *The Book of Ecclesiastes*, New International Commentary on the Old Testament (Grand Rapids, MI: Eerdmans, 1998), 7. Yet from looking at what the text itself says about the author (see 1:1–2, 12, 16; 2:1–12, 15, 17, 20; 4:13; 7:25–29; 8:2–5; 10:16–17, 20; 12:9–10)—especially calling him "the son of David" and "king in Jerusalem" (1:1; there are only so many men who would fit that description literally), and then describing his wisdom (1:12–18; 2:12; cf. 7:25), wealth (2:1–11), and literary achievements (12:9–10; cf. Prov. 1:1)—I find no reason that we shouldn't call the author of Ecclesiastes "Solomon." Moreover, as Longman points out, "the verb *qahal*, on which the name Qoheleth is formed, occurs a number of times in 1 Kings 8, which is Solomon's speech at the dedication of the Temple." *Ecclesiastes*, Cornerstone Biblical Commentary (Carol Stream: IL: Tyndale, 2006), 253.

3. How perfect is James Limburg's classroom illustration! He shares: "When I have taught the book of Ecclesiastes in a classroom, at this point I reach into my pocket and pull out a cigar. I carefully remove the cellophane wrapper, strike a match, light the cigar, take a deep draw, and blow out a puff of smoke. 'That,' I say, 'is something like what the writer of Ecclesiastes means when he says *hevel*. It means a breath, a vapor, a cloud of steam, like a puff of smoke. Observe two things about that puff of smoke: (1) It is without substance. You can't grab onto it. (2) It is not lasting. Now we see the puff of smoke; in a few seconds we will no longer be able to detect it.'" *Encountering Ecclesiastes: A Book for Our Time* (Grand Rapids, MI: Eerdmans, 2006), 11. Samuel Beckett's play *Breath* (a play that lasts a mere thirty-five seconds) is another great example. As Philip Ryken summarizes: "As the curtain opens, there is a pile of rubbish on the stage, illuminated by a single light. The light dims and then brightens a little before going completely out. There are no words or actors in the drama, only a sound track with a human cry, followed by an inhaled breath, and exhaled breath, and another cry." *Ecclesiastes: Why Everything Matters*, Preaching the Word (Wheaton, IL: Crossway, 2010), 274.

4. Read Mark Twain's vivid description of this in his *Life on the Mississippi*, Library of America (New York: Literary Classics of the United States, 1982), 227–28.

5. See Longman, *The Book of Ecclesiastes*, 70.

6. Jerome put it this way: "What is more vain than this vanity: that the earth, which was made for humans, stays—but humans themselves, the lords of the earth, suddenly dissolve into the dust?" Quoted in J. L. Crenshaw, *Ecclesiastes*, Old Testament Library (Philadelphia: Westminster, 1987), 63.

7. This is a quote from Lennon's famous interview with Maureen Cleave of the London *Evening Standard* on March 4, 1966.

8. Do the names Elbridge Gerry, George Dallas, Hannibal Hamlin, Schuyler Colfax, and Alben Barkley ring a bell?

9. Sidney Greidanus illustrates in this way: "People have had mountains named after them, but a following generation changes the names. People have had their names etched into buildings, but in time the buildings will be demolished and the names forgotten. People write books to be remembered by posterity, but in time the books will be replaced by other books and the authors will be forgotten." *Preaching Christ from Ecclesiastes: Foundations for Expository Sermons* (Grand Rapids, MI: Eerdmans, 2010), 47.

10. According to my count, death is named or alluded to twenty-one times in the book: 3:2, 19–22; 4:2–3; 6:3, 12; 7:1–2; 8:8, 10; 9:3–5, 10; cf. 1:4, 11; 2:14–18, 20–21; 4:16; 5:15–16, 20; 7:14; 8:13; 11:8; 12:1–7. Cf. Westminster Shorter Catechism (Q. 19) which speaks of mankind, due to the fall, being "made liable to all miseries in this life, [and] to death itself."

11. One of my favorite Billy Collins's poems is "Forgetfulness," which, to my point above, begins, "The name of the author is the first to go / followed obediently by the title, the plot, / the heartbreaking conclusion, the entire novel / which suddenly becomes one you have never read, never / even heard of." *Sailing Around the Room: New and Selected Poems* (New York: Random House, 2001), 29.

12. Carl Jung wrote: "About a third of my cases are suffering from no clinically definable neurosis, but from the senseless and emptiness of their lives. This can be described as the general neurosis of our time." Quoted in Harold Kushner, *When All You've Ever Wanted Isn't Enough: The Search for a Life That Matters* (New York: Summit, 1986), 18.

13. Tolstoy, quoted in Timothy Keller, *The Reason for God: Belief in an Age of Skepticism* (New York: Dutton), 201.

14. Sartre, quoted in Ibid., 127.

15. As summarized by Bart D. Ehrman, *God's Problem: How the Bible Fails to Answer Our Most Important Question—Why We Suffer* (New York: HarperOne, 2008), 11–12.

16. For my sermon on Ecclesiastes 12:13–14, see chap. 4.

17. Having contemplated what the tyranny of time does to our work—nothing new; nothing remembered—we turn now, in the language of Ecclesiastes, to "consider the work of God" (7:13a; 8:17; 11:5).

18. Every deed Jesus did, we might say, was *justifying "wisdom"* (Matt. 11:19). Wisdom's "deeds" (11:2) here allude to Jesus's deeds in 11:5 (cf. chaps. 8–9), which pave the way for the identification of Jesus as wisdom incarnate ("come to me" in 11:28–30). See Craig S. Keener, *Matthew*, IVP New Testament Commentary Series (Downers Grove, IL: IVP Academic, 1997), 220.

19. Duane A. Garrett, *Proverbs, Ecclesiastes, and Songs of Songs*, New American Commentary (Nashville: Broadman, 1993), 288.

20. In 1 Corinthians 15, Paul argues that the verifiability (through eyewitness testimony) of the resurrection should lead to the validity of our work. Note the "therefore" in verse 58: "Therefore, my beloved brothers, be steadfast, immovable, always abounding in the work of the Lord, knowing that in the Lord your labor is not in vain."

21. It is worth adding here an insight made by Bryan Chapell at Hudson T. Armerding's memorial service (December 12, 2009). After Chapell read, "For the righteous will never be moved; he will be remembered forever" (Ps. 112:6), he asked, "How? How will the righteous man be remembered?" Chapell answered, "By having his name written by God in the book of life" (see Phil. 4:3; Rev. 3:5; 13:8; 17:8; 20:12, 15; 21:27).

22. Note especially Jesus's hyperbolic language in Matthew 7:23. Jesus says he does not *know* the "*workers* of lawlessness."

23. As William Manchester notes, "The most baffling, elusive, yet in many ways the most significant dimension of the medieval mind were invisible and silent. One was the medieval man's total lack of ego [that is an exaggeration from an overall very exaggerated but interesting book]. Even those with creative powers had no sense of self. Each of the great soaring medieval cathedrals, our most treasured legacy from that age, required three or four centuries to complete. Canterbury was twenty-three generations in the making; Chartres, a former Druidic center, eighteen generations. Yet we know nothing of the architects or builders. They were glorifying God. To them their identity in this life was irrelevant." *A World Lit Only by*

Fire: The Medieval Mind and the Renaissance; Portrait of an Age (Boston: Little, Brown, 1992), 21.

Chapter 4: Repining Restlessness

1. Augustine, *Confessions*, trans. R. S. Pine-Coffin (New York: Penguin, 1961), 21.

2. Tremper Longman argues that Ecclesiastes is a "reflective autobiography." See especially his *Fictional Akkadian Autobiography* (Winona Lake, IN: Eisenbrauns, 1991).

3. On authorship, see chap. 3, n2.

4. "Yet let him keep the rest, / But keep them with repining restlessness: / Let him be rich and weary, that at least, / If goodness lead him not, yet weariness / May toss him to my breast." From the last line of George Herbert's "The Pulley." *The Complete English Works*, Everyman's Library (New York: Knopf, 1995), 156.

5. I italicized "see" because nearly fifty times in this short book we read of what Solomon *sees*, *saw*, or *has seen*.

6. See chap. 3 on Ecclesiastes 1:1–11, "Why Work?"

7. See Mary Oliver, "The Orchard," in *Red Bird* (Boston: Beacon, 2008), 20–21. For two other excellent modern poems on this theme, see "Temptation," in Czeslaw Milosz, *Selected Poems, 1931–2004* (New York: HarperCollins, 2006), 140; and the second stanza of John Updike's "Hospital 11/23–27/08," in *Endpoint and Other Poems* (New York: Knopf, 2009), 22: "God save us from ever ending, though billions have. / The world is blanketed by foregone death, / small beads of ego, bright with appetite, / whose pin-sized prick of light winked out, / bequeathing Earth a jagged coral shelf / unseen beneath the black unheeding waves."

8. A. J. Jacobs, *The Know-It-All: One Man's Humble Quest to Become the Smartest Person in the World* (New York: Simon & Schuster, 2004), 369. Also of interest is Daniel Tammet's story. In his memoir, *Born on a Blue Day: Inside the Extraordinary Mind of an Autistic Savant* (New York: Free Press, 2006), one of today's most brilliant minds recalls, "I still remember vividly the experience I had as a teenager lying on the floor of my room staring up at the ceiling. I was trying to picture the universe in my head, to have a concrete understanding of what 'everything' was. In my mind I traveled to the edges of existence and looked over them, wondering what I would find. In that instant I felt really unwell and I could feel my heart beating hard inside me, because for the first time I had realized that thought and logic had limits and could only take a person so far. This

realization frightened me and it took me a long time to come to terms with it" (223–24). This is no little admission, for he "recited 22,514 digits of pi without error in a time of five hours and nine minutes to set a new British and European record" (185). Tammet came to terms with wisdom's limits by arriving at "an intellectual understanding of God and Christianity" (224). The concept of the Trinity, he writes, "was something I could picture in my head and that made sense to me" (224).

9. Although he misjudged (or was it false modesty?) his own significance, Charles Darwin understood this reality. In his autobiography, he wrote, "My books have sold largely in England, have been translated into many languages, and passed through several editions in foreign countries. I have heard it said that the success of a work abroad is the best test of its enduring value. I doubt whether this is at all trustworthy; but judged by this standard my name ought to last for a few years." *The Autobiography of Charles Darwin* (Cambridge: Icon Books, 2003), 74–75. John Updike, in his book/poem *Endpoint*, begins the subsection "The Author Observes His Birthday, 2005," lamenting "a life poured into words." He laments not only because his words won't be remembered, but because perhaps people "in that unthinkable future" will no longer read, that the "printed page was just a half-millennium's brief wonder" (8).

10. "Job learned about the vanity of this world by *losing* it all; the Teacher [i.e., Solomon] saw it by *having* it all." Mark Dever, *The Message of the Old Testament: Promises Made* (Wheaton, IL: Crossway, 2006), 536. John Donne uses this engaging analogy: "Therefore *Solomon* shakes the world in peeces, he dissects it, and cuts it up before thee, that so thou mayest the better see, how poor a thing, that particular is, whatsoever it be, that thou sets thy love upon in this world. He threads a string of the best stones, of the best Jewels in this world, knowledge in the first Chapter, delicacies in the second, long life in the third, Ambition, Riches, Fame, strength in the rest, and then he shows you an Ice, a flaw, a cloud in all these stones, he layes this infamy upon them all, *vanity, and vexation of spirit.*" *The Sermons of John Donne*, ed. George R. Potter and Evelyn M. Simpson, 10 vols. (Berkeley: University of California Press, 1953–62), 3:48.

11. Duloxetine, branded as Cymbalta, is the most popular antidepressant sold today. It is the second best-selling drug in the United States.

12. Gordon J. Keddie, quoted in T. M. Moore, *Ecclesiastes: Ancient Wisdom When All Else Fails* (Downers Grove, IL: InterVarsity, 2001), 91.

13. Peter J. Leithart gives another image: "We can no more give permanent form to the world than we can guide the wind into a paddock for

the night. We can no more give permanent form to the world than we can sculpt the evening breeze into solid shapes. Our projects are not sandcastles on the beach. That image, for Solomon, would suggest something far too solid and permanent. Our projects are cloud castles on a windy day." *Solomon among the Postmoderns* (Grand Rapids, MI: Brazos, 2008), 68.

14. What Jacques Ellul wrote concerning Ecclesiastes 12:13 is fitting: "To believe in God is to see the facts of the world are not the end of the matter." *Reason for Being: A Meditation on Ecclesiastes*, trans. Joyce Main Hanks (Grand Rapids, MI: Eerdmans, 1990), 213.

15. Contra J. L. Crenshaw, who claims 12:13 "is alien to anything Qohelet has said thus far." *Ecclesiastes*, Old Testament Library (Philadelphia: Westminster, 1987), 192. I side with H. C. Leupold, who speaks of this summary (12:13–14) as being "met with repeatedly in one form or another throughout the book." *Expositions of Ecclesiastes* (Grand Rapids, MI: Baker, 1952), 300. Daniel C. Fredericks adds: "This is not 'changing the subject'; it *is* the subject of Ecclesiastes." *Ecclesiastes and the Song of Songs*, Apollos Old Testament Commentaries (Downers Grove, IL: IVP Academic, 2010), 251.

16. Some scholars—e.g., Sheppard, Murphy, Fox—have shown how this "dual injunction" is found throughout the book of Sirach (1:26–30; 2:16; 10:19; 23:27). See Roland Murphy, *Ecclesiastes*, Word Biblical Commentary (Nashville: Nelson, 1992), 126.

17. Here is one of my favorite quotes from all my studies on the Wisdom Literature: "Before the God who is both transcendent and immanent, Creator and Redeemer, the only appropriate human posture is prostration before His majesty. The Psalms are frequent witness to the truth that personal happiness and inner security are found in the praise of God. The recognition that human destiny is fixed in direct proportion to the praise of God will free the heart to soar to Him, oblivious of personal gain. For only when God is exalted does man find his rightful place in the universe. Wisdom has its own term for this dimension of faith, the 'fear of the Lord.'" C. Hassell Bullock, *An Introduction to the Old Testament Poetic Books* (Chicago: Moody, 1988), 67.

18. Some scholars make too much of Ecclesiastes' use of "fear God" instead of "the fear of the LORD," for such language while uncommon is not unprecedented (see especially Job 1:9 and Gen. 22:12; cf. Job 40:1–2). Ecclesiastes was written by a Hebrew sage who surely understood "God" as "the LORD"—"the God of Abraham, the God of Isaac, and the God of Jacob" (Ex. 3:6). Moreover, this "God" in Ecclesiastes (named forty

times in the book) certainly acts like the God of the Pentateuch (see 2:26; 3:9–18; 5:1–6, 18–20; 6:1–2; 7:13–14; 8:16–9:1; 9:2–12; 11:5, 9; 12:1, 7). Cf. Daniel J. Estes, *Handbook on the Wisdom Books and Psalms: Job, Psalms, Proverbs, Ecclesiastes, Song of Songs* (Grand Rapids, MI: Baker Academic, 2005), 382. Estes argues that the term "fear Elohim" rather than "fear Yahweh" is used in Ecclesiastes because the book was "written to a universal audience" (i.e., not just Israel).

19. It is found structurally at key places in Proverbs (1:7), Job (28:28), and Ecclesiastes (12:13). Cf. Roland E. Murphy, *The Tree of Life: An Exploration of Biblical Wisdom Literature*, Anchor Bible Reference Library (New York: Doubleday, 1990), 16.

20. John Calvin speaks of this concept in this way: "Therefore, let the fear of the Lord be for us a reverence compounded of honor and fear." *Institutes of the Christian Religion*, Library of Christian Classics, ed. John T. McNeill, trans. Ford Lewis Battles (Philadelphia: Westminster, 1960), 3.2.26.

21. See chap. 1, "The Beginning of Wisdom," where I define the fear of the Lord in Proverbs as a continual (23:17) humble and faithful submission to Yahweh, which compels one to hate evil (8:13) and turn away from it (16:6) and brings with it rewards better than all earthly treasures (15:16)—the rewards of a love for and a knowledge of God (1:29; 2:5; 9:10; 15:33), and long life (10:27; 14:27a; 19:23a), confidence (14:26), satisfaction, and protection (19:23).

22. See also the Westminster Confession of Faith, 14.2, which speaks of "this faith . . . yielding obedience to the commands."

23. For the connection between Wisdom and Torah, see Craig G. Bartholomew, *Ecclesiastes*, Baker Commentary on the Old Testament Wisdom and Psalms (Grand Rapids, MI: Baker Academic, 2009), 84–93, 370, 372. Cf. Berry G. Webb, *Five Festal Garments: Christian Reflections on the Song of Songs, Ruth, Lamentations, Ecclesiastes, and Esther*, New Studies in Biblical Theology (Downers Grove, IL: InterVarsity, 2000), 97.

24. Cf. Graeme Goldsworthy, *Gospel and Wisdom: Israel's Wisdom Literature in the Christian Life*, Biblical Classics Library (London: Paternoster, 1995), 157; Michael V. Fox, *Ecclesiastes*, JPS Bible Commentary (Philadelphia: Jewish Publication Society, 2004), *ix*.

25. Duane A. Garrett, *Proverbs, Ecclesiastes, and Song of Songs*, New American Commentary (Nashville: Broadman, 1993), 345.

26. Albert Camus, *The Myth of Sisyphus and Other Essays*, trans. Justin O'Brien (New York: Knopf, 1967), 123.

27. The idea here is that of biblical "shalom": the blessing of God which brings peace and joy in all circumstances (e.g., the Beatitudes).

28. John Wesley's journal entry for January 2, 1777, makes this point: "I began expounding, in order, the book of Ecclesiastes. I never before had so clear a sight either of the meaning or the beauties of it. Neither did I imagine that the several parts of it were in so exquisite a manner connected together; all tending to prove that grand truth, that there is no happiness out[side] of God." *The Works of John Wesley: Journals from September 13, 1773 to October 24, 1790* (1872; repr., Grand Rapids, MI: Baker, 2007), 4:91.

29. Walter C. Kaiser, *Ecclesiastes: Total Life*, Everyman's Bible Commentary (Chicago: Moody, 1979), 59.

30. "Men, why are you doing these things? We also are men, of like nature with you, and we bring you good news, that you should turn from these vain things to a living God, who made the heaven and the earth and the sea and all that is in them. In past generations he allowed all the nations to walk in their own ways. Yet he did not leave himself without witness, for he did good by giving you rains from heaven and fruitful seasons, *satisfying your hearts with food and gladness*" (Acts 14:15–17).

31. Douglas Wilson notes, "What is the hallmark of wisdom in this fallen world? The answer is *joy* at the end of the tether. But before we can learn joy at the end of the tether, we must learn the strength of that tether. The Lord is God and we are not." *Joy at the End of the Tether: The Inscrutable Wisdom of Ecclesiastes* (Moscow, ID: Canon, 1999), 38. For the possible connection between the verbs—*eat, drink, rejoice*—and Old Testament worship, see Leithart, *Solomon Among the Postmoderns*, 168. Leithart argues that Solomon, like Moses in Deuteronomy 14:26, is "calling us to worship."

32. Eugene Peterson's translatation of 9:7–8 captures the spirit of the idea: Seize Life! Eat bread with gusto, / Drink wine with a robust heart. / Oh yes—God takes pleasure in your pleasure! (MESSAGE).

33. I think the Lord's Supper is a tangible representation of the Preacher's theology in this way: Jesus said to take ordinary bread and wine (food and drink) and to celebrate his work for us. Joy in God's work in the midst of human inability to conquer death—sound familiar? The church fathers saw this, associating the commands of joy with the Eucharistic celebration. Yet sadly, through their erroneous allegory, they taught that Ecclesiastes encouraged ascetic separation from the world.

34. Based on a concept from von Rad—"Like a pedal-point [a sustained bass note running through an organ composition or portion of a

composition] this word [hevel] runs through the entire book," *Weisheit in Israel*, 304 (Limburg's translation)—James Limburg uses a helpful musical analogy: "It is true that *hevel, hevel* sounds throughout the book like a pedal point on an organ. But while important, the pedal point, the sustained note in the bass, is never the main focus of the musical composition. Over against the pedal point, in full awareness of it, there is a melody, perhaps a sturdy chorale, or maybe even an exciting, even joyful counterpoint. I suggest that this counterpoint, the 'joy' theme in Ecclesiastes, is really what it is all about. A New Testament writer who does have affinities with the wisdom tradition, started out his letter in a manner which could summarize the theme of Ecclesiastes: 'Count it all joy, my brothers and sisters' (Jas 1:2)." *Encountering Ecclesiastes: A Book for Our Time* (Grand Rapids, MI: Eerdmans, 2006), 137.

35. Leland Ryken, *Words of Delight: A Literary Introduction to the Bible* (Grand Rapids, MI: Baker Academic, 1992), 321.

36. Ibid.

37. For an excellent summary of this theme, see Martin Luther's introduction to his commentary on Ecclesiastes, in *Luther's Works: Ecclesiastes, Song of Solomon, Last Words of David 2 Samuel 23:1–7* (St. Louis: Concordia, 1972), 15:7–11.

38. As Thomas à Kempis famously phrased it: "'Vanity of Vanities,' and 'all is vanity,' unless we serve God and love him with our whole heart (*Eccles* 1, 2). Oh, this is the highest and safest wisdom, that by contempt of the world we endeavor to please God." *The Following of Christ*, ed. J. van Ginneken (New York: American Press, 1937), 14.

39. In summary of this theme, Murphy rightly states that the Preacher "hardly merits" R. N. Whybray's title, "Preacher of Joy." Yet Murphy admits, "There are several passages in the book that can be advanced in favor of the gospel of enjoyment." Roland E. Murphy, *The Tree of Life*, 53, 55. On an interesting historical note: The Masoretes of the Middle Ages assigned a Jewish feast to each of the Five Megilloth—Song of Songs (Passover), Ruth (Pentecost), Lamentations (Fast of the Ninth of Ab), and Esther (Purim) and—drum-roll please—Ecclesiastes (Feast of Tabernacles). Yes, that joyous harvest celebration—like our Thanksgiving—they paired (rightly so!) with Ecclesiastes.

40. See C. L. Seow, "'Beyond Them, My Son, Be Warned': The Epilogue of Qohelet Revisited," in *Wisdom, You Are My Sister: Studies in Honor of Roland E. Murphy, O. Carm., on the Occasion of His Eightieth Birthday*, ed. Michal L. Barre, Catholic Biblical Quarterly Monograph Series 29

(Washington DC: Catholic Biblical Association of America, 1997), 139. Seow notes, "It is probable that an eschatological judgment is meant in 12:14."

41. If needed, reread Job 38–41.

42. Fox says, "In some Masoretic editions, and in public readings, verse 13 is repeated, so that the book not end with a threat." *Ecclesiastes*, 85.

43. I am indebted to Peter Leithart for his thoughts on this verse and others like it (e.g., 3:16–17; 11:9). See *Solomon Among the Postmoderns*, esp. 100–101, 163, 166–67.

44. See Matt. 25:41–46; Rev. 2:23; 22:12; cf. Rom. 2:6–8; 2 Thess. 1:8; 2 Tim. 4:14; 1 Pet. 1:17; Rev. 20:12–13, listed in Bruce K. Waltke, *Book of Proverbs, Chapters 1–15*, New International Commentary on the Old Testament (Grand Rapids, MI: Eerdmans, 2005), 131.

45. Rudolf Schnackenburg notes that "find rest for your souls" means "not peace of mind but, using biblical speech (Isa. 28:12; Jer. 6:16), the satisfaction of the salvific longing of the entire human being (cf. 1 Peter 1:9; Heb. 3:11–4:11). Wisdom's invitation is transferred to Jesus." *Gospel of Matthew*, trans. Robert R. Barr (Grand Rapids, MI: Eerdmans, 2002), 111. Cf. Michael Green, who writes, "[Jesus] offers 'rest,' not cessation from toil, but peace and fulfillment and a sense of being put right. We have only to come, to entrust ourselves to him, and we shall find rest." *Message of Matthew*, Bible Speaks Today (Downers Grove, IL: IVP Academic, 2000), 143.

46. "This pearl of price, this tree of life, this spring, / Who is possessed of shall reign a king. / Nor change of state nor cares shall ever see, / But wear his crown unto eternity. / This satiates the soul, this stays the mind, / And all the rest, but vanity we find." From Anne Bradstreet, "The Vanity of All Worldly Things," in *Chapters into Verse: Poetry in English Inspired by the Bible*, ed. Robert Atwan and Laurence Wieder (New York: Oxford University Press, 1993), 1:354.

Chapter 5: The Devil's Question

1. Jonathan Edwards, *The Works of Jonathan Edwards*, ed. Edward Hickman (repr., Carlisle, PA: Banner of Truth, 1992), 1:*clxxiii*. The language and theology here is surprisingly similar to Calvin: "The history written here shows us how we are in the hands of God, and that it is for him to order our life, and to dispose of it according to his good pleasure, and that our duty is to make ourselves subject to him in all humility and obedience; that it is right that we are entirely his, whether to live or to die; and that, even when it pleases him to lift his hand against us, even when we do not

understand for what reason he does so, nevertheless we should glorify him always, confessing that he is just and fair; and that we should not murmur against him, that we should not enter into dispute with him, knowing that we would always be overcome in any contest with him" (Job 1.1). Quoted in David J. A. Clines, "Job and the Spirituality of the Reformation," in *The Bible, the Reformation, and the Church*, ed. W. P. Stephens (Journal for the Study of the New Testament: Supplement Series 105), 49–72. Sheffield: Sheffield Academic Press, 1995), 68–69.

2. Edwards, *The Works of Jonathan Edwards*, 1:*clxxix*.

3. Conveying a similar thought, the Heidelberg Catechism reads: "Health and sickness . . . yea, all things, come not by chance but by [God's] fatherly hand" (A. 27).

4. J. H. Green, *The Argument of the Book of Job Unfolded* (Minneapolis: Klock, 1977), 74.

5. I will usually use the name "Satan" (as used in Job), not "Devil." Yet when I use the two names interchangeably, I do so intentionally, for I am not of the opinion, like some Old Testament scholars, that there is little or no correlation between the "Satan" of Job and the "Devil" of the New Testament. The New Testament not only uses the titles interchangeably (Rev. 12:9; 20:2), but Satan's activity in both Testaments is strikingly similar (see esp. Matt. 4:1–11; Acts 10:38; Rev. 12:10). So, while I agree with Daniel J. Estes that "the book of Job is an adumbration of the doctrine of Satan that is developed much more clearly in the New Testament" (*Handbook on the Wisdom Books and Psalms: Job, Psalms, Proverbs, Ecclesiastes, Song of Songs* [Grand Rapids, MI: Baker Academic, 2005], 26), nevertheless I think there is nothing pre-evolutionary, if you will, about Satan's person, power, and ploys.

6. The psychsoanalyst Carl Jung thought this dialogue and decision (recorded in Job 1:6–12) was diabolical; that it was a "crude representation of a divinity who cruelly permits the torture of his creation." See R. A. F. MacKenzie and Roland E. Murphy, "Job," in *New Jerome Biblical Commentary*, ed. Raymond E. Brown, et al. (Englewood Cliffs, NJ: Prentice Hall, 1990), 467. Such a view is nearsighted, for the Bible teaches that divine love can show itself through suffering, and trials and testings can authenticate or refine faith. God ordained and allowed the trials of Job, just as he did Jesus's temptations in the wilderness, not because he wants to *know* if Job will continue to honor him (for God knows all things, even the future), but rather because God wants to *show* that Job will honor him despite his circumstances. God tests Job not to see if Job will succeed or

fail but to reveal the essence of authentic faith and to demonstrate that his divine power is made perfect in human weakness.

7. I use the word *perfect* to reflect the obvious numerology of verse 3:10: 1,000, 10,000.

8. *Ecclesiasticus* or the Wisdom of Jesus Son of Sirach summarizes nicely this idea: "My child, when you come to serve the Lord, prepare yourself for testing. Set your heart right and be steadfast, and do not be impetuous in time of calamity" (Sir. 2:1–2).

9. Timothy Keller notes "a tragic string of suicides" that followed the economic crisis of 2009–2010, including the acting chief financial officer of Freddie Mac, the chief executive of Sheldon Good, and a Bear Stearns's executive. See *Counterfeit Gods: The Empty Promises of Money, Sex, and Power, and the Only Hope that Matters* (New York, Dutton, 2009), *ix–x*.

10. For how her impatience is contrasted with his patience, see Meredith Kline, "Job," in *Wycliffe Bible Commentary,* ed. Charles F. Pfeiffer and Everett F. Harrison (Chicago: Moody, 1962), 463.

11. Christopher Ash comments that the three different places named represent "the wisdom of the world gathering to this sufferer." *Out of the Storm: Grappling with God in the Book of Job* (Vancouver: Regent College, 2004), 28.

12. Derek Thomas notes, "Thomas Aquinas theorized that Satan had spared her in his opening salvo against Job in order to use her against Job." *The Storm Breaks: Job Simply Explained*, Welwyn Commentary Series (repr., Webster, NY: Evangelical Press, 2005), 54.

13. See ibid.

14. For textual evidence supporting my view that the scorn of Job's friends (and his household!) should also be considered a "test," see 5:14; 16:20; and 19:13–22.

15. "Victory before truth" is a line from George Sandys's poem "A Paraphrase Upon Job," in *Chapters into Verse: Poetry in English Inspired by the Bible,* ed. Robert Atwan and Laurance Wieder, 2 vols. (New York: Oxford University Press, 1993), 1:289: "Against thee, and thy two associates, / My anger burns, and hastens to your fates; / Since you, unlike my servant Job, have erred, / And victory before the truth preferred."

16. Dennis R. Magary notes how rhetorical questions dominate the poetic dialogue. See "Answering Questions, Questioning Answers: The Rhetoric of Interrogatives in the Speeches of Job and His Friends," in *Seeking Out the Wisdom of the Ancients: Essays Offered to Honor Michael V. Fox on the*

Occasion of His Sixty-fifth Birthday, ed. Ronald L. Troxel, Kelvin G. Friebel, and Dennis R. Magary (Winona Lake, IN: Eisenbrauns, 2005), 283–98.

17. "As the drama unfolds, the three friends who have claimed to speak for God are discredited and their doctrine of retribution proven inadequate. And Elihu, the abrasive [and angry] young champion of orthodoxy, adds nothing to their arguments." William J. Dumbrell, "The Purpose of the Book of Job," in *The Way of Wisdom: Essays in Honor of Bruce K. Waltke*, ed. J. I. Packer and Sven K. Soderlund (Grand Rapids, MI: Zondervan, 2000), 91. On the best summary I have read on Elihu, see Christopher Ash's chapter, "A Surprising New Voice," in *Out of the Storm*, 81–88.

18. Of all the exceptional poetry, satire, and irony scattered through the book of Job, my favorite lines are Job's witty responses to his friends' accusations. But to him, of course, it is no laughing matter.

19. In his short story "The Anatomy of Loneliness" Thomas Wolfe writes, "The most tragic, sublime and beautiful expression of loneliness which I have ever read is the Book of Job." In *The Complete Stories of Thomas Wolfe*, ed. Francis E. Skipp (New York: Simon & Schuster, 1987), 494.

20. See Dumbrell, "The Purpose of the Book of Job," 97, who summarizes, "According to 42:7b–8, therefore, it seems that Job was right to question God in the dialogues, that he was acting correctly in raising the question of divine justice" (98). Later he adds, "Job's words have been audacious, accusatory, and defamatory, but he is right!" (101).

21. What Jacques Ellul wrote concerning Ecclesiastes 12:13 is apropos here: "To believe in God is to see the facts of the world are not the end of the matter." *Reason for Being: A Meditation on Ecclesiastes*, trans. Joyce Main Hanks (Grand Rapids, MI: Eerdmans, 1990), 213.

22. The medieval Jewish commentator Rashi faults Job for talking too much. See James L. Crenshaw, "The Book of Job" (1992) in *Urgent Advice and Probing Questions: Collected Writings on Old Testament Wisdom* (Macon, GA: Mercer University Press, 1995), 443.

23. Susan E. Schreiner, *Where Shall Wisdom Be Found? Calvin's Exegesis of Job from Medieval and Modern Perspectives* (Chicago: University of Chicago, 1994), 29.

24. Yes, as Derek Thomas puts it: Job's sufferings foreshadowed the fact that "union with Christ brings with it a union with his sufferings," and that "pain only dissipates in heaven." *The Storm Breaks*, 18.

25. The second line in the article "Divine Providence" in *The Catholic Encyclopedia* expresses this idea: "As applied to God, Providence is God Himself considered in that act by which in His wisdom He so orders all

events within the universe that the end for which it was created may be realized." Leslie J. Walker, "Providence, Divine," in *The Catholic Encyclopedia*, ed. Charles G. Herbermann, et al., 15 vols. (New York: Robert Appleton, 1911), 12:510.

26. Timothy Keller, *The Reason for God: Belief in an Age of Skepticism* (New York: Dutton, 2008), 23.

27. Ibid.

28. Ibid., 23–24.

29. Cf. Daniel 3:16–18a: "Shadrach, Meshach, and Abednego answered and said to the king, 'O Nebuchadnezzar, we have no need to answer you in this matter. If this be so, our God whom we serve is able to deliver us from the burning fiery furnace, and he will deliver us out of your hand, O king. But *if not* . . . '"

30. On the theme of life after death or immortality in the Old Testament, see C. Hassell Bullock's excellent summary of fairly recent scholarship: "A Recognizable Immortality," *An Introduction to the Old Testament Poetic Books* (Chicago: Moody, 1988), 59–63. See especially, Mitchell Dahood, *Psalms*, 3 vols., Anchor Bible (Garden City, NY: Doubleday, 1970), 3:*xlvi–li*. Dahood argues that, along with other Old Testament texts, there are thirty-three passages in the Psalms and eight passages in Proverbs that support the doctrine of an afterlife. Cf. Bruce K. Waltke, "Does Proverbs Promise Too Much?" *Andrew University Seminary Studies* 34 (1966): 319–36.

31. Roland E. Murphy translates "redeemer" as "vindicator" and thinks it references Job's vindicating vision in 42:5. *The Tree of Life: An Exploration of Biblical Wisdom Literature*, Anchor Bible Reference Library (New York: Doubleday, 1990), 40. I like Murphy's translation because I believe (contra his exegetical suggestion) that it supports my exegesis of 19:26: Job will be vindicated only on the last day, after he has died and risen again (in the flesh no less).

32. Is it possible that "at the last" has an eschatological reference, speaking of what Jesus called "the last day," the day of the resurrection and then the judgment? (See John 6:39, 40, 44, 54; 11:24, 12:48; see also "the day of wrath" in the Wisdom Literature—Job 20:28; 21:30; Prov. 11:4.)

33. This theme of eschatological justice is not as uncommon in the Wisdom Literature. See "Second Motivation: Judgment" in chap. 4.

34. According to Thomas Aquinas, Job insisted upon and asserted the truth of the resurrection by pointing to the inequalities within history. Job reasoned as follows: either God's rule is unjust (because it appears so from a

mere observation of life), or there is an afterlife that guarantees the justice of divine governance. See Schreiner, *Where Shall Wisdom Be Found?* 81, 160.

35. We could better deal with the hardship of this perishable, defiled, fading world if, like Peter, we hoped for "an inheritance that is imperishable, undefiled, and unfading, kept in heaven for [us]" (1 Pet. 1:4). We could also better rejoice that "though now for a little while, if necessary, [we] have been grieved by various trials, so that the tested genuineness of [our] faith—more precious than gold that perishes though it is tested by fire—may be found to result in praise and glory and honor at the revelation of Jesus Christ" (1:6–7).

Chapter 6: My Servant

1. Certainly the word *why* is found on Job's lips: "Why does a just God not punish injustice in this world?" (see 21:7; 24:1); "Why does God contend against me?" (see 10:2; 13:24; 19:22); and "Why was I born if only to suffer like this?" (see esp. 3:11–22; cf. 10:18). Yet, God does not answer directly any of those *why* questions. The more important interrogatives in the book of Job are *who* and *where*, as used in God's two speeches: Job, *who* are you to speak of me? Job, *where* were you when I created the world?

2. Robert W. Yarbrough, "Christ and the Crocodiles" in *Suffering and the Goodness of God*, ed. Christopher W. Morgan and Robert A. Peterson (Wheaton, IL: Crossway, 2008), 24.

3. William J. Dumbrell agrees: "It is often maintained that the main problem addressed in Job is the problem of suffering. Yet we note that the divine speeches contain no allusion to suffering, making it clear that suffering is not the central problem of the book. This conclusion is reinforced by the observation that the fundamental issue with which the book deals . . . is raised before Job's suffering begins (1:6–12) and that his problem is resolved immediately prior to his restoration (42:10–16)." "The Purpose of the Book of Job," in *The Way of Wisdom: Essays in Honor of Bruce K. Waltke*, ed. J. I. Packer and Sven K. Soderlund (Grand Rapids, MI: Zondervan, 2000), 91.

4. My view is contra scholars who think the book of Job is merely an iconoclastic attack on traditional wisdom (i.e., that Deuteronomic theology advocated in the book of Proverbs). I agree with Murphy, who summarizes, "It is important to recall that [Job's friends] echo ideas that are fully in accord with other parts of the Bible." Roland E. Murphy, *The Tree of Life: An Exploration of Biblical Wisdom Literature*, Anchor Bible Reference Library (New York: Doubleday, 1990), 38. Cf. Tremper Longman III, *How*

to Read Proverbs (Downers Grove, IL: InterVarsity, 2002). Longman speaks of how the thought of Job's friends "could be supported by proof texts from the book of Proverbs" (81), yet how the book of Job is "a canonical corrective" to reading Proverbs with a mechanical application which always makes the connection "between wise behavior and material reward" (87).

5. There are only slight differences in Paul's usage and the Hebrew (MT), which is perhaps due to his own Greek translation.

6. While Job 42:7–9 clearly asserts that Job's friends spoke wrongly, we should be open to a more gracious reading of Job's friends (or, more gracious in part) based on New Testament usage of their quote-worthy words (as we would for our reading of Lot in Genesis based on Peter's seemingly overly gracious words in 2 Pet. 2:7–9). So what Gregory the Great wrote of Job's friends is fair: "[M]any things that they say are admirable, were they not spoken against the afflicted condition of the holy man." Gregory I (the Great), *Libri XXXV Moralium*. Patrologia Latina 75, 5.11.27. And Calvin's summary appropriate: "There is nothing in their speeches that we may not receive as if the Holy Spirit had spoken it." *On Job* 1.1.

7. Robert L. Alden comments: "Things that they said were true enough standing out of context, but as those statements pertained to the case of Job and God, they were wrong." *Job*, New American Commentary (Nashville: Broadman, 1993), 411.

8. Even though God ultimately reproved Job's friends for speaking wrongly of Job and God, it does not mean that God rebuked their theology per se. We misread this difficult middle section of the book if we think Job's friends were theologically unorthodox. A brief glance of the Old Testament, especially the Wisdom Literature, demonstrates their theology and rhetoric as biblical. Proverbs 13:21 (NIV), e.g., says, "Misfortune pursues the sinner, but prosperity is the reward of the righteous." Or what Eliphaz says to Job, "As I have seen, those who plow iniquity and sow trouble reap the same" (4:8), sounds quite similar to what Paul says to the Galatians, "Do not be deceived, God is not mocked; for whatever a man sows, this he will also reap" (6:7 NASB). Their issue was that they saw God's providence to be mathematical, not mysterious. Cf. R. A. F. MacKenzie and Roland E. Murphy, "Job," in *New Jerome Biblical Commentary*, ed. Raymond E. Brown, et al. (Englewood Cliffs, NJ: Prentice Hall, 1990), 467.

9. Leland Ryken, *Words of Delight: A Literary Introduction to the Bible* (Grand Rapids, MI: Baker Academic, 1992), 342.

10. The basic universal principle in biblical wisdom is that "the physical and moral universe operates by the law of cause-effect." C. Hassell

Bullock, *An Introduction to the Old Testament Poetic Books* (Chicago: Moody, 1988), 57. Cf. Ulrich Luz, *Matthew 8–20*, Hermenia (Minneapolis: Fortress, 2007), 27. I phrase it this way: sin has awful consequences; righteousness is rewarded.

11. "Suffering may be retributive, testing, discipline, or it may in the end be largely inexplicable." Norman K. Gottwald, *A Light to the Nations: An Introduction to the Old Testament* (New York: Harper & Row, 1959), 485. What is said of Ecclesiastes could also be said of Job's friends: "The warning for us here is that we should avoid the mistake of using proverbial wisdom as timeless general rules." Graeme Goldsworthy, *Gospel and Wisdom: Israel's Wisdom Literature in the Christian Life*, Biblical Classics Library (London: Paternoster, 1995), 112.

12. I'll add here an extra word of application: while we need to stand firmly upon the foundation of orthodoxy, part of the purpose of the Wisdom Literature is to help us leap from that box (not off the box, but above it). Neither Job nor his friends were willing (until the theophany) to leap. There was no development in their knowledge of God and no desire for discovery, to learn more about God so they might better know, love, and obey him.

13. Archibald MacLeish, *J.B.* (Boston: Houghton Mifflin, 1986), 153. This same theme is picked up in a number of "postmodern" movies, including the 1952 Japanese film *Ikiru* (trans. "to live"), where the main character Kanji Watabe sings (as he dies) the lyrics from a 1920s love song: "Life is so short / Fall in love, dear maiden / While your lips are still red / Before you can no longer love— / For there will be no tomorrow." For insightful comments on this film and others in this category, see Robert K. Johnston, *Useless Beauty: Ecclesiastes through the Lens of Contemporary Film* (Grand Rapids, MI: Baker Academic, 2004), 47.

14. For a great novel on the unresolved tension of this theme—the silence of God—read Shusaku Endo, *Silence*, trans. William Johnston (New York: Taplinger, 1980).

15. On God's creatorship and the coherence of creation in Wisdom Literature, see Derek Kidner, *The Wisdom of Proverbs, Job and Ecclesiastes: An Introduction to Wisdom Literature* (Downers Grove, IL: IVP Academic, 1985), 12–14.

16. This is my partial paraphrase of 38:4–18.

17. The alchemist says, "God created the world so that, through its visible objects, men could understand his spiritual teachings and the marvels of his wisdom." Paulo Coelho, *The Alchemist*, trans. Paulo Coelho (San Francisco: HarperSanFrancisco, 1993), 133.

18. Susan E. Schreiner, *Where Shall Wisdom Be Found? Calvin's Exegesis of Job from Medieval and Modern Perspectives* (Chicago: University of Chicago Press, 1994), 141.

19. Ibid.

20. Seen in part as a polemic against pagan myths, Robert S. Fyall contends that Behemoth represents the figure of death, and Leviathan symbolizes Satan. See *Now My Eyes Have Seen You: Images of Creation and Evil in the Book of Job*, New Studies in Biblical Theology (Downers Grove, IL: IVP Academic), 2002. Accepting this interpretation, Christopher Ash writes, "The issue in the Lord's speeches is, 'How strong is God?' And in particular it is the question 'Is he strong enough to control evil and keep it on a leash?' . . . [God says] 'You cannot begin to take on the problem of evil, Job. And you know that.'" *Out of the Storm: Grappling with God in the Book of Job* (Vancouver: Regent College, 2004), 89, 96.

21. Francis I. Anderson summarizes well Job's emotions: "He is at once delighted and ashamed." *Job*, Tyndale Old Testament Commentaries (Downers Grove, IL: IVP Academic, 1976), 291.

22. With a title that might be fitting for Job himself, Y. A. Hoffman labels the book of Job a "blemished perfection." She explains: "My conclusion was that the unique feature of the book of Job is its blemished perfection. While this formulation may sound absurd, in reality it is not so. Like any paradox, it seems vague and provocative. If 'blemished,' then in what sense can it be 'perfect'? Yet such, to the best of my judgment, is the book of Job. My claim that its perfection is achieved, not in spite of its blemishes, but precisely because of them relates both to the figure of Job as a believer and to the literary character of the book itself." *Blemished Perfection: The Book of Job in Context*, Journal for the Study of the Old Testament Supplement Series 213 (Sheffield: Sheffield Academic Press, 1996), 9.

23. From Blake's poem "The Everlasting Gospel."

24. Carl Schultz, "Job," in *Evangelical Commentary on the Bible*, ed. Walter A. Elwell (Grand Rapids, MI: Baker, 1989), 365.

25. Ibid.

26. Robert Alter writes: "God's poetry enables Job to glimpse beyond his human plight an immense world of power and beauty and awesome warring forces. This world is permeated with God's ordering concern, but as the vividness of the verse makes clear, it presents to the human eye a welter of contradictions, dizzying variety, energies and entities that man cannot take in. Job surely does not have the sort of answer he expected, but he has a strong answer of another kind. Now at the end he will no longer presume to

want to judge the Creator, having been brought through God's tremendous poetry to realize that creation can perhaps be sensed but not encompassed by the mind—like that final image of the crocodile already whipping away from our field of vision, leaving behind only a shining wake for us to see." *The Art of Biblical Poetry* (New York: Basic Books, 1985), 110.

27. H. H. Rowley, *Job*, New Cambridge Bible Commentary, rev. ed. (repr., Grand Rapids, MI: Eerdmans, 1980), 265.

28. Cf. Ps. 73:25–28; Hab. 3:17–19.

29. John E. Hartley, *Book of Job*, New International Commentary on the Old Testament (Grand Rapids, MI: Eerdmans, 1988), 537.

30. Rowley, *Job*, 266.

31. In chapter 42 a spark has turned into a flame, then a flame into a vast fire which consumes the "deep darkness." The term "deep darkness" is used nine times in the dialogues (3:5; 12:22; 16:16; 22:13; 24:17 [twice]; 28:3; 34:22; 38:17). The word "dark" and its derivatives are used thirty-eight times in chaps. 3–37. Then (very interestingly), the Lord's speech begins, "Who is this that *darkens* counsel by words without knowledge?" (38:2).

32. As Jesus was doing here, Jews categorized the Hebrew Scriptures in three parts—the Law, Prophets, and Psalms, or sometimes called the Torah, Prophets, and the Writings. The Writings begin with the book of Psalms and include what we commonly call "the Poetic Books"—Psalms, Job, Proverbs, Ecclesiastes, and the Song of Solomon. Of additional interest, note James 5:10–11a: "As an example of suffering and patience, brothers, take *the prophets* who spoke in the name of the Lord. Behold, we consider those blessed who remained steadfast. You have heard of the steadfastness of *Job*." Is James claiming prophetic status to the person of Job? In some ancient arrangements of the Hebrew Bible, Job is placed within the prophetic books.

33. Our tendency is to have a "reluctant christology" when we come to the Wisdom Literature. I borrow this phrase from Derek Thomas's chapter "A Christological Focus?" in *Calvin's Teaching on Job: Proclaiming the Incomprehensible God* (Ross-shire, Scotland: Mentor, 2004), 305–34. According to Thomas, in Calvin's sermons on Job, Calvin was surprisingly "not at all preoccupied with a christological agenda" (306).

34. Might the book of Job speak equally about God's love and forgiveness as it does God's transcendence, sovereignty, and justice? James applies it this way: "Behold, we consider those blessed who remained steadfast. You have heard of the steadfastness of Job, and you have seen *the purpose of the Lord, how the Lord is compassionate and merciful*" (James 5:11).

35. To be clear, it is not Job but his three friends who offer the sacrifice. The Hebrew word is clear: "And you [second person, masculine, *plural*] sacrifice" (42:8). Yet, I like how the ESV blurs the whole action together— their sacrifice and Job's mediatorial prayer in God's one act of atonement for sin: "Now therefore [you three] take seven bulls and seven rams and go to my servant Job and offer up a burnt offering for yourselves. And my servant Job shall pray for you, for I will accept his prayer not to deal with you according to your folly." Bruce K. Waltke, however, speaks of Job offering the sacrifice: "Job mediates for his abusive friends and restores the relationship through serving as their priest. He offers up the atoning sacrifice that they bring him, and he prays that they be saved from the wrath they deserve (Job 42:8). They humble themselves by acknowledging as their priest the one they wronged." *An Old Testament Theology: An Exegetical, Canonical, and Thematic Approach* (Grand Rapids, MI: Zondervan, 2007), 945.

36. Cf. what is taught in 1 John 1:5–10, which reminds me of a good gospel tract: (1) God is light/holy, (2) we are sinful, (3) the blood of Jesus cleanses us from sin, (4) we should confess our sins and God will be faithful to forgive.

37. See Acts 2:23; cf. John 8:44.

38. I add the adjective *perfect* because there was the perfect number of animals sacrificed—"seven bulls and seven rams" (42:8). On this Thomas Aquinas writes, "Now seven is the number of totality. Hence, a seven-fold sacrifice is suitable for the expiation of grave sins." *The Literal Exposition of Job: A Scriptural Commentary Concerning Providence,* trans. Anthony Damico, American Academy of Religion, Classics in Religious Studies, (Atlanta: Scholars Press, 1989), 471.

39. On this, Derek Thomas writes: "The sacrifice is costly: seven bulls and seven rams (42:8). Only royalty could afford such an offering. The sacrifice is referred to as a 'burnt offering,' the commonest offering in the Old Testament. As part of the ritual, hands were laid on the animal's head, firstly to identify the victim with the worshipper, but also, and more importantly, to signify a representative and substitutionary significance in the act that followed. Of all the sacrifices offered, the burnt offering demonstrated most clearly God's anger poured out against sin in that the victim of the sacrifice was totally consumed. The offering, which represented and was a substitute for the offerer, quite literally went up in smoke!" *The Storm Breaks: Job Simply Explained*, Welwyn Commentary Series (repr., Webster, NY: Evangelical Press, 2005), 316. Also note here

in the epilogue—in one of many parallels to the prologue—how Job has moved from sacrificial offerings for general sins to a sacrifice for specific sins. He has also gone from being the priest for his family to those beyond his family.

40. We might add here: Part of that vindication is the defeat of Satan, who, so dominant a figure in the prologue, is nowhere to be found in the epilogue. Has God restrained the Devil's power? Or, to use the language of Job 1:12, has Satan's *hand* been cosmically slapped?

41. In a (sadly) rare christological comment from Job commentators, David Atkinson writes, "Once again, the book of Job is pointing beyond itself to the Mediator between God and human beings, the man Christ Jesus who gave himself as an offering for sins and now ever lives to make intercession for us." *The Message of Job*, Bible Speaks Today (Downers Grove, IL: IVP Academic, 1991), 158.

42. Job demonstrates no lack of outward integrity in word or deed. In this way he was a "blameless" man (6:10, 30; 9:21; 10:6–7). Moreover, he was "blameless" when it came to his friends' accusations. And yet he admits being a "sinner" in a general sense, perhaps due to committing minor (unknown?) sins (see 7:20; 13:26). Is not Luther's famous term apropos for Job—*simul justus, simul peccator*?

43. And Job's story ends with his death (42:17), not resurrection, ascension, etc.

44. In his *Moralia in Job*, Gregory the Great spoke of Job as "an anticipation of the Redeemer in his passion." See Manlio Simonetti and Marco Conti, eds., *Job*, Ancient Christian Commentary on Scripture (Downers Grove, IL: IVP Academic, 2006), 11.

45. In this way the story of Job is like the story of Jonah—they are both "signs" of what we should expect: "Then some of the scribes and Pharisees answered him, saying, 'Teacher, we wish to see a sign from you.' But he answered them, 'An evil and adulterous generation seeks for a sign, but no sign will be given to it except the sign of the prophet Jonah. For just as Jonah was three days and three nights in the belly of the great fish, so will the Son of Man be three days and three nights in the heart of the earth. The men of Nineveh will rise up at the judgment with this generation and condemn it, for they repented at the preaching of Jonah, and behold, something greater than Jonah is here. The queen of the South will rise up at the judgment with this generation and condemn it, for she came from the ends of the earth to hear the

wisdom of Solomon, and behold, something greater than Solomon is here'" (Matt. 12:38–42).

46. Contra Dumbrell's conclusion in his otherwise excellent essay: "Perhaps the purpose of the book of Job will continue to elude us." See his "The Purpose of the Book of Job," in *The Way of Wisdom*, 104. Also contra S. E. Porter, "The Message of the Book of Job: 42:7b as Key to Interpretation," *Evangelical Quarterly* 63 (1991): 291–304. Might Job 42:8, as I am suggesting here, be the key?

47. It is used only seventy-five times in the Old Testament, all but eight times as a title.

48. The title "my servant" is used of the following: Abraham (1); Caleb (1); Naaman (1); Eliakim (1); Isaiah (1); Zerubbabel (1); the Branch (1); Nebuchadnezzar (3); Moses (6); Job (6); Jacob/Israel (8); the servant of Isaiah 43–52 (13); David (24). The word *servant* is used thirty-eight times for David.

49. See esp. Isa. 42:1–4; 49:4–9; 52:13–53:12.

50. Perhaps of further significance: this is also the same chapter where Jesus speaks of his wisdom being greater than Solomon's (12:42).

51. The poet William Blake illustrates well my thought here. In 1825 Blake made twenty-one engravings of the book of Job. The eighteenth is a picture of Job with his hands raised horizontally—like a cross. His three friends are kneeling at the altar, as the flame and smoke from the sacrifice (which is set behind Job's cross-like stance) rise into the sun. The inscription below reads: "And my Servant Job shall pray for you." Similarly, Taddeo Gaddi (1300–1366), the Florentine artist, painted a fresco of Job praying for his friends. Job is depicted like a king. There is a throne and a royal crown and other symbols that seek to connect Job to the royal righteousness of Christ. For a fuller description and photograph of the painting, see Samuel E. Balentine, "My Servant Job Shall Pray for You," *Theology Today* 58 (2002): 505–6. Also, read H. Wheeler Robinson, *The Cross in the Old Testament: The Cross of Job; The Cross of the Servant, and the Cross of Jeremiah* (London: SCM, 1955), 51–54. Robinson speaks of the book of Job as "a first draft of the Gospel story" (54). He writes of Jesus, who "clearly identified Himself in the synagogue at Nazareth with the Servant of Yahweh" and drank "the cup which His Father held to his lips . . . in the attitude of Job" (51).

52. They should have acted like the Bereans, who "received the word [i.e., the gospel] with all eagerness, examining the Scriptures daily to see if these things were so" (Acts 17:11).

Chapter 7: How Shall Wisdom Be Preached?

1. Pope Innocent III, *Between God and Man: Six Sermons on the Priestly Office*, trans. Corinne J. Vause and Frank C. Gardiner (Washington, DC: Catholic University of America Press, 2004), 6.

2. Not only are there few studies on the topic of *preaching* the Wisdom Literature, but there are almost none on *preaching Christ* from the Wisdom Literature. See n. 3 in the preface.

3. By "theology," I mean, strictly speaking, our view of God. By "ethics" I refer to what the New Testament most often does with Wisdom Literature's ethical exhortations; namely, it answers the question, "How should we live in light of God's judgment?"

4. Prov. 26:11 as quoted in 2 Pet. 2:22.

5. Note that Ecclesiastes is not quoted in the New Testament (although it is perhaps alluded to in Matt. 6:7; 11:17; Luke 12:19; John 3:8; Acts 2:46; Rom. 3:10; 8:20; 2 Cor. 5:10; Col. 4:1; 1 Tim. 6:7; and James 1:19; and twice in the early Christian book *The Shepherd of Hermas*). Also note, as is typical, how the New Testament writers take liberty with their use of the Old Testament—using the LXX (I quote above from Brenton's translation), paraphrasing the Hebrew, changing pronouns, etc. See G. K. Beale and D. A. Carson, eds. *Commentary on the New Testament Use of the Old Testament* (Grand Rapids, MI: Baker Academic, 2007), 679, 680–81, 703–4, 985–87, 1041–43, 1057.

6. In sum: (a) God is beyond our complete understanding (Rom. 11:35; Job 41:11); (b) God will judge all people (1 Pet. 4:18; Prov. 11:31); (c) therefore, fear the Lord.

7. "But *this is that* which was spoken by the prophet Joel" (Acts 2:16 KJV). For examples of predictive prophecies, see Matt. 1–4; John 19:24–36.

8. E.g., see Prov. 3:34 and 1 Pet. 5:5.

9. E.g., see Prov. 25:21–22 and Rom. 12:20.

10. E.g., see Prov. 3:11–12 and Heb. 12:6.

11. Most of the New Testament allusions to the Wisdom Literature involve ethics, notably holy living; e.g., see Matt. 5:44; 23:12, 25:40; Luke 1:52; Rom. 12:16; Eph. 6:4; 1 Thess. 5:22; 1 Tim. 6:9; James 1:19; 2:1; 4:10; 1 Pet. 2:17; 4:8; 5:6.

12. G. K. Beale, "Positive Answer to the Question Did Jesus and His Followers Preach the Right Doctrine from the Wrong Texts?" in *Right Doctrine from the Wrong Texts: Essays on the Use of the Old Testament in the New*, ed. G. K. Beale (Grand Rapids, MI: Baker Academic, 1994), 387–404.

13. Here I refer especially to God's sovereignty, incomprehensibility, and justice.

14. To clarify, let me give you an example of what I mean. Let's say Proverbs says, "Guard your tongue." Here's what the poor preacher does with this theme: "Well, we all know we can't bite our tongues, but thank God for sending Jesus. He alone lived the perfect life. He alone sinned not with his mouth. He alone died for all our sins," and so on. Proverbs in this way is used like a pedagogy, which is never how Proverbs is used (in quotations or allusions) in the New Testament. In my lecture for the Charles Simeon Trust, "Preaching the Gospel Genre" (see the Simeon Course on Biblical Exposition, http://www.simeoncourse.org) I illustrated this by talking about the preacher who preaches only a "justification by faith alone clarification sermon" on Matthew 25:31–46. While it is important to show how Scripture interprets Scripture, to use the doctrine of *sola fide* to remove or lessen the "moral weight" of the necessity of obedience, good works, perseverance, or holiness (see Westminster Confession of Faith 13:1–16:7) is not only exegetically wrong, but it produces the opposite effect of what is intended in God's Word. As I said then, I write now: remember, many of Paul's letters were written before the Gospels, and the Gospel writers didn't see the need to package things tightly and clear up any potential theological misunderstandings. We shouldn't feel the pressure to do so in each and every sermon.

15. The best summary I have found of what I am seeking to explain comes from Sidney Greidanus. He shows how the New Testament church centered on Jesus Christ, "but not in the narrow sense of focusing only on Christ crucified, nor in the broadest sense of focusing only on the Second Person of the Trinity or the eternal Logos. The New Testament Church preached the birth, ministry, death, resurrection, and exaltation of Jesus of Nazareth as the fulfillment of God's old covenant promises, his presence today in the Spirit, and his imminent return. In short, 'preaching Christ' meant preaching Christ incarnate in the context of the full sweep of redemptive history." *Preaching Christ from the Old Testament: A Contemporary Hermeneutical Method* (Grand Rapids, MI: Eerdmans, 1999), 4.

16. Cf. J. I. Packer, "Theology and Wisdom," in *The Way of Wisdom: Essays in Honor of Bruce K. Waltke*, ed. J. I. Packer and Sven K. Soderlund (Grand Rapids, MI: Zondervan, 2000), 1–14. Packer speaks of four main ways in which New Testament wisdom moves beyond its Old Testament counterpart: (1) epistemological, (2) christological, (3) soteriological, and (4) behavioral. For his words on behavior or what I'm calling "ethics," see p. 9.

17. "Gospel" ethics implies divine provision (i.e., grace that comes from what God has done and will do for us in Christ), Jesus who saves *and sanctifies*. So, to be clear, I am not advocating anthropocentric ethics, what Bryan Chapell humorously calls, *sola bootstrapsa*—"Take hold of those bootstraps and pick yourself up so that God will love you more." *Christ-Centered Preaching: Redeeming the Expository Sermon*, 2nd ed. (Grand Rapids, MI: Baker Academic, 2005), 289. Cf. Jay E. Adams, *Preaching with Purpose: A Comprehensive Textbook on Biblical Preaching* (Grand Rapids, MI: Baker, 1982). Adams states the same idea in this way: "Edificational preaching must always be evangelical; that is what makes it moral rather than moralistic" (147).

18. Graeme Goldsworthy gives a good summary of this first tip: "[The Wisdom Literature] complements the perspective of salvation history. Indeed, we should go further than that and say that wisdom is *a theology of the redeemed man living in the world under God's rule* [emphasis mine]. It is thus as much an aspect of kingdom theology as salvation history is." *Gospel and Kingdom: A Christian Interpretation of the Old Testament* (Exeter: Paternoster, 1983), 142. Cf. Duane A. Garrett, "Preaching Wisdom," in *Reclaiming the Prophetic Mantle: Preaching the Old Testament Faithfully*, ed. George L. Klein (Nashville: Broadman, 1992), 108–10.

19. There are a number of excellent summaries of the gospel: see John Chapman, *Know and Tell the Gospel: Help for the Reluctant Evangelist* (London: St. Matthias, 1981), 18–28; John Stott, *Romans: God's Good News for the World* (Downers Grove, IL: InterVarsity, 1994), 46–54; Graeme Goldsworthy, "The Gospel," in *New Dictionary of Biblical Theology*, ed. T. Desmond Alexander and Brian S. Rosner (Downers Grove, IL: IVP Academic, 2000), 521–24. I include here, however, Matt Newkirk's definition, given to me via e-mail in his first edit of this chapter: "I think of the gospel as the good news that the kingdom of God is being brought to the earth and that freedom has been obtained for his exiled people to enter that kingdom, by virtue of Jesus' life, death, resurrection, and exaltation. This kingdom citizenship comes only through faith in Jesus, that is, allegiance to the King (the means of entry into the kingdom) and is to be reflected in the way his people live (the ethics of the kingdom)."

20. Goldsworthy summarizes well the method I used above: "Homiletic applications to us and our contemporaries must be arrived at via the person and work of Christ." *Gospel-Centered Hermeneutics: Foundations and Principles of Evangelical Biblical Interpretation* (Downers Grove, IL: IVP Academic, 2006), 257.

21. Chapell's definition is this: "Typology as it relates to Christ's person and work is the study of the correspondences between persons, events, and institutions that first appear in the Old Testament and preview, prepare, or more fully express New Testament salvation truths." *Christ-Centered Preaching*, 281.

22. Typology is also, as David L. Larsen points out, "the basic hermeneutic of Hebrews." See "Preaching the Old Testament Today," in *Preaching the Old Testament*, ed. Scott M. Gibson (Grand Rapids, MI: Baker, 2006), 176.

23. I like how Larsen phrases this idea in one of his subheadings: "The Old Testament . . . So Poignantly Provides a Rich Pictorialization of God's Plan." Ibid., 177.

24. Graeme Goldsworthy, *Gospel and Wisdom: Israel's Wisdom Literature in the Christian Life*, Biblical Classics Library (Carlisle, UK: Paternoster, 1995), 149.

25. Roland E. Murphy writes, "Despite the pretense of exegetical precision, exaggeration and uncontrolled fantasy seem to be flaws endemic to allegorical exposition." *The Song of Songs*, Hermeneia (Minneapolis: Fortress, 1990), 93.

26. For a fair critique of patristic exegesis of Proverbs 8, see Bruce K. Waltke, *The Book of Proverbs, Chapters 1–15,* New International Commentary on the Old Testament (Grand Rapids, MI: Eerdmans, 2004), 127–31. On allegory in the Song of Solomon, see Marvin H. Pope, *Song of Songs*, Anchor Bible (New York: Doubleday, 1977), 89–210. See also my thesis, *Walking on "the Ashes of God's Saints": John Donne's Interpretation of the Song of Songs and the Origenist Exegetical Tradition* (Trinity International University, 2001).

27. My introduction to biblical theology was through reading Jonathan Edwards's wonderful book (my favorite of his), *The History of Redemption*. However, typical of Puritan exegesis, Edwards sees more in the text than what is exegetically viable. He exaggerates the connections between Joseph and Jesus. So, while I agree with his opening statement concerning Joseph—"This salvation of the house of Israel, by the hand of Joseph, was upon some accounts very much a resemblance of the salvation of Christ"— I disagree with the number of resemblances. See Jonathan Edwards, *The Works of Jonathan Edwards*, ed. Edward Hickman (repr., Carlisle, PA: Banner of Truth, 1992), 1:545.

28. Goldsworthy, *Gospel-Centered Hermeneutics*, 252.

29. Sidney Greidanus speaks of two "types" in Ecclesiastes. One is the figure of "King Solomon" in 1:12–2:26; the other is the "one Shepherd"

of 12:11. Of the first type, he writes: "Solomon . . . the king of peace, rules wisely in the city of peace (Jeru-*salem*). King Solomon is a type of the great King of peace; he prefigures Jesus Christ." Of the second type, he writes: "The phrase 'one shepherd' is used only three times in the Hebrew Bible, once here in Ecclesiastes and twice in Ezekiel. In Ezekiel the LORD promises Israel a glorious future under 'one shepherd,' another like David. [He then quotes in full Ezekiel 34:23–24; 37:24–25]. . . . Assuming that the editor of Ecclesiastes had these passages in mind, his references to 'one shepherd' would function as a type of the coming Davidic shepherd king. The New Testament identifies Jesus not only as another King David . . . but also as the shepherd king [I add for support: Matt. 25:31–46; cf. 1 Cor. 4:5; 2 Cor. 5:10; Heb. 4:12–13; 2 Pet. 3:7–13]. Jesus himself said, 'I am the good shepherd. . . . So there will be one flock, *one shepherd*' (John 10:11–16; cf. Heb 13:20)." *Preaching Christ From Ecclesiastes: Foundations for Expository Sermons* (Grand Rapids, MI: Eerdmans, 2010), 56, 301–2. Cf. Nicholas Perrin, "Messianism in the Narrative Frame of Ecclesiastes?" *Revue Biblique* 108 (2001): 51–57.

30. See my forthcoming volume on Song of Solomon in the Preaching the Word series (Wheaton, IL: Crossway, forthcoming).

31. E.g., see the section "The End of Fools" in my sermon on Proverbs 1:1–7 (chap. 1).

32. Here's another possible example: Peter's "satanic" response to Jesus's mission (Matt. 16:22–23) is similar to Satan's testing of Job. Like Satan in Job, Peter in Matthew thinks suffering will trip up the faithfulness of the man of God and thus thwart the plans of God.

33. Or we can add: If we are struggling to set the wisdom text in the full context of Scripture (the redemptive-historical story line), or if we've done that earlier and/or often in our sermon series.

34. Greidanus summarizes: "Although the teaching of Christ could be considered part of the work of Christ, Jesus' teaching is often overlooked in discussions on preaching Christ from the Old Testament. . . . The teaching of Jesus is an indispensable component for preaching Christ from the Old Testament, for the Old Testament was Jesus' Bible, and he based his teaching on it. Jesus' teaching included not only teaching about himself (Son of Man, Messiah), his mission, and his coming again but also teachings about God, God's kingdom, God's covenant, God's law (e.g., Matt 5–7), and the like." *Preaching Christ from the Old Testament*, 8–9.

35. James M. Efird summarizes: "[Jesus] called an intimate group to be around him so that he could teach them, much like the leader of a wisdom

school. His teachings, as one can readily learn by examination of the texts, consist of short pithy sayings, parables, a few allegories, and many figures of speech usually characterized by the element of hyperbole." *Biblical Books of Wisdom: A Study of Proverbs, Job, Ecclesiastes, and Other Wisdom Literature of the Bible* (Eugene, OR: Wipf & Stock, 2001), 84.

36. To be clear, I am not stating here that every ethical instruction in the Wisdom Literature needs some sort of explicit New Testament counterpart to validate it. The Wisdom Literature stands alone as part of God's inspired and authoritative Word, and as such each text can be used *as is* to teach, reprove, correct, and train us in righteousness (2 Tim. 3:16). What I am saying, however, is that the person and work (including teachings) of Christ sheds new light on the old texts.

37. I used the fourth appendix in NA27: "Loci Citati vel Allegati."

38. Two examples of christological connections (not teachings directly from Jesus): (1) Prov. 3:4: "So you [my son] will find favor . . . in the sight of God and man"; Luke 2:52: "And Jesus increased in wisdom . . . and in favor with God and man"; (2) Job 4:9: "By the breath of God they perish"; 2 Thess. 2:8: "The Lord Jesus will kill [the lawless one] with the breath of his mouth."

39. Other possibly linguistic connections (not all related to the teachings of Christ) include: Prov. 1:16 with Rom. 3:15–17; Prov. 1:23 with John 7:39; Prov. 2:3–6 with James 1:5; Prov. 2:13 with John 3:19–20; Prov. 3:7 with Rom. 12:16; Prov. 4:18 with Matt. 5:14; Prov. 4:19 with John 12:35 (cf. 11:10); Prov. 6:27 with Matt. 5:28; Prov. 8:15 with Rom. 13:1; Prov. 8:17 with John 14:21; Prov. 10:12 with 1 Pet. 4:8; Prov. 10:24 with Matt. 5:6; Prov. 11:24 (cf. 22:9) with 2 Cor. 9:6; Prov. 16:16 (cf. 23:2) with Matt. 13:44; Prov. 16:33 with Acts 1:26; Prov. 18:4 with John 7:38; Prov. 19:18 (cf. 22:6) with Eph. 6:4; Prov. 20:8 with Matt. 3:12; Prov. 20:20 with Matt. 15:4; Prov. 20:22 with 1 Thess. 5:15; Prov. 21:15 with Rev. 19:1–8; Prov. 22:11 with Matt. 5:8; Prov. 24:21 with 1 Pet. 2:17; Prov. 25:6–7 with Luke 14:8–10; Prov. 27:1 with James 4:13–14; Prov. 28:10 with Matt. 15:14; Prov. 28:13 with 1 John 1:9; Prov. 30:5 with Heb. 1:1–2; Prov. 30:8 with 1 Tim. 6:8; Eccles. 1:2 with Rom. 8:20; Eccles. 5:15 and Job 1:20 with 1 Tim. 6:7; Eccles. 7:20 with Rom. 3:10–12; Eccles. 11:5 with John 3:8; Eccles. 12:14 (and Prov. 10:9) with Matt. 10:26 (cf. 2 Cor. 5:10); Job 2:6 with 2 Cor. 12:7; Job 5:11(cf. 12:19) with Luke 1:52 (James 4:10); Job 9:8 with Matt. 14:26; Job 12:14 with Rev. 3:7; Job 12:7–9 (as well as chaps. 38–41) with Rom. 1:20; Job 23:10 (cf. Prov. 17:3) with 1 Pet. 1:7; Job 34:19 with James 2:1; and Job 38:3 with Luke 12:35.

40. See E. Jacob's categories in Goldsworthy, *Gospel-Centered Herme-neutics*, 246. By "progressive," I refer to progressive revelation. Cf. Geer-hardus Vos, *Biblical Theology* (Grand Rapids, MI: Eerdmans, 1975), 5.

41. See also 1:8–10; 2:1–5; 3:1–4, 11–12; 4:20–22; 7:1–5; 13:24–25; 19:18; 20:7; 22:15; 22:28; 23:13; 29:17.

42. See also 12:26; 13:20; 14:7; 15:17; 16:29; 17:12; 22:24–25; 23:20–21; 24:1–2; 27:17.

43. Here I am not suggesting that we randomly illustrate when exegeti-cally stumped. I am merely suggesting we allow our exegetical imagina-tion some room to roam. While patristic and medieval exegesis of the Old Testament may be rightly accused of unwarranted "roaming," I favor the fathers and schoolmen's christological sensibilities above much of modern spiritually straightjacketed exegesis.

44. Other possible examples include the use of similes throughout Prov-erbs (esp. 25:8–26:28) and Jesus's use of the word "like" in the parables of the kingdom (Matthew 13); what God "hates" in Prov. 6:16–19 and Jesus's hatred of hypocrisy, injustice, selfishness, pride (Luke 11:42–44), and false teaching (Rev. 2:6); the Proverbs on the uselessness of (and pos-sible injuries) caused by correcting a scoffer, and Jesus's teaching on not throwing "pearls before pigs, lest they trample them underfoot and turn to attack" (Matt. 7:6); the many Proverbs on the tongue (e.g., 10:19–21) as Jesus's words on that theme (e.g., Matt. 12:34). Cf. Prov. 15:29 and John 9:31; Prov. 19:11 and Matt. 5:44; Prov. 20:2 (cf. 24:29) and Matt. 5:39; Prov. 21:2 and Luke 16:15; Prov. 21:3 and Matt. 9:13 (cf. 23:23); Prov. 21:26 and Matt. 5:42; Prov. 25:8 and Matt. 5:25; Eccles. 7:20 and John 2:24–25 (cf. Mark 7:20–23).

45. Two other possible examples include: (1) the theme of man's unrigh-teousness (Eccles. 7:20, 22; cf. Rom. 3:10) and the man Jesus Christ as our righteousness (1 Cor. 1:23–24, 30); and (2) Ecclesiastes' thoughts on nothing "new" under the sun, and how Jesus makes or will make every-thing new—new creatures and new creation (see 2 Cor. 5:17; Rev. 21:5).

46. Charles Jennens captured this perfectly in his remarkable compilation of Scripture, which is the text of George Frideric Handel's beloved oratorio *Messiah*. "I Know That My Redeemer Liveth," one of the best-known arias from *Messiah*, juxtaposes Job 19:25–26 and 1 Cor. 15:20.

47. Other possible examples include the theme of *time* in Eccles. 3:1–8 and Jesus's coming in "the fullness of time" (Gal. 4:4–5) to fulfill God's perfectly timed plan of salvation (see Mark 1:15; John 7:30; 13:1; cf. Rom. 5:6). Let me also add a few from the book of Job: Job's desire for an advocate

and Jesus as our advocate before God (1 John 2:1–2; cf. Heb. 4:14); In Job (as elsewhere in the Old Testament) the sea is viewed as an evil force, due to its unruly nature, and thus only God can control it. Jesus is depicted in the Gospels as one who has dominion over the sea (Matt. 8:23–27; 14:22–32); Job's faith in a resurrection (Job 19:25) and our knowledge that our redeemer lives—"He has risen" (Mark 16:6); Job did not know that the way of God might involve suffering for righteousness' sake. Yet Christ did (Matt. 16:21; 26:39), and he has taught his followers to expect suffering for following him (Matt. 10:16–23, 34–39; John 16:2; 2 Cor. 1:3–11). Thus Christians can rejoice even in suffering (Acts 5:41; 16:25; James 1:2) as they long for deliverance and vindication (Rev. 6:10).

48. Tremper Longman III, *How to Read Proverbs* (Downers Grove, IL: InterVarsity, 2002).

49. Dennis E. Johnson summarizes the issue well: "Wisdom Literature poses special challenges for Christ-centered preaching." *Him We Proclaim: Preaching Christ from All the Scriptures* (Phillipsburg, NJ: P&R, 2007), 303.

50. Or why not compare God's rebuke of Job's friends and their false wisdom to Jesus's many rebukes of the Pharisees and their false wisdom in the Gospels?

51. The reference to the east in Job 1:3 likely refers to Job living east of the Jordan River, anywhere between Edom (Judg. 6:3) and Haran (Gen. 29:1).

52. New Testament parallels, as listed above, are great for illustrations. But to be clear I am not advocating we supplant the Old Testament text we are preaching with whatever New Testament text we are using as an illustration. The main "voice" of my sermon on Job 1–2, for example, should be Job's cries on the ash heap, not Jesus's in the garden. For other possible illustrations from Proverbs, there are many: Prov. 1:16 and Mark 3:6 (cf. Rom. 3:15–17); Prov. 3:28 and Luke 11:5–13; Prov. 8:15 and Matt. 28:18; Prov. 10:25 (cf. 12:7) and Matt. 7:24–27; Prov. 11:28a and Matt. 19:16–24; Prov. 14:35 and Matt. 25:14–30; Prov. 24:20 and Matt. 25:1–13; Prov. 22:9 and Luke 14:1; Prov. 25:6–7 and Luke 14:7–11; Prov. 26:23 and Luke 11:39; Prov. 27:6 and Matt. 26:49; Prov. 27:1 and Luke 12:19–20 (cf. James 4:13–16); Prov. 27:23 and John 10:3; Prov. 28:3 and Matt. 18:28; Prov. 28:19 and Matt. 25:21; Prov. 29:7, 14 and Matt. 11:4–5. For other possible illustrations from Ecclesiastes, I suggest the following five: (1) John 15:10–11 is a great summary of the whole book. (2) The theme of not knowing in 3:12–14, 22 can be contrasted with the blind man's confession of Jesus's power: "One thing I do know . . ." (9:25). (3) The admonition to "let your words be few" in prayer because "God is in heaven

and you are on earth" fits well with Jesus's teaching on prayer (Matt. 6:5, 7) and his example prayer—the Lord's Prayer (6:9–13), a very short prayer addressed to "our Father *in heaven.*" (4) The teaching on the benefits of companionship—"two are better than one"—and Jesus's sending of the disciples out "two by two" (Mark 6:7). (5) The call in Eccles. 12:1–8 (and we might say throughout Proverbs) to the young to remember their creator (before it's too late) and Jesus's call for repentance (before it's too late), with his illustration of the falling tower of Siloam (Luke 13:1–5). For possible illustrations from Job, I have come up with these: Job 2:11 (Job's three friends) and Mark 14:32–42 (Jesus's three disciples); Job's testing by God via Satan and Jesus's being driven into the wilderness by the Spirit (Mark 1:12–13); Bildad associates Job with the wicked (Job 18), and the Jewish religious leaders think Jesus is working for the Devil (Mark 3:20–30); the friends "God will bless or judge now" theology contrasted with the parable of the wheat and weeds (Matt. 13:24–30); Job's accusations against his friends (6:27; 13:2–11; 19:1–6, 20–22; 21:1–6, 28–34) and Jesus's woes to the scribes and Pharisees (Matthew 23); the divine speeches in Job 38–41 and Jesus's transfiguration (Matt. 17:1–5); Job's isolation and *why* question to God (Job 19:13–24) and Jesus's abandonment by his friends and his *why* cry from the cross: "My God, my God, why have you forsaken me?" (Mark 15:34); Job's vindication and God's people being vindicated as Satan is cast into the lake of fire (Rev. 20:10; cf. 12:10; 1 John 3:8); Job's (assumed) forgiveness of his ignorant friends (Job 42:9) and Jesus's plea for forgiveness on the cross: "Father, forgive them, for they know not what they do" (Luke 23:34).

53. While Paul taught on the gospel's inherent efficacy (see Phil. 1:18), he also spoke about "how we lived among you" (1 Thess. 1:5 NIV), and encouraged believers to conduct themselves "in a manner worthy of the gospel" (Phil. 1:27 NIV). Chapell summarizes my point here perfectly: "No truth calls louder for pastoral holiness than the link between a preacher's character and a sermon's reception." *Christ-Centered Preaching,* 38.

Appendix A

1. Martin Luther, "Letter to Eoban Hess, 29 March 1523," in *Luthers Briefwechsel,* D. Martin Luthers Werke, 120 vols. (Weimar: Böhlhaus, 1883–2009), 3:50.

2. While the prophets use the freer form of prose, their language at times is rightly labeled "poetry." As Sidney Greidanus notes, "In general we can say that prophetic speeches are mostly in the form of poetry." *The*

Modern Preacher and the Ancient Text: Interpreting and Preaching Biblical Literature (Grand Rapids, MI: Eerdmans, 1988), 240. See also, Gerhard von Rad, *Old Testament Theology*, trans. D. M. G. Stalker, 2 vols. (repr., New York: Prince, 2005). He states, "While there are exceptions, the prophets' own way of speaking is, as a rule, in poetry" (2:33).

3. See my book, *God's Lyrics: Rediscovering Worship through Old Testament Songs* (Phillipsburg, NJ: P&R, 2010).

4. Gen. 4:23–24, 49:2–27; Num. 21:14–15, 27–30; 23:7–10, 18–24; 24:3–9, 15–24; Josh. 10:12–14; Phil. 2:5–11; Col. 1:15–20; 1 Tim. 3:16; and possibly John 1:1–5, 9–11; Rom. 10:9ff.; 1 Cor. 12:3; Eph. 5:14; 2 Tim. 2:5–6; Heb. 1:3; 1 Pet. 3:18c–19.

5. Robert Lowth, *Lectures on the Sacred Poetry of the Hebrews*, trans. G. Gregory (London: Tegg, 1839).

6. For the Ryken and Bullock books, see "Six Helpful Resources" at the end of this Appendix.

7. See books and/or articles by Michael Patrick O'Conner, Terrence Collins, Douglas K. Stuart, Pieter van der Lugt, Robert Alter, Stephen A. Geller, Adele Berlin, T. Carmi, David L. Peterson, and Mary Watkins.

8. While the Masoretes vocalized the poetic books, it is still conjecture (by them and us) as to how the Hebrew originally sounded. There is no contemporary scholarly consensus on meter in Hebrew poetry. Thus, Duane Garrett, for this reason and others, writes: "For myself, I doubt that meter existed in Hebrew poetry and more strongly believe that if it did exist, we have not yet figured out how it worked. The preacher, in my opinion, should disregard references to meter in commentaries on the psalms [and other poetical books]." Duane A. Garrett, "Preaching From the Psalms and Proverbs," in *Preaching the Old Testament*, ed. Scott M. Gibson (Grand Rapids, MI: Baker, 2006), 113. T. Witton Davies adds, "Biblical Hebrew poets were less conscious as poets than western poets, and thought much less of the external form in which they expressed themselves. Biblical poetry lacks therefore close adherence to formal rules as that which characterizes Greek, Arabic or English poetry. The authors wrote as they felt and because they felt, and their strong emotions dictated the forms their words took, and not any objective standards set up by the schools. Hebrew poetry is destitute of meter in the strict sense, and also of rhyme." See "Hebrew Poetry," *The International Standard Bible Encyclopedia* (1915).

9. Douglas Stuart, *Old Testament Exegesis: A Handbook for Students and Pastor*, 3rd ed. (Louisville: Westminster, 2001), 19.

10. On the use of rhyme and sound in Hebrew poetry, see esp. Wilfred G. E. Watson, *Classical Hebrew Poetry: A Guide to Its Techniques*, Journal for the Study of the Old Testament Supplement Series 26 (Sheffield: JSOT Press, 1984), 222–50. See also, his chapter "Poetic Devices," 273–348, which explains the functions of repetition, envelope figure, keywords, the refrain, allusion, ellipsis, irony, oxymoron, hyperbole, merismus, hendiadys, enjambment, rhetorical questions, and other poetic devices.

11. Richard G. Moulton, *Literary Study of the Bible* (Boston: Heath, 1898), 150.

12. All poetry uses various forms of repetition. English poetry, for example, uses repetition of sound (rhythm, meter, rhyme, assonance, alliteration), repetitions of sense (refrains, puns, ambiguities, metaphor, irony), repetitions of context (quotations, the use of proper names or specialized words from a particular literary tradition), and repetition of variations of the prose order (hypallages, inversions, zeugma). See F. W. Bateson, *English Poetry and the English Language* (Oxford: Oxford University Press, 1973), 18 n29. Hebrew poetry uses the literary device of repetition as well, and most notably (and uniquely when compared to English poetry) parallelisms.

13. In his commentary on the Song of Solomon, Andrew E. Hill writes: "Rhythm of thought is the balancing of ideas in a structured or systematic way. The primary vehicle for conveying this thought rhythm is word parallelism, in which similar or opposite ideas are offset in the lines of poetry (e.g., earrings/strings of jewels, 1:10; mountains/hills, 2:8; opened/left, gone, 5:6). Sometimes this poetic parallelism arranges ideas synthetically or climatically in that each idea in the successive lines of the verse builds on the previous one (e.g., wall/windows/lattice, 2:9)." *Evangelical Commentary on the Bible*, ed. Walter A. Elwell (Grand Rapids, MI: Baker, 1996), 452.

14. Norman Gottwald labels these three terms as "repeated, contrasted, and advanced." The full quote is worth including here: "The fundamental formal feature of canonical poetry is the correspondence of thought in successive half lines, known as parallelism of members. The thought may be repeated, contrasted, or advanced; it may be figurative, stairlike, or inverted. The parallelism may be both within lines and between lines." *Interpreter's Dictionary of the Bible*, vol. 3 (Nashville: Abingdon, 1976), 839.

15. It should be noted that synonymous parallelisms are "very seldom precisely synonymous," that is, the second line "does not simply repeat what has been said but enriches it, deepens it, and transforms it by adding fresh nuances and bringing in new elements," which in turn "renders it more concrete and vivid and telling." James Muilenburg, quoted in Greidanus,

The Modern Preacher and the Ancient Text, 62. Robert Alter calls this "focusing." See his *Art of Biblical Poetry* (New York: Basic Books, 1987), 2–26, 62–84. Others also call it "climactic" parallelism.

16. For other examples, see 1 Sam. 18:7; Pss. 15:1; 24:1–3; 25:5; 36:5; Eccles. 10:18; Isa. 2:4; 6:4; 13:7; Amos 5:24; Mic. 4:3. See also, the famous poem of Eccles. 3:1–8.

17. For other examples, see Pss. 20:8; 30:6; 37:9; Eccles. 10:12; Isa. 54:7; cf. Prov. 10:5; 16:9; 27:2; 29:27.

18. For other examples, see Ex. 15:6; Pss. 1:3, 15:4; 19:8ff.; Prov. 1:7.

19. E.g., Psalms 121, 139.

20. E.g., Psalms 10, 35, 38, 51, 54, 74, and 77. Concerning the five elements of laments, see Leland Ryken, *Words of Delight: A Literary Introduction to the Bible*, 2nd ed. (Grand Rapids, MI: Baker Academic, 1992), 240–41.

21. See esp. Psalm 119; cf. Psalms 9–10, 15, 25, 34, 37, 111, 112, 145; Lamentations 1–4; Nah. 1:1–10.

22. An English or Shakespearean sonnet has the following pattern: a-b-a-b, c-d-c-d, e-f-e-f, g-g. The poem is fourteen lines long, falling into three coordinate quatrains and a concluding rhyming couplet. An ode—like John Keats's "Ode on a Grecian Urn"—is a lengthy poem written to a set structure.

23. What Ryken says of Psalm 121 (*Words of Delight*, 201), I say of Hebrew poetic form in general.

24. Note that 8:4 excludes the oath found in 2:7 and 3:5, "by the gazelles or the does of the field."

25. Like the Song of Solomon, Psalm 107 uses both a strict (vv. 8, 15, 21, 31) and a variant refrain (vv. 6, 13, 19, 28).

26. Martin Buber, "Leitwort Style in Pentateuch Narrative," in *Scripture and Translation*, ed. M. Buber and F. Rosenzweig, trans. L. Rosenwald and E. Fox (Bloomington, IN: Indiana University Press, 1994), 114. While made in the context of Pentateuchal narrative, Buber's definition works in general with Hebrew poetry as well.

27. For some of these examples, see Watson, *Classical Hebrew Poetry*, 287–88.

28. Kneeling is optional; praying is not.

29. Stuart, *Old Testament Exegesis*, 19.

30. The definition of "alliteration" comes from the *Concise Oxford English Dictionary*, 11th ed. (New York: Oxford University Press, 2004), 35.

31. C. Hassell Bullock, *An Introduction to the Old Testament Poetic Books* (Chicago: Moody, 1988), 40.

32. See Ryken's concluding remarks in *Words of Delight*, 180. See also his helpful resource, *Dictionary of Biblical Imagery* (Downers Grove, IL: IVP Academic, 1998).

33. Ryken, *Words of Delight*, 183.

34. Stuart, *Old Testament Exegesis*, 19.

35. See Duane A. Garrett, "Preaching From the Psalms and Proverbs," 102, 111–12.

36. Ibid., 102.

37. Ibid., 103.

38. See, e.g., my sermon on Proverbs 31:10–31 in chap. 2.

39. Matthew Arnold, *Literature and Dogma: An Essay Towards a Better Apprehension of the Bible* (New York: MacMillan, 1914), *xiii*.

40. Ryken, *Words of Delight*, 210.

41. The first term was used by architect Ludwig Mies van der Rohe, the second by industrial designer Dieter Rams.

42. Ryken, *Words of Delight*, 207.

Appendix B

1. For extended introductions on each book, see the *ESV Study Bible*.

2. *ESV Children's Bible* (Wheaton, IL: Crossway, 2005), 776.

3. Ibid., 811. I also like the summary to Ecclesiastes in the *ESV Journaling Bible* (Wheaton, IL: Crossway, 2006): "Ecclesiastes contains reflections of an old man, the 'Preacher,' as he considers the question of meaning in life. He looks back and sees the futility ('vanity') of chasing after even the good things this life can offer, including wisdom, work, pleasure, and wealth. Even if such things are satisfying for a time, death is certain to end this satisfaction. In fact, God's judgment on Adam for his sin (Gen. 3:17–19) echoes throughout the book (especially 12:7). Yet the person who lives in the fear of the Lord can enjoy God's good gifts. Young people, especially, should remember their Creator while they still have their whole loves before them (12:1). Traditionally interpreters of Ecclesiastes have identified the 'Preacher,' who is also called 'the son of David, king in Jerusalem' (1:1), as Solomon (tenth century B.C.)" (1052).

4. In Ecclesiastes, the word "good/goodness" is repeated fifty-one times and "vanity" thirty-eight.

5. *ESV Children's Bible*, 625.

6. Tremper Longman III, *How to Read Proverbs* (Downers Grove, IL: InterVarsity, 2002), 117.

7. Also, don't feel limited to stay within 10:1–22:16. Pillage all of Proverbs.

8. Often 22:17–24:22 is viewed as "thirty sayings of the wise," and 24:23–34 as "five more sayings." I join them together, for I see them connected by the key words "do not."

9. This is part of the "Do Not" series. How could I resist?

10. Or you can use the title I used for chap. 2, "Imperishable Beauty."

11. These sixteen preaching units are based on old class lectures and a current draft for my commentary on Ecclesiastes in the Reformed Expository Commentary series (Phillipsburg, NJ: P&R, forthcoming). I will not preach through Ecclesiastes until early 2012. Perhaps then I will be persuaded by other more careful and thoughtful divisions of the text: e.g., Sidney Greidanus, *Preaching Christ from Ecclesiastes: Foundations for Expository Sermons* (Grand Rapids, MI: Eerdmans, 2010), *viii–ix*; and Philip Graham Ryken, *Ecclesiastes: Why Everything Matters*, Preaching the Word (Wheaton, IL: Crossway, 2010), 7–8.

12. Here, in one overview sermon, I suggest focusing on 2:11–13 but adding key concepts from the three cycles of speeches.

GENERAL INDEX

SCRIPTURE INDEX